NUCLEAR AUTHORITY

NUCLEAR AUTHORITY

The IAEA and the Absolute Weapon

ROBERT L. BROWN

Georgetown University Press
Washington, DC

Library of Congress Cataloging-in-Publication Data

Brown, Robert L. (Robert Louis), author
Nuclear authority : the IAEA and the absolute weapon / Robert L. Brown.
   pages cm
  Includes bibliographical references and index.
  ISBN 978-1-62616-182-5 (hardcover : alk. paper)—ISBN 978-1-62616-183-2 (pbk. : alk. paper)—ISBN 978-1-62616-184-9 (ebook)
   1. International Atomic Energy Agency.   2. Nuclear nonproliferation.
3. Nuclear weapons—Safety measures.   4. Nuclear industry—Security measures.
I. Title.
JZ5675.B76   2015
327.1'747—dc23
                                                                    2014024871

This book is printed on acid-free paper meeting the requirements of the American National Standard for Permanence in Paper for Printed Library Materials.

20 19 18 17 16 15   9 8 7 6 5 4 3 2 First printing

Printed in the United States of America

Cover design by Anne C. Kerns, Anne Likes Red, Inc.

Contents

Illustrations

Preface

THIS BOOK is about the power of the International Atomic Energy Agency to affect the nuclear policy choices of states. This is not a book that argues whether states should disarm themselves of nuclear weapons or make their use of nuclear energy safer by eliminating the technology or giving control over it to a supranational actor. Some may find it disappointing that I do not take a normative position on the role of nuclear power or weapons in our world. If this were a book about the International Monetary Fund, would you expect the author to reveal that she hates money? Or reveres it?

This book is about why authority relationships emerge at the global level to govern a transnational issue. There are individual and collective actors that appear to desire radical change in policy outcomes in order to realize alternative futures that better meet their interests. In this book state and nonstate actors are described as working through iterative processes to achieve a variety of nuclear policy outcomes as goals in themselves and as means to other ends. The International Atomic Energy Agency, usually referred to by its abbreviation, "the IAEA," or even more simply "the Agency," is only one strategy that some states use to achieve their goals. I do not argue that more or less IAEA authority is good or bad for international politics generally, or for the United States specifically. I believe the first task of political science is to help actors who do have normative goals make good choices by explaining patterns of political behavior: how do actors and their environment interact to cause the observed variation political cal outcomes?

In exploring why the power of the IAEA to affect behavior has changed over time, I talk about "authority" but have tried carefully to not talk about "sovereignty." Discussing sovereignty immediately opens up politicized debates over delegation versus abdication. My wife told me about a case—she's a lawyer—in which agents of the court convinced one woman to willingly transfer responsibility over her children to another woman. Now, having done this, these agents are trying to change the purpose of this transfer from one that was temporary to one that is permanent. Whereas she had originally agreed to allow another woman to raise her children for the short term and with the hope of eventual reunification with her children, these agents now wish to allow the other woman to make this relationship permanent through adoption. Did the mother—ultimately, one principal served by the court through a long chain of delegation—abdicate her authority in her initial decision to delegate? Is the transfer truly permanent, or can she at some future point choose to challenge her abdication of responsibility over these children?

Scholars of international relations will see this case of adoption as an analogy for the choices being made by some states with respect to their international organizations. I have limited my claims to the authority that international organizations may have over states, and more narrowly over nuclear issues, but these relationships are not fundamentally different from those within states. I have avoided in this book making the simple statement that states are losing sovereignty, but something is occurring that is affecting the power of states not only over their foreign policy behavior but also over outcomes at the domestic level. In short, I believe this book is as much about the IAEA and nuclear policy cooperation as it is about the fundamental political relationships that provide our society with order.

The subject of political authority at the international level has been my theoretical interest in political science since I began working on my dissertation at UC San Diego in 2003. In the space of a few months I finished my coursework, defended my qualifying exams, attended a four-week multidisciplinary Public Policy and Nuclear Threats (PPNT) summer "boot camp," and attended a book conference for what became *States, International Organizations, and Principal-Agent Theory* (2006). These experiences motivated my dissertation, *Nonproliferation through Delegation*, explaining why since the 1950s we can observe states delegating resources and autonomy to an international organization to advance their cooperation on nuclear weapons, but similar cooperation would not occur on chemical weapons until the 1990s, and not at all for biological weapons.

This puzzle had contemporary relevance as I and other graduate students at UC San Diego sought to understand the US decisions to invade Afghanistan and Iraq after al-Qaeda attacked the United States on my second day of graduate school: Lindsay Heger and Wendy Wong were each trying to understand how organizational structure affected the influence of nonstate actors, Laura Wimberly examined how governance costs should affect a powerful state considering war against a weaker state, and I wanted to understand the choice to use international organizations rather than some other multilateral or unilateral strategy to control access to weapons of mass destruction.

When I finally began to write *Nuclear Authority*, I knew I wanted to focus on the most puzzling aspect of delegation to control the threat from weapons of mass destruction: the International Atomic Energy Agency. One purpose of writing a book rather than an article is to create sufficient space for the reader to suspend disbelief long enough to be receptive to the argument and evidence available. This one particular international organization was among the few, if not the only, international security institutions that had independent agency to affect international politics. States appeared to make decisions about war and peace on the basis of the Agency's judgments. But the authority puzzle matters because the IAEA is not the only international organization to grab the attention of international relations scholars or foreign policy analysts and policymakers.

Since this is my first book, it is my best opportunity to formally thank a number of people and institutions. This project benefited much from the advice I received during graduate school at UC San Diego, and I want to single out for their support and guidance my dissertation committee, David Lake (chair), Miles Kahler, Bob Powell, Kristian Gleditsch, and Phil Roeder. Lindsay Heger, Danielle Jung, Laura Wimberly, and Wendy Wong helped focus my ideas and writing in our dissertation reading group. I also benefited from the opportunities and guidance I received from ongoing participation in the PPNT program as a graduate student. As director of the Institute on Global Conflict and Cooperation (IGCC), Susan Shirk convinced the National Science Foundation to fund this IGERT project and then mentored many of us through our graduate programs. Susan helped me find financial and intellectual resources at many stages of my graduate career, including sending me to Bob Einhorn, who gave me a paid summer internship as a graduate student at the Center for Strategic and International Studies and gave me access to an immense wealth of policymaker experience on nuclear policy, including Clark Murdock's Project on Nuclear Issues. David and Susan are a continuing source of advice and assistance.

A number of institutions and individuals have helped make possible *Nuclear Authority*. As director of the PPNT program from 2007–13 I had the incredible opportunity to interact with many speakers, students, and collaborators. Linton Brooks has been a constant source of policy wisdom and professional guidance. I also want to thank for the contributions of their intellectual capital to PPNT, and to me personally even if they didn't know it, George Anzelon, Jay Davis, Zach Davis, Matt Gardner, Erik Gartzke, Huban Gowadia, Bob Kelley, Hans Kristensen, Matt Kroenig, Jim Larrimore, Mike May, Michael Nacht, Joe Pilat, Brad Roberts, Laura Rockwood, Scott Sagan, Mark Schanfein, Larry Scheinman, Etel Solingen, Rick Wallace, and the late Herb York. It was humbling to have the opportunity to discuss my work with and be exposed to these individuals, as well as the many other speakers and students who allowed me to access their wealth of anecdotes, experience, and suggestions on all aspects of nuclear technology, policy, and politics. Many people at IGCC made this possible: Susan Shirk and Tai-Ming Cheung provided me with much advice, and

Laura Martin, Helen Olow, Heidi Knuff Serochi, Lynne Bush, Eva Thiveos, and Marie Thiveos provided the most incredible administrative support one could ask for. Laura helped me get through the many summers of running the boot camp, and I couldn't, and wouldn't, have done it without her. Thank you also to Neil Narang and Bethany Goldblum for taking over PPNT so I had the time to write this book.

Nuclear Authority benefited from my spending the 2011–12 academic year as a junior faculty research fellow at Harvard's Belfer Center for Science and International Affairs thanks to a Stanton Nuclear Security Fellowship. The Managing the Atom program was wonderful, and I want to thank Matthew Bunn, Trevor Findlay, Olli Heinonen, Susan Lynch, Marty Malin, Steve Miller, Will Tobey, and others who made this an incredibly rewarding experience. This project benefited from research assistance from a number of graduate students at Temple University, including Taylor Benjamin-Britton, Gorana Draguljic, Lauren Farmer, and Arnold Kim. Undergraduate students in several of my courses at Temple University also contributed as they wrote research papers in my nuclear policy courses and prepared policy briefs as a component of simulations of the IAEA Board of Governors forced upon them in my introductory international politics and nuclear policy courses.

For reading drafts, and helping me to focus my ideas, I want to thank Chad Rector, Neil Narang, Jeff Kaplow, David Lake, Mark Pollack, Trevor Findlay, and Laura Martin. Portions or aspects of this book were also presented to, and benefited immensely from, the 2012 and 2013 PPNT summer boot camp, Temple University, the University of Delaware, UC Berkeley, and the Harvard Belfer Center. Aspects of this book were also presented at Annual Meetings of the American Political Science Association and International Studies Association, the PPNT Winter Conferences, the Nuclear Science and Security Consortium 2013 summer school, and the 2014 National Nuclear Security Administration University and Industry Technical Interchange. I also wish to thank Don Jacobs and the other staff at Georgetown University Press, as well as several anonymous reviewers who provided input on how this book could be improved.

While I am incredibly thankful for the advice and support of these many people as I worked on this book, only I am responsible for the end result. Any of its remaining weaknesses, errors, or other omissions are my own fault. My apologies also to anyone I left out.

On a more personal note, I couldn't have completed this book without the ongoing support of many people outside of academic and policy circles. For helping me maintain something of an even psychological keel and teaching me much about teaching and mentoring, I want to thank the many hapkido friends, mentors, and students at UC Berkeley, UC San Diego, Temple, and Harvard: it helps put life in perspective to do a few extra burpees, shrimps, or spin kicks, or take a few extra lumps being punched, kicked, or thrown. Especially if delivered with "fiendish cackles of glee." My family has been incredibly supportive throughout this project, including my mother, father, brother, wife, daughter, son, and all the other members of the extended Brown and Hashima clans. My wife, Sandy, especially stuck by me, read chapters, and dished out her own lumps when I needed it.

1

The Absolute Weapon

WHEN BERNARD BRODIE (1946, 21) described the atomic bomb as "the absolute weapon," his hyperbole was intended to emphasize for US policymakers the importance of quickly adapting to the new and dangerous world they had created. The idea that the United States should work with others to reduce the danger from nuclear weapons predated the first nuclear weapon test and the first use of nuclear bombs against Japan that instantly killed tens of thousands of people at Hiroshima and Nagasaki in the summer of 1945. But Winston Churchill, prime minister of the United Kingdom, and Franklin Roosevelt, president of the United States, rejected approaching the Soviet Union over the international control of atomic power during the Second World War. And after the war, when President Harry Truman's emissary Bernard Baruch proposed the international control of atomic power to the United Nations, it was rejected. The Soviet Union wanted first to ban and destroy all nuclear weapons before it would accept a control system, which the West rejected. The major powers had abandoned plans for international nuclear controls before it was clear the spread of nuclear bombs would force even them to completely reconsider how they could provide for their national security.

The first success at imposing any international controls on the spread and use of nuclear energy did not occur until the creation of the International Atomic Energy Agency (IAEA 1957). The United States hoped the IAEA would spur peaceful exploitation of atomic power by supplying nuclear assistance in exchange for safeguards against that assistance being misused for nuclear weapons. The IAEA has come quite far from its origins as a failed provider of civilian nuclear energy services, from the 1960s when many questioned whether it could implement the global verification system called for in the impending Nuclear Non-Proliferation Treaty (NPT), and even from the early 1990s, when, after the Gulf War, the IAEA was heavily criticized for missing Iraq's nuclear weapons program. The Secretariat, a bureaucracy of 2,500 staff, is best known today for verifying in over 180 countries that some or all their nuclear materials are exclusively in peaceful uses, including negotiating the international treaties that constitute safeguards agreements and define for states when and how they must open to verification. It supplies hundreds of international nuclear technical assistance and training programs each year and is the trusted agent of the international community for verifying disarmament in states that committed under the NPT to forgo nuclear weapons. The Secretariat also participates in the international governance of nuclear counterterrorism, nuclear trade, nuclear transport security, and nuclear safety by hosting international conferences, issuing standards, and conducting review missions.

The IAEA's Board of Governors oversees the Secretariat's programs. Usually by consensus, the thirty-five states represented by governors recommend to its General Conference of all members the annual budget and who should be appointed as the Secretariat's director general. It also approves the slate of technical assistance projects and individual safeguards agreements. Less routine, very political, and sometimes decided by a straight majority vote are decisions imposing stronger verification standards and judging whether states like Iran, North Korea, and others are in compliance with their nonproliferation treaty commitments or should face sanctions or be reported to the UN Security Council for noncompliance. These decisions are informed by, if not initiated by, reports from the Secretariat, but the Board can also impose such decisions because many of the governors represent the same states that dominate the UN Security Council, the International Monetary Fund (IMF), and the World Bank.

This book makes the empirical claim that the IAEA has acquired the independent power to issue rules and make commands in some areas of nuclear policy with which states feel pulled to comply. Efforts to control "the absolute weapon" have relied upon a hodgepodge of unilateral policies and multilateral arrangements, but only the IAEA is the agent of the 162 members of its General Conference, and of the 190 parties to the 1970 NPT, arguably the most important modern international security treaty, and of several regional nuclear weapon-free zones. The IAEA judges compliance with the NPT but also issues the rules by which compliance is judged, verifies compliance, demands that states found in violation return to compliance, and sanctions states for their violations. And beyond the area of nonproliferation, it also contributes to international nuclear disarmament, safety, security, and supply.

This power is actually a separation of powers between the two agents of the IAEA's members: the Board and the Secretariat. This relationship has historically worked well although their occasional discord shows them to increasingly be distinct actors on the international stage. One salient example is the conflict that erupted between the Board and then–director general Mohamed ElBaradei. After the Secretariat was proven right about the state of Iraq's nuclear program in 2002–3 and then received the Nobel Prize for Peace in 2005, ElBaradei refused for years to declare that Iran was in non-compliance with its NPT commitments. Then, after winning reappointment to a third term despite opposition by the United States, the Agency's most powerful supporter and the contributor of more than one-third of its resources, he criticized the Board for financially starving the Agency. He warned, reports Kerr (2007), that its proposed 2008 budget "does not by any stretch of the imagination meet our basic, essential requirements." A leaked US government cable by Schulte (2009) described ElBaradei's 2009 intervention into the debate as a "backlash." ElBaradei said they "would eventually 'reap what they sowed'" and that forcing the IAEA to increasingly subsist on voluntary contributions "was a 'bastardization' of an important international organization" (Schulte 2009). This supposed servant of the Board survived repeatedly challenging his masters, telling them that they, not he, would be held responsible for the dire consequences of failing to heed his warnings.

How did this international organization acquire the power to issue rules and commands over sensitive national security issues like nuclear nonproliferation and disarmament, with which states expect each other to comply? This book presents the theoretical claim that the power acquired by the IAEA is political authority, a form of power that arises out of the persistent demand for agency gains with successful supply by an agent. I argue that states are demanding political authority when they find collective action persistently impeded by policy uncertainty or conflicts of interest, but an agent's authority is contingent upon its demonstrated, repeated ability to supply this cooperation. This contingency means all authority is continually contested as states and other actors advance their own more or less divergent interests and their own claims to authority.

This power is part of a larger puzzle about the effects of international organizations. Deployed to solve complex cooperation problems, their effects are difficult to disentangle from the complex strategic interaction in which they are embedded. Often the demand for agency gains is weak, short-lived, or easily isolated from other issues, allowing delegations to international organizations to be highly circumscribed in function or time. Often, states are unsure whether an agent is effective for their needs and delegation is a conditional policy experiment from which states can escape with little penalty.

THE NUCLEAR AUTHORITY PUZZLE

Months before the nuclear bomb was first used against Japan, demonstrating to the world the incredible power of this "absolute weapon," deliberations were under way in the US government over how nuclear weapons could or should be used. The US internal conversation presaged the wider international debate that emerged after the world learned of the atom bomb's destructive power.[1] On the one hand, even though the horrors of World War II had desensitized many from immediately considering the moral question of mass civilian death and destruction, Sims (1990) and Wittner (1993, 61) argue that the fear of the cataclysmic effects of nuclear weapons fed a strong desire for complete and general disarmament and "world government." These ideas seem idealistic now, but in the world of the late 1940s, with two world wars and a global economic depression in the immediate past and another global conflict over Communism on the horizon, dramatic solutions seemed the only way to prevent another world war. Scientists involved in developing America's first nuclear weapons in the Manhattan Project called on President Franklin Roosevelt before the bomb's use and then afterward were joined by many others inside and outside the United States in pressing President Harry Truman to internationalize all aspects of the atomic program (Wittner 1993, esp. chap. 4).

On the other hand, even Brodie's (1946) early writings show it was hard to ignore the potential technological, economic, and coercive value of the US monopoly on atomic technology. Although US military strategists disagreed whether nuclear weapons were most effective for destroying Soviet cities or destroying the Soviet military capabilities that could launch a Pearl Harbor–style surprise attack, the monopoly appeared to deter any further Soviet incursion into Europe or Asia (Freedman 2003, 41).[2] Many inside the United States opposed any steps toward abandoning this leverage. Continuing nuclear science research also promised new technological developments that could further advance US power or quality of life. To dissuade others from pursuing nuclear weapons, President Truman was convinced within days of the Hiroshima and Nagasaki bombings to release the Smyth Report (1945), a public relations campaign that described in just enough detail the scientific and engineering difficulty of nuclear weapons. Redirection toward peaceful uses was also the purpose of the US Acheson–Lilienthal proposal for internationalization of the atom presented by Bernard Baruch to the new United Nations in 1945. Known as the Baruch Plan (1946), it called for the "managerial control or ownership of all atomic-energy, activities potentially dangerous to world security" by an international atomic development authority. The plan was rejected by the Soviet Union, in part because US disarmament would be delayed until others had accepted verification but also because Baruch proposed to eliminate the permanent member veto at the Security Council over this agency's activities.

Although debate continued for decades over how the United States should use nuclear weapons, Brodie had made the point early, and publicly, of the vulnerability of Western democracies if their enemies acquired nuclear weapons. James Goodby (2006) argues that the compromise within the United States, and then between the United States and the United Kingdom, was to hope to maintain the US atomic monopoly through secrecy. The 1943 Quebec Agreement between Canada, the United Kingdom, and the United States was extended to continue their agreement to not communicate any information about nuclear technology without the consent of the others. The Coordinating Committee for Multilateral Export Controls was then formed in January 1950 to extend a wider range of export controls by more Western states against the USSR and its Eastern Bloc allies. By now many states wanted nuclear arsenals for their assumed military utility, for technological advancement, or simply for the prestige of being an atomic power.

The Soviet Union became the second member of the atomic club in 1949 and only slowly embraced the disadvantages of further proliferation. The United States and the Soviet Union supported the proliferation of peaceful uses that could aid nuclear weapons programs and were themselves engaged in a rapid vertical proliferation toward ever-larger stockpiles, but they also worked independently to reduce demand for nuclear weapons by their respective allies. They offered alliances, conventional arms, and other security assurances. They were unsuccessful in stopping France and China from stockpiling nuclear weapons, but their unilateral efforts became more robust toward stopping South Korea, Taiwan, East and West Germany, and others. The effectiveness of these policies at reducing demand for nuclear weapons is the foundation of many arguments today for continuing to maintain a robust US nuclear arsenal.

When the United States finally entered the growing international market for nuclear supply in 1954, it did so because it feared both being left out of its commercial promise and seeing that market develop without proper constraints. US president Dwight Eisenhower's Atoms for Peace program allowed US exports but made them conditional upon "safeguards"— assurances that US assistance would not be used to produce nuclear weapons, including certain rights of inspection and the right to later recall the assistance. The United Kingdom, France, and even the Soviet Union soon followed with their own bilateral safeguards systems. The primary focus of international cooperation, though, was on the supply side of the problem:

limiting access to the equipment, knowledge, and materials needed for nuclear weapons.

Eisenhower's "Atoms for Peace" speech to the UN General Assembly also included another proposal for an international solution to the perceived danger of more nuclear states. Believing that converting fissile materials after their diversion from peaceful uses was "an elaborate and expensive process of a magnitude which would be very difficult to carry out without its becoming known" (US Senate 1957, 79), Eisenhower proposed creating an international atomic agency to underwrite the development of peaceful nuclear uses. With no immediate commercial prospects for nuclear energy, Eisenhower believed a little international encouragement could keep scarce national nuclear resources focused on civilian applications and unavailable for military uses. The IAEA that emerged from US-sponsored negotiations in 1957 held the promise of becoming a global supplier of nuclear materials and facilities but with safeguards against their subsequent diversion to military uses.

Superpower coercion, supplier constraints, and IAEA incentives to focus on civilian efforts offered parallel tactics for stopping new nuclear powers from emerging. However, they were also applied unevenly. And the United Nations was failing to offer more universal and permanent solutions. From the Baruch Plan to the UN General Assembly's "First Committee," created to negotiate complete and general disarmament, the threat of another use of atomic weapons did not abate. Enthusiasm for comprehensive solutions to the threat of another world war—complete and general disarmament and even limited nuclear disarmament—waned through the 1950s.

International efforts instead shifted to a more minimal strategy of "nonproliferation," first in the form of a test ban. Popular support in many countries, explain Wittner (1997) and York (1987), came more from the fear of radioactive fallout from nuclear testing than from the belief that testing enabled the proliferation of nuclear weapons in ways that could destabilize the delicate US–Soviet strategic balance. A moratorium among the three nuclear powers provided some space for negotiating a ban on all tests until France "broke" the moratorium with its first test. But a complete ban on testing was already proving impossible to achieve for the United States and United Kingdom as long as the Soviet Union refused to accept the verification measures they thought necessary to confirm the absence of underground nuclear testing. Even then, explains Goodby (2005), it took the near spasm into nuclear war over Cuba in 1962 before they could conclude the 1963 Limited Nuclear Test Ban Treaty.[3] Although "limited," the treaty solved the fallout problem and relieved enough pressure on the superpowers that a comprehensive test ban would take another three decades to conclude. France and China, however, rejected the Limited Nuclear Test Ban

Treaty, believing that as long as their support would reduce pressure for more comprehensive measures by the United States and Soviet Union, they might as well avoid constraints on their own programs and continue testing.

The nonproliferation successes of the 1950s and 1960s were successes of the various national nonproliferation efforts. The IAEA as a collective effort, though, was largely a failure. The Agency was a new agency facing all the struggles of newly stood-up bureaucracies but also tasked with creating a global safeguards system from scratch when even the United States safeguards system was rudimentary. These natural challenges were made worse when the main nuclear supplier states failed to give the Agency the nuclear materials it needed to become a supplier of nuclear fuel. Then commercial nuclear power began to take off, ending the market failure before it could carve out a peaceful supply niche. Supplier states, especially the United States, were also quite slow to transfer to the Agency the implementation of bilateral safeguards.

To fill the gap left by a disappointing IAEA, states began pursuing regional nuclear weapons–free zones (NWFZ) and a global nonproliferation agreement. NWFZs were more intended to keep superpower nuclear weapons out, after the Cuban Missile Crisis, than they were to prevent proliferation by regional actors. The NPT legalized a commitment to the nonproliferation of nuclear weapons with what is now described as a grand bargain between members of the nuclear club and the non–nuclear weapons states (NNWS). In exchange for promises of progress on complete and general disarmament, including nuclear disarmament by nuclear weapons states (NWS), and promises that no party would restrict access to nuclear materials and peaceful technologies, the NNWS parties would accept "comprehensive safeguards" by the IAEA on their civilian nuclear programs.[4] In contrast to the voluntary nature of the regular IAEA safeguards system, these comprehensive safeguards would be mandatory for all NNWS parties to the NPT.

The international community now views this bargain as the keystone of the nonproliferation regime, but it was unclear if the Agency could handle the expected increase in its responsibilities or if many states of interest could be encouraged to accept the NPT. Several had ruled out ratifying the NPT at all, including China, France, and India. Many holdout states argued the NPT was discriminatory because it did not make nuclear weapons illegal to have or use. Others worried the NPT would not make them more secure because it did not establish mechanisms or timelines for disarmament, because the future verification system was unclear, and because it did not include explicit security guarantees by NWS to those forgoing the security benefits of nuclear weapons. After India's subsequent test of a "peaceful nuclear explosive" in 1974, the nuclear supplier states finally formed an informal cartel, the Nuclear Suppliers Group, to force even non-NPT states to accept IAEA safeguards as a condition of nuclear supply.[5] The United States failed to get a formal consensus among the Nuclear Suppliers Group to agree to not sell sensitive fuel cycle technologies, but no members subsequently did.

This was the basic structure of the nuclear nonproliferation regime for the rest of the Cold War. Most states of concern for proliferation were convinced to ratify the NPT, helping the IAEA grow as it implemented safeguards in more states; 148 states had acceded to the NPT by 1989, a phenomenal share of the 159 states then in the United Nations. The legitimacy of the norms and rules of the nonproliferation regime was reinforced by the limited number of states acquiring nuclear weapons after the NPT entered into force, many fewer than the "15 or 20 or 25" that John F. Kennedy (1963) thought possible.[6] This includes the norm of accepting the safeguards system designed by the Board and then negotiated into bilateral treaties and implemented by the Secretariat. Although IAEA membership is not necessary to accept IAEA safeguards, many joined the Agency to have a voice in its affairs and to benefit from its support for peaceful uses, bringing its total membership to 109 by 1989. The Agency's assistance programs offered consulting on energy projects for developing states but also the research, development, and implementation of radiation-based medical diagnostic, disease eradication, and agricultural efficiency programs. In the wake of the 1986 reactor meltdown in the Soviet city of Chernobyl, the Agency also attempted to expand its safety-related codes, training programs, and consultation missions.

The end of the Cold War brought new signs of internalization of the norms and rules of the nonproliferation regime. Many new states acceded to the NPT and joined the IAEA, but several former Soviet republics that found themselves to be nuclear armed upon their independence (Belarus, Kazakhstan, and Ukraine) took some convincing to disarm and accept IAEA comprehensive safeguards on their remaining nuclear programs. Then, in the space of just two years, the IAEA was faced with several incredible challenges. While implementing the armistice agreement between the United Nations and Iraq after the 1991 Gulf War, the IAEA discovered that Iraq had pursued nuclear weapons not through undetected diversions from a declared program but with an entire undeclared parallel program. And when South Africa sought to leave its apartheid legacy behind and accede to the NPT, not only did the Secretariat find itself verifying the accuracy of South Africa's declaration for its peaceful nuclear energy program but the Board also ordered it to verify its "completeness."[7] Then IAEA ad hoc inspections to verify the accuracy of North Korea's safeguards declaration almost immediately revealed inconsistencies that suggested it also had a military goal in mind. And the Secretariat unexpectedly was asked by South

Africa to verify the just-completed dismantlement of its nuclear weapons program.

Iraq and North Korea would present a continuing political challenge to the international nonproliferation regime for years. They resisted the IAEA's resolution of their nuclear status but the ongoing demand by the international community for independent verification provided an opportunity for the IAEA to grab the international stage. The IAEA emerged from the post–Cold War era buoyed by its demonstration of expertise on nuclear monitoring and on disarmament, which almost no state by then possessed, but also unencumbered by the political biases apparent in many of its most powerful members states. This stature only increased when its strengthened safeguards system revealed that more states were engaging in undeclared nuclear activities. The most significant of these in recent years is Iran, which many suspect has aspirations to acquire nuclear weapons, but states as diverse as South Korea, Egypt, Iraq, and Libya also found themselves needing the IAEA to verify the peacefulness of their nuclear programs.

Reliance by the nuclear nonproliferation regime upon the IAEA and the UN Security Council has resulted in a few high-profile failures. Iraq obstructed verification for years and evicted UN and IAEA inspectors without penalty in 1998 and would probably still be unresolved if the United States had not invaded and ousted the regime in 2003. Despite IAEA protestations and negotiations, and despite UN Security Council sanctions and concerted Western pressure, Iran continues to resist opening to the verification regime to which it had committed. North Korea, after renouncing the NPT and withdrawing from the IAEA, has also refused to freeze its program and has tested nuclear weapons multiple times, despite international sanctions and criticism even by its closest supporter, China. The Agency's assistance programs may also have been contributing to nuclear proliferation (Brown and Kaplow 2014).

That many see these as failures of the Agency reflects its increased significance and salience to global security problems. Since the end of the Cold War, the IAEA has played a pivotal role through continually verifying nonproliferation by almost all states, verifying if not implementing disarmament in several states that acquired nuclear weapons, and offering the opportunity for peaceful resolution to a few hard cases like Iraq, North Korea, and Iran. It strengthened its comprehensive safeguards regime when weaknesses were revealed, a collaborative effort by both the Board and the Secretariat but undertaken without guidance or approval by the parties to the NPT and various NWFZs that rely on safeguards. Its nuclear safety expertise has been expected in nuclear accidents even when it has little legal autonomy to act. New roles are likely for the Agency in nuclear security, nuclear safety, and future nuclear arms control regimes. And yet, as the confrontations with Iran and over Iran have so far alluded to, this is not without conflict among its members, between members and the Board and the Secretariat, and between the Board and the Secretariat. These are failures of the regime, though, where responsibility is shared by the IAEA, the parties to the NPT, and the major powers of the UN Security Council.

IAEA rules and commands are often contested by states that challenge its specific findings on compliance, by members that dispute its focus on the regulatory aspects of safeguards instead of its mandate for the promotion of peaceful uses, by states that hold nuclear safety and security to be sovereign concerns, and by states that hold the entire nonproliferation regime to be discriminatory. Its power over nuclear safety, nuclear security, and peaceful nuclear assistance is weaker than its effect on nuclear nonproliferation and disarmament. Though the IAEA is not all-powerful, it has acquired the power to issue rules and make commands on some range of nuclear issues with which states feel obligated to comply.

As important as the IAEA is to many contemporary international political conflicts, it is woefully understudied. There are a few older histories of the IAEA (Bechhoefer 1959; Scheinman 1985; Blix 1997; Fischer 1997) and memoirs by former directors general Hans Blix (2004) and Mohamed ElBaradei (2011) that supplement studies of arms control more generally (e.g., Sims 1990; Wittner 2003). There remains, unfortunately, very little systematic analysis of the Agency's development. At least through the mid-1970s, the literature is torn between those that argue the Agency was weak and insignificant. Some of them observed it had little technical capacity because it limited its reach to minor technical assistance, standards development, and international technical conferences (Goldschmidt 1982; Scheinman 1987), while others argued the Agency achieved buy-in for its programs by compromising on the scope of its safeguards (Bechhoefer 1973). Some saw its focus on expertise, professionalism, and political insulation from broader Cold War conflicts as a source of strength (Pendley, Scheinman, and Butler 1975; Scheinman 1987) while others saw this as a by-product of norms of nonproliferation being spread by the IAEA's professional staff (Brewer 1978) and more broadly (Wittner 1997).

Most contemporary analyses of the IAEA come from policy practitioners who are incredibly knowledgeable about the day-to-day activities of the IAEA.[8] These analysts stand too close to the daily events of a single organization, however. Their analyses often fail to note the institutional change over time from a newly born IAEA with only a handful of members, staff, and dollars to an established international organization that today has 162 members and receives more than $750 million each year for direct spending to support activities by more than 2,500 employees. They remark on increasing politicization of the Board's debates while neglecting to note that the Board, and not its individual members, is the only legitimate judge of compliance with the nonproliferation regime. They complain when the director general fails to report to the Board that a state is in noncompliance, but they ignore that the Board refuses to act without such a report from the Secretariat. Lost in current policy debates is the fact that the Agency has evolved from a small, limited agent for nuclear supply into an international organization with the power to affect the terms and pace of debate on core international security that rival even the most powerful states in the system.

Nuclear policy analysts also miss how the evolution of the IAEA could be part of a larger puzzle: is there a broader evolution of state sovereignty and world governance as international organizations reach further into states to solve the problems between them? The Security Council appears more often to shift from reacting to asserting a forward-looking legislative role (Rosand 2004). Negative attention on the IMF, first in the 1998 Asian financial crisis and more recently with Greece, occurs more often as it intervenes more often, and with greater effect, in transnational monetary issues.[9] The specific challenge here, though, is to demonstrate and explain the evolution of the IAEA. If an international organization can issue rules and make commands to states that in the absence of the threat or use of violence elicits their compliance, then it has power. Koppell (2008, 180) argues that the routinization of subordination to an actor's power is authority, but this does not explain authority. How has the IAEA acquired power to issue rules on nuclear policy and make commands with which states must obey?

INTERNATIONAL NUCLEAR AUTHORITY

International organizations may be pushed on a community of states by a hegemonic power imposing its own most preferred outcomes (Mearsheimer 1994) or acting as a public goods provider (Kindleberger 1973; Krasner 1999; Lake 2009). State leaders may feel pulled into delegating because they believe this strategy, or the policies that the international organization represents, are more appropriate or legitimate (Katzenstein 1996; Finnemore and Sikkink 1998; Wendt 1999; Checkel 2005). States may also choose to delegate resources and autonomy to an international agent when simpler strategies—informal groupings, paper contracts, or diffuse norms of behavior—appear unable to produce the collective action they desire (Kiewiet and McCubbins 1991; Pollack 1997; Hawkins et al. 2006a; Bradley and Kelley 2008a). The process by which states negotiate and accede to a contract that creates delegation provides information to others about their commitment to accepting the policies supplied by the agent (Fearon 1994; Schultz 1999; von Stein 2005). The principals rarely must approve or decide whether to fund each specific action by the agent, pushing onto the full community the distributional economic and political costs that would otherwise fall on a few of any specific policy outcome. Members of the international organization then renew their initial commitment by participating in governance and paying regularized contributions. Delegation therefore serves as a signal of commitment by states to collective outcomes, a means of "tying hands" (Fearon 1997) that makes it more costly for them to choose alternative strategies in the future.

As various as the causes of creation of such agents may be, still other factors may be important to understanding their ultimate effects upon state behavior. First, the ability of an international organization to affect outcomes seems to relate to its size (Brown 2010). Following cartel theory, international organizations may gain greater control over the political market by increasing the number of states that use it to cooperate. For example, the number seeking IAEA membership (and being welcomed by the other members) or accepting IAEA comprehensive safeguards because they choose to accede to the NPT (see figure 1.1) may increase IAEA control over nuclear policy with fewer states operating outside the institution. The ability to affect outcomes might also increase with the size of the regular budget and the number of staff (see figure 1.2).

Second, the design of an international organization is also an important source of variation in the ability to identify, select, monitor, and implement

Figure 1.1. Number of States in UN, IAEA, and NPT

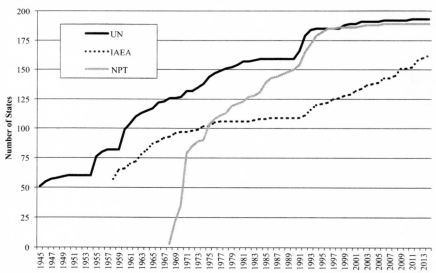

Data Sources: IAEA, "Member States of the IAEA" (Vienna: International Atomic Energy Agency, 2014); UNODA, "Treaty on the Non-Proliferation of Nuclear Weapons: Status of the Treaty" (Geneva: United Nations Office for Disarmament Affairs, 2014); and United Nations, "Member States of the United Nations" (New York: United Nations, 2014).

Figure 1.2.   IAEA Budgetary Resources

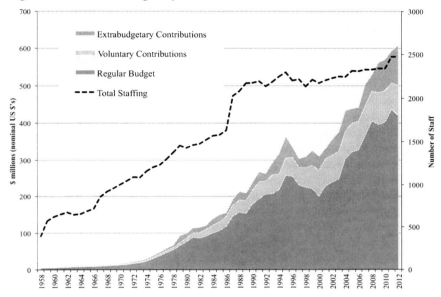

Data Sources: IAEA (1958–2012). The Annual Report. Vienna, The International
Atomic Energy Agency.
IAEA (1960–2012). The Agency's Accounts. Vienna, The International Atomic Energy
Agency.

solutions to complicated policy questions (Hawkins et al. 2006b; Koremenos 2008; Brown 2010). Delegation can be structured to create or exploit
a set of assets—materiel, but also processes and expertise—that are necessary or specific to supplying particular policy outcomes. Especially if states
were otherwise unable or unwilling to invest in the specific assets required
for cooperation, delegation can enable agents to supply the investment
economies of scale needed to create expertise, monitor behavior, or compel
compliance (Hawkins et al. 2006b). The Intergovernmental Panel on Climate Change was explicitly created to gather the scientific expertise and
incentivize it to judge whether climate change was occurring and, if so, its
possible causes and effects.

International economies of scale can be created, however, with little or
no delegation—and they often are. The United States led the creation of
the International Space Station, for example, because of "the advantages of
sharing the risks and rewards of undertaking such a monumental effort"
and because "cost [would have been] prohibitive even to the wealthiest
nation on its own" (Manzione 2002, 509). The Group of 8 meeting of the

leaders of the largest industrial democracies can coordinate multilateral cooperation on the international economy and the Nuclear Suppliers Group does coordinate nuclear export controls, both without creating an international bureaucracy. Bilateral arms control agreements, private satellite imagery firms, and financial markets also work quite well without creating international agents.

While international organizations can overcome hold-up problems that prevent collective investments necessary for some multilateral cooperation, this book argues that an international agent can acquire power over the international community on an issue area if it supplies states with two particular agency gains. First, collective investment can enable an agent to create new knowledge about a policy area, and this expertise can create a substantial informational advantage relative to its principals (McCubbins and Schwartz 1984). When policy expertise is combined with incentives to use expertise to achieve particular policy goals, an agent acquires policy partiality. The IMF and the International Bank for Reconstruction and Development acquired substantial leverage over the states that seek their loans because these organizations have developed specialized models and acquire specialized information to guide their lending and consulting, partiality that is especially powerful when other economic actors can use their judgments as investment signals (Barnett and Finnemore 2004; Gould 2006b). The IAEA has invested in policy partiality by creating procedures that deploy its expertise toward identifying nuclear proliferation whenever it observes proliferation occurring. By design, this agent is also partial to supplying policy whenever possible to improve international nuclear safety, nuclear security, and access to peaceful nuclear technology.

Second, an agent's resource and information advantages provide the greatest value to the international community, argue Barnett and Finnemore (2004, 18), when the agent's design contributes to its developing "prescribed rules and operating procedures that eliminate arbitrary and politicized influences." Rule-governed administration of policy by trained and neutral officials—the hallmark of Max Weber's modern civil service—fosters policy that benefits from what Barnett and Finnemore (2004) term "bureaucratic impersonality." Impersonality constrains an agent to achieving specific goals using specific processes identified in advance by its principals. This elicits compliance because it minimizes the opportunity for the agent to advance alternative goals even when doing so might better satisfy the shifting, short-term interests of individual bureaucrats or powerful individual principals.[10]

The IAEA appears designed not only to be biased toward identifying proliferation when it occurs (policy partiality) but also to seek proliferation irrespective of an actor's interests and actions on unrelated issues (e.g., human rights, economic policy, political ideology). Delegation for behavioral impersonality to the IAEA is valuable because most states lack sufficient expertise about nuclear proliferation, safety, or security, and because many states cannot be trusted to ignore their religious, economic, historic, or other political biases. The United States has been among the strongest supporters of the nonproliferation regime but has repeatedly compromised its nonproliferation principles to obtain other foreign policy goals.

This book argues that the persistent demand for the benefits of delegation within an issue area is demand for a political authority to supply that which states cannot themselves provide. The ability of an international organization to supply policy partiality and behavioral impersonality successfully and over time is the source of its power to issue rules and commands within an issue area with which others expect they must comply: international political authority. That authority is diminished by its contingency, contestation, or limits does not dismiss the reality of its effects.

Observing the authority of international organizations and its effects upon state behavior poses an inference problem. While it may be possible to observe the development of black-letter law and formal institutions within the nonproliferation regime, including the delegation of rights and responsibilities to the IAEA, other factors are only partially observable. The size of the IAEA's budget and staff are largely observable as indicators of its capacity, as discussed earlier, but these indicators may not be directly comparable to complementary or competitive efforts by states and other nonstate actors. Powerful states make some of their contributions opaque, including how they support the IAEA. Concepts such as autonomy, nuclear norms, and authority have also long resisted measurement despite their apparent importance, forcing scholars to rely on potentially tenuous analogies, plausibility probes, and indirect inference.[11] Chapter 2 elaborates on the concept of political authority and hypothesizes on the processes that may cause political authority in international organizations.

To test the power of the theory of political authority and the alternatives, the body of this book divides the nuclear age into four periods of observation. Chapter 3 corresponds roughly to the birth of the nuclear age through the birth of the Agency (pre-1961), chapter 4 examines the adolescence of international nuclear cooperation (1962–85), chapter 5 demonstrates the effect of a series of intense nuclear policy challenges (1986–98), and chapter 6 explains the emergence at the IAEA of international nuclear authority (1998–2013). The divided but extended historical treatment creates the opportunity to incorporate diverse sources of evidence when tracing the causes and effects of specific choices of individual and collective actors both inside and outside the Agency as they respond to a series of technical and political challenges to the existing nuclear policy architecture. This allows a rich exploration of how and why the IAEA has changed over time, including the importance of the relationship between the IAEA's political and bureaucratic organs, of key personalities, and of political conflicts in the broader international environment. Process tracing also allows the analysis to incorporate changes in the broader international structure, changing perceptions of nuclear weapons, and the changing technological context to explicitly test alternative explanations. In short, this research design allows me to explain why the IAEA has evolved into a potent but also independent force in international politics.

Nuclear policy encompasses a wide range of areas in which delegation to and the authority of the IAEA may be more or less significant. To increase the power of the analysis by combining process tracing with cross-case comparisons, this study also divides the "nuclear policy" landscape into four issue areas for observation:

1. *Nonproliferation* describes strategies used to dissuade actors from acquiring the capability to construct a nuclear weapons arsenal or destroying those capabilities before the actor is successful. Historically nonproliferation strategies have included supply controls, safeguards against improper use (verification), and coercive counterproliferation, including economic and military sanctions for proliferation-related behavior.
2. *Disarmament* covers any strategies, including arms control, implementing and verifying the destruction of an actor's demonstrated capacity to develop, construct, and deliver deployable nuclear weapons. This implies a qualitative shift in the cooperation problem has occurred when actors have demonstrably acquired capabilities with "military dimensions" or deployable devices.
3. *Safety and security* encompasses strategies intended to maintain the safe use of nuclear materials and technologies. These include the safe operation of nuclear facilities, the safe transport and storage of nuclear materials, and the protection of facilities and materials against misuse by nonstate actors. Succinctly, safety strategies protect from genuine accidents while security strategies protect from theft, misuse, or deliberate accidents.
4. *Promotion of peaceful uses* supports developing and exploiting nonmilitary uses of nuclear science. This includes electricity production but also the use of radioactive materials for other industrial, medical, agricultural, or other scientific purposes. Though now in disfavor, there was also extensive research into using peaceful nuclear explosives for digging harbors or canals and for fossil fuel and mineral extraction.

Given the many areas of nuclear policy, it should not be surprising that states have chosen a variety of strategies for pursuing each of them. The

NPT and IAEA are core elements of the nonproliferation regime, for example, but also important are Nuclear Suppliers Group export controls, interdiction under the Proliferation Security Initiative, regional NWFZs, UN Security Council resolutions (especially #1540), and the multiple test ban treaties (from "Limited" and "Threshold" to "Comprehensive"). These strategies comprise an overlapping network of unilateral, microlateral/plurilateral, multilateral, and international attempts to treat the symptoms that occur when states demand nuclear weapons.

The pursuit of all the areas in some ways also appears contradictory. For example, promotion efforts may complicate the nonproliferation problem but also safety and security concerns to the extent the alternatives to nuclear are better. The Acheson–Lilienthal Plan proposed international control of peaceful uses and of nuclear devices, while the IAEA statute focused foremost on promotion and secondarily on safety and safeguards against proliferation, a set of priorities that was to change over time. International cooperation and governance may vary across forms by the number and type of actors involved, by the breadth of their policy cooperation (number of areas), and by the depth of cooperation in each area. An additional challenge of this book, then, is not only to explain how the IAEA became an international political authority for only some nuclear issues but also to explain decisions to support the IAEA rather than the many alternatives that also appear in this study.

The data derive from archival research of documents from governments and international organizations, open-source data on national nuclear energy and weapons programs, and secondary histories of the nonproliferation regime. The analysis also benefits from dozens of interviews over the past decade with former and current officials of various national governments and several international organizations, including the IAEA, the United Nations, the Comprehensive Test Ban Treaty Organization, and the Organization for the Prohibition of Chemical Weapons. In many cases, however, the interviews are reported anonymously to protect those individuals who wished to provide candid perspectives and, sometimes, confidential information.

CONCLUSION

This book explicates the rise of political authority at international organizations by analyzing the change over time in the international demand for and IAEA supply of collective action on nuclear policy: facilitating international bargaining, monitoring nuclear behavior, and supplying nuclear policy outcomes from standards setting and development assistance to enforcement of the nonproliferation regime. The IAEA may offer economies of scale in monitoring and provide a forum for policy negotiations, but it emerges as a politically significant actor with the authority to issue rules and make commands with which states feel pulled to comply. The nuclear authority of the IAEA varies, though, across issue areas in ways that provides additional opportunities to understand the causes of political authority.

This work is significant for offering the first institutional analysis of the expanding authority of an understudied international organization that is pivotal to contemporary international security issues: the IAEA. By explaining cooperation on one of the most important international security issues—the proliferation of nuclear weapons—we can learn much about the weaknesses of the nonproliferation regime and its prospects for reform and reinvigoration. Understanding international nuclear authority is one corner of a research agenda that scholars must undertake collectively if we are to understand why international organizations sometimes possess the power to issue rules or commands with which states expect they must comply. This book will therefore also help us understand the role of the other international institutions that may now be evolving from multinational meetings into agents of global governance, including the IMF, World Health Organization, and UN Security Council.

There are three implications of this analysis for international politics more generally. First, international institutions do not just exist in the world but must be created by specific actors to accomplish specific goals and are costly to change. International organizations are constructed when cooperation is necessary but other forms of cooperation are insufficiently appropriate or effective for producing the desired outcomes. The design of these international agents is important to their ability to bias outcomes in favor of these goals. Second, once international organizations are created, they become actors in their own right with some autonomy, authority, and legitimacy to intervene in political interactions, though they vary in these qualities just as states are more or less sovereign. Third, the proliferation of an array of global problems that defy easy solution, including but not limited to nuclear proliferation, calls into question an international system predicated upon the freedom of states from accountability—sovereignty—in these problem issue areas. The authority of international organizations offers solutions but also challenges for their principals (directly, states, and indirectly, the citizens of these states) when the design of these international organizations means they may not be fully accountable to all their principals.

NOTES

1. Nuclear physicists bemoan the use of the term "atomic" because everything contains atoms. A nuclear bomb is "nuclear" because nuclear processes are responsible for creating the energy released.

2. There is an extensive literature debating the effectiveness of deterrence, either nuclear or conventional, as well as a "revisionist" camp of historians who argue that the Soviets were not deterred because they had no aggressive intentions, only defensive concerns.

3. "Treaty Banning Nuclear Weapon Tests in the Atmosphere, in Outer Space and Under Water" (1963). Also referred to as the Partial Test Ban Treaty, or PTBT.

4. An NWS is defined in Article IX of the treaty as any state that "manufactured and exploded a nuclear weapon or other nuclear explosive device prior to 1 January 1967."

5. The founding seven members of the London Club were Canada, France, the Federal Republic of Germany (West Germany), Japan, the Soviet Union, the United Kingdom, and the United States, though another eight states joined by 1978 (Thorne 1997).

6. India was believed to have put away its nuclear program after demonstrating in 1974 that it had a nuclear capability, leaving only Israel and South Africa as strongly suspected of having successful nuclear weapons programs.

7. The directive to verify the accuracy and completeness of South Africa's declaration precedes its inclusion for the implementation of North Korea's safeguards agreement; see von Baeckmann, Dillon, and Perricos (1995). South Africa did not ask the IAEA to verify its disarmament until 1993.

8. See, for example, Aloise (2011), Findlay (2003, 2012a), Goldschmidt (2008a), Hibbs and Persbo (2009), and Lewis (2011).

9. See, for example, Lavigne, Maier, and Santor (2009), Martin (2003), and Steinwand and Stone (2008).

10. This description is similar to that used by Barnett and Finnemore (1999, 707), who argue impersonality "is 'rational' in that it deploys socially recognized relevant knowledge to create rules that determine how goals will be pursued."

11. See, for example, Brown (2009), Lake (2009), and Tannenwald (2007).

2

Theory of Authority

GIVEN THE RESILIENCE of international anarchy and state sovereignty, it would be surprising if the IAEA has power over any area of state behavior at all. The theory of political authority argues, first, that international nuclear authority is in demand when persistent conflicts of interest and nuclear policy uncertainty prevent states from coordinating to supply collective action on nuclear issues. Second, an international organization acquires nuclear authority only when it aggregates and successfully deploys resources and expertise through impersonal procedures to supply the nuclear policy outcomes desired by the international community. Political authority is more than a conduit for multilateral coordination or great power collusion. Neither is it the shadow of hegemonic interests or compelling norms of behavior. This does not mean the authority of an international organization is complete or uncontested, but it is observable as the contingent power, in the absence of a coercive capacity, to elicit accommodation and compliance by other actors with its rules and commands.

NUCLEAR COLLECTIVE ACTION PROBLEMS

If one thing is clear in recent discussions by Robert Rauchhaus, Matthew Kroenig, and Erik Gartzke (2011) and Scott Sagan (2011), nuclear scholars are only beginning to understand the causes and consequences of nuclear proliferation. Nuclear weapons, argue John Mearsheimer (2001) and Kenneth Waltz (2002), may create conditions for peace by making war with a nuclear weapon state too costly to consider. Nuclear weapons may also bring great international prestige, bolster the political power of individual leaders or substate groups, or feed civilian technological and industrial achievements (Sagan 1996–97; Solingen 2007; Rublee 2009). Faced with these powerful incentives, more than twenty states have seriously explored nuclear weapons, and ten have successfully built them: first the United States, then the Soviet Union (now Russia), followed by the United Kingdom, France, China, Israel, India, South Africa, Pakistan, and, most recently, North Korea.[1]

While many states lack the domestic capacity or the right friends, dozens of states have chosen to not pursue nuclear weapons, some because they believe they would be more secure if neither they nor their neighbors possessed nuclear weapons (Sagan 2002). Others believe they would face a greater risk if crises occurred in the shadow of nuclear war (George and Smoke 1974; R. Powell 2003). Practicing self-restraint exposes individual states to the fundamental challenge of the security dilemma: How can states avoid the unilateral pursuit of security, pondered Jervis (1978), if doing so will leave them all worse off?

Some oppose nuclear proliferation by others because of serious doubts about a state's ability to control the use of such dangerous weapons (Sagan 2002; Brown 2007–8). And a few states have voluntarily disarmed, giving up their weapons. Did their security conditions change, or did nuclear weapons bring only unwanted attention and social opprobrium, as Rublee (2009) and Tannenwald (2007) argue? Controlling access by others to the "absolute weapon" similarly exposes states to the free rider problem: Which states should pay to enforce restraint by others while some happily avoid the costs?

While states have unilaterally pursued proliferation and counterproliferation, cooperative efforts to increase the cost of acquiring nuclear weapons fall into the general category of nonproliferation. The demand for nonproliferation is a function of the demand for nuclear weapons, which is affected by arms control and disarmament agreements (Schelling 1960; Jervis 1978); alliance politics, such as for the North Atlantic Treaty Organization (Koremenos 2001; Kydde 2001); and the strength of norms of nuclear deterrence (Scoblic 2001; Waltz 2002). Some strategies focus on blocking supply (nonproliferation) and others on destroying capabilities (counterproliferation) or attenuating demand ("positive" and "negative" security assurances). Attempts to limit access began long before the creation of the IAEA, but today's nonproliferation regime includes norms, formal treaties, informal supplier control arrangements, and the nearly universal commitment through the Nuclear Non-Proliferation Treaty (NPT) to open to IAEA verification. The complexity of this interconnected web makes it difficult to define the scope of "nonproliferation." There is also incredible variation in who participates, and the costs are imposed more on some than others. The distributional effects of blocking supply are greater, for example, for supplier states, their recipients, and potential proliferators than for states not active in the nuclear marketplace or uninterested in proliferating.

Nuclear disarmament poses an additional challenge. Destroying the industrial infrastructure and credibly verifying the absence of weapons and the capability to make them is very difficult. International inspectors spent years trying to determine if the weapons program was dismantled in South Africa, a country that was lauded for its cooperation and transparency (von Baeckmann, Dillon, and Perricos 1995). The process did not go nearly so smoothly in Iraq, where efforts began in the summer of 1991, but IAEA director general Hans Blix reported his conclusion only in 1998 that the program was dismantled. If a state was so politically, militarily, or socially insecure that it sought nuclear weapons as a solution, what must change for others to believe promises to disarm are credible? The profound technical challenge makes it necessary for states to also prove their interests have changed from when they were motivated to seek nuclear weapons in the first place.

The independent pursuit of nuclear weapons requires acquiring other nuclear technologies. The reactors that make electricity and the isotopes needed for medicine, agriculture, or industry require fissile materials as fuel. Some reactors run on natural uranium (0.07 percent Uranium-235), which requires mining and processing uranium ore into a metal form. Others require that the uranium fuel be purified or "enriched" to 3 percent to 5 percent Uranium-235, sometimes called low-enriched uranium (LEU). Enrichment on a scale suitable for supplying energy or weapons programs can be accomplished using any of several incremental processes, of which gas centrifuges are currently most popular, but states have also historically used magnetic separation and gaseous diffusion. Some reactors, especially early research reactors, run on uranium enriched above 20 percent or highly enriched uranium (HEU). Enriching uranium above 80 percent, however, makes it also suitable for nuclear weapons. Weapons-grade uranium can be a direct product of the enrichment process, or fresh reactor fuel can be diverted and the enriched uranium chemically extracted. Reactor fuel once "spent" still contains most of its original stock of fissile material as well as radioactive waste products and can be reprocessed to extract plutonium for reactor fuel or nuclear weapons. These technologies are inherently "dual-use," facilitating both nuclear weapons and peaceful applications.

Many states also fear other potential transborder effects of peaceful nuclear uses. Preventing accidents through nuclear safety includes the preventive and response measures for safely operating, transporting, and storing nuclear materials. In the early years of the nuclear age, this meant protecting local populations from radiation-releasing accidents. Recently safety has expanded to include also providing for the secure exploitation of nuclear technology: protecting it from theft or other misuse by insiders, terrorists, or enemy states. Many of the same processes improve both, but there is now a policy distinction between preventing accidents (nuclear safety) and preventing deliberate actions (nuclear security).

The normative, political, and technological overlap between the four nuclear issue areas complicates effective collective action on any one without adversely affecting interests on each other, much less other issues. States have different interests on each, and other issues, as well as a varying capacity to contribute to collective action. Unfortunately, states have little objective means to evaluate the effectiveness of the many, and sometimes competing, strategies. They are also trying to apply strategies against a growing and evolving population as political fragmentation, economic globalization, technological development, and the proliferation of nuclear technologies make new actors relevant. In short, the absence of a consensus within or among the four nuclear issue areas on appropriate goals and effective strategies has persistently interfered with attempts to collectively bargain, monitor, and implement nuclear policy.

THE SUPPLY OF NUCLEAR COOPERATION

Despite these recurring barriers to cooperation on nuclear policy issues, we do observe extensive collective action. The alphabet of nonproliferation institutions illustrates its great variation, including test ban treaties (limited, or LTBT; peaceful nuclear explosives, or PNET; threshold, or TTBT; and comprehensive, or CTBT), export controls (Coordinating Committee for Multilateral Export Controls, or COCOM; and the Nuclear Suppliers Group, or NSG), the NPT, several nuclear weapon–free zones (NWFZ), and the Proliferation Security Initiative (PSI). In addition to the most well-known institutions, a search of the United Nations Treaty Collection Database finds more than five thousand records describing "nuclear" or "atomic" bilateral and multilateral agreements for supply of technology or materials, promotion of nuclear science, arms control, verification, legal liability frameworks, and safety protocols.

The IAEA stands out, however, because of its centrality to international nuclear diplomacy. How do we explain the possibility that this international organization has acquired the power to issue rules and make commands to states over nuclear nonproliferation? Why has it not acquired equal authority over other nuclear issues? The possibility that any international organization has acquired independent political authority over any policy area is a challenge to the way that many scholars explain the causes and effects of international organizations.

Structural Constraints

Structural theories of international politics argue that international organizations have little independent influence over state behavior once we account for the material and social factors that exist outside individual political interactions, constraining the set of strategies available to individual actors and therefore the possible outcomes. For structural realists such as Kenneth Waltz (1979), the distribution of material power in the system is the structural condition that drives the most important international outcomes we observe. The absence of an overarching political authority—anarchy—makes any cooperation, but especially on security issues, hard to achieve or sustain "for fear that the other side will cheat on the agreement and gain a relative advantage" (Mearsheimer 1994, 13). Randall Stone (2011) argues that key design features of the International Monetary Fund (IMF) are compromised if some principals possess extraordinary formal or informal influence over its actions. The United States used its exceptional informal influence in the 1940s and 1950s to impose conditions for lending to force recipient states into economic reforms (until other members formally accepted "conditionality"; see Brown 2010) and now periodically compels the bureaucracy to ignore these rules (Stone 2011, 197–200). The United States also now uses its formal voting power to block important changes at the IMF, including any changes that would erase its veto over those changes.

International organizations exist and have effects, realists conclude, because they are imposed on weaker states by more powerful ones when it is in their self-interest to do so (Wallander, Haftendorn, and Keohane 1999). International organizations, they believe, can have effects independent of their great power masters only if they can be observed forcing these powerful states to behave in direct violation of their self-interest. However, because it is easy to identify examples in which the order they attempt to supply is violated by self-interested great powers, international organizations do not have independent effects or, therefore, authority. If true, however, why do powerful states go through the exercise (and cost) of creating them in the first place? And why do they persist despite the weakening of their sponsors or end of their ostensible purpose?

Social constructivists argue, as James Fearon and Alexander Wendt (2002) summarize, the effects of international organizations are largely products of the norms, beliefs, and identities constructed in social processes that define the behaviors and outcomes that are more or less appropriate for populations of states and other actors. March and Olsen (1999) describe an ongoing interaction between states, international organizations, and other nonstate actors that constructs and reconstructs how constructions of "appropriate" are defined. These norms, beliefs, and identities are often issue specific and support specific strategies or outcomes as more or less appropriate, such as those governing how states fight wars (Johnstone 2008a) or treat their own citizens (Finnemore 1996; Greenhill 2010). Following social constructivist arguments, the IAEA's influence over states could be a by-product of the increasing coercive effect of two types of norms.

First, norms about appropriate policy processes may support the employment of particular institutional forms (Meyer and Rowan 1977; Eyre and Suchman 1996). Stronger international procedural norms of multilateralism (Finnemore 1996) and internationalization (Avant, Finnemore, and Sell 2010; Mitchell and Powell 2011), especially when encountering the weakening appropriateness of state sovereignty (Caporaso 1996), should make international organizations the appropriate way for states to pursue their foreign policy interests. International organizations, they argue, became preferred over other multilateral and unilateral options because they were negotiated by accepted processes (Hathaway 2002, 1958; Hurd 2007), designed to be procedurally and substantively similar to domestic institutions (Mitchell and Powell 2011), and actively consented to and maintained by states (Franck 1992; Bodansky 2008). Hurd (2007), for example, argues that international organizations can exercise "sovereign authority" if states internalize the belief that they "ought to be obeyed." Further, Meyer and Rowan (1977) argue that the professionalization of international behavior, from the employment of regular state representatives to bureaucratization, may also contribute to the construction that international organizations are "modern" responses, much as international conferences were in the late nineteenth century. Internalization of procedural norms of internationalization is undermined, Barnett and Finnemore (2004, 303–35) argue, to the extent that international bureaucracies are perceived to be more weakened than national bureaucracies by politically expedient excessive or illogical limitations on action, unreliable funding, and stochastic intervention by their principals. The Security Council's authority, therefore, is undermined when it fails to act as others believe it should (Rosand 2004).

Second, international rules and contracts only formalize the appropriate norms, principals, and identities already being constructed and internalized in the international social environment (Bull 1977; Wendt 1992; Finnemore and Sikkink 1998; Buzan and Little 2000). While international treaties and standards prescribe nonproliferation behaviors, most states agree and comply because they have already internalized the belief that proliferation is disreputable, illegitimate, or psychotic (Tannenwald 1999; Rublee 2009). Several scholars have identified a "nuclear taboo," a norm of non-use that "stigmatized nuclear weapons as unacceptable weapons" despite there being no legal prohibition against using them (Tannenwald 2007, 2).[2] These norms slowly replaced the prestige and power nuclear weapons had earlier conferred upon states (Sagan 1996–97). However, they have not replaced alternative security norms about the appropriateness of nuclear deterrence (Scoblic 2001; Waltz 2002), despite its many critics (Wilson 2008; Walker 2011). These competing nuclear norms affect security behavior but also exist alongside environmental norms affecting nuclear testing and nuclear energy (Wittner 1993; Freedman 2003).

In short, particular nuclear and procedural norms compete as they are internalized and transmitted (advocated) by state leaders, societal groups, and epistemic communities in ways that attribute and maintain perceived authority. If social structure is causal, the IAEA could be only one venue for construction of international norms that constrain how people value nuclear weapons, nuclear energy, and nuclear safety and security. It may simply be a social environment for behavioral and procedural norm socialization as IAEA bureaucrats and diplomats compete over, internalize, and transmit home new intersubjective understandings of appropriate nuclear behavior (Adler and Barnett 1998; Moravcsik 2000; Checkel 2005). The IAEA may also sometimes fail to perform as expected when norm competition creates conflicting expectations (Chayes and Chayes 1993). Its successes and failures may also affect broader beliefs in the international community about the legitimacy of internationalization.

The waxing and waning strength of these norms, beliefs, and identities as they compete makes it hard to determine which are dominant among any set of actors for nuclear issues, especially when any individual actor may hold mutually contradictory ideas at any one time. For example, although civil servants appear to prioritize the prestige of their organizations over personal gains, believing its actions and missions are legitimate, it is unclear if they do so because they have already internalized particular norms or are subsequently socialized by interactions within the international organization (Carpenter 2010, 55).

The coercive effects of social structure, structuralists argue, means that much about the IAEA and its alternatives—their design, their processes and outputs, and the individuals who work for or against them—are largely meaningless as actors attempt to bargain, monitor, and implement collective action on nuclear policy.

Delegation Relationships

Rational institutionalists focus on how international organizations, because they employ an international bureaucracy, differ from other strategies for producing individual or joint gains for their state masters. Like other international institutions, international organizations are discreet contracts among a group of states that lower the future costs of collective action, Frieden, Lake, and Schultz (2009) and Abbot and Snidal (1998) argue, if they create rules to guide behavior, forums for reducing the costs of joint decision making (including dispute resolution and enforcement), and mechanisms for producing information useful to making decisions (including verifying compliance). These contracts are assumed to be an efficient translation of the interests of the cooperating states, weighted by their bargaining power (Downs, Rocke, and Barsoom 1996; Koremenos, Lipson, and Snidal 2001). Excluding some of the relevant but more problematic states or requiring fewer or smaller compromises of them can ease these barriers to cooperation but also compromises the effectiveness of the institution. While the Convention on the Law of the Seas may be mostly effective without US ratification, for example, a climate agreement would appear hollow if the United States, China, or India refuses to join.

International institutions become more difficult to directly negotiate, verify, and enforce, however, as the number of relevant states increases, as uncertainty over state's interest in solution increases, or as uncertainty about the nature of a problem and its effective solution increases.[3] It helps, argue Olson and Zeckhauser (1966) and Keohane (1984), if a hegemon is willing to leverage its influence to produce social order.[4] Great powers have tremendous influence in the negotiations that set and adjust the institutions, but they are also constrained by their norms and rules (Krasner 1991; Steinberg 2002; Lake 2009; Schneider 2011). Lake (2009), for example, argues that weaker states negotiate and join international institutions and organizations to signal their consent to the hierarchy or "rightful rule" of a strong state. Dominant and subordinate states are both constrained only as long as the relationship efficiently supplies political order that is mutually beneficial. However, these authority relationships assume a dominant actor who already possesses an incredible coercive capacity and that authority ultimately resides in the strong state and not the international organization that appears to be implementing the contract.

International organizations differ from other institutions by employing an external agent to help states when cooperation is particularly difficult (Hawkins et al. 2006a).[5] The UN Charter created several executive "organs," including the Security Council and a secretariat, and the Statute of the IAEA created its Board of Governors and Secretariat. Contracting with or creating from scratch an executive agent for collective action requires, first, that the individual states form themselves into a collective principal. For example, the UN Charter also creates the UN General Assembly as its collective principal, and the Statute of the IAEA creates the IAEA's General Conference. Lake and McCubbins (2006) argue these contracts establish how the principals relate to each other when managing their agent.[6]

Second, a delegation contract is established between the collective principal and an external agent if it transfers to the agent the resources it needs to make decisions or take actions on their behalf (McCubbins, Noll, and Weingast 1987; Rogowski 1999). Pooling national fiscal support and issue-specific materiel and human resources can create assets specific to collective action on a specific issue. The UN Security Council, for example, not only approves peacekeeping interventions but also pools the troops and other resources needed to implement these interventions.

A delegation contract is also established when a collective principal transfers to the agent some level of autonomy or discretion to deploy resources toward the bargaining, monitoring, or implementation of collective action (Brown 2010). The traditional functionalist view focused on international organizations as technocratic bureaucracies, separated by their limited autonomy from the political disputes that normally prevented states from cooperating, that could supply economies of scale and some policy specialization (Mitrany 1948; Imber 1989). Rational institutionalists argue, however, that successful international organizations actively manage the political effects of international policy outcomes, facilitate collective decision making, create policy bias, and enhance the credibility of commitments for political actors (Hawkins et al. 2006a). This requires that the delegation contract somehow obligate the principals in some respect to accommodate their agent.[7] The UN Charter, for example, specifies conditions under which the collective membership, individual members, or other actors must follow the decisions of the Security Council.

Delegation is therefore risky if an agent has the autonomy to make decisions that differ from those its principals would prefer, becomes trapped in inefficient bureaucratic routines, or engages in mission creep (Barnett and Finnemore 2004). This autonomy may constrain the formal influence even of powerful states (Rector 2009; Schneider 2011). However, it may also open bureaucrats to excessive influence by powerful states (Urpelainen 2012), especially if resources are not exclusively allocated through the collective principal or the collective principal cannot agree to hold its agent accountable (Lake and McCubbins 2006).[8] For example, disagreements mounted among Security Council states in the mid-1990s over the UN Special Commission for Iraq (UNSCOM), criticized for bias in part because UNSCOM's intelligence, inspectors, and materiel flowed primarily from major Western powers. However, principals appear generally successful at limiting "agency slack" through a combination of screening potential agents, limiting autonomy in advance, and rewarding or punishing based on performance (McCubbins, Noll, and Weingast 1987; Hawkins and Jacoby 2008, 4).

Some are critical of the delegation metaphor because, as Thomas Risse (2000) argues, most effects connected to international organizations actually occur outside them. For example, Erica Gould (2006a) finds that states often accept IMF conditions as a cover for implementing domestically unpopular policy goals, and Beth Simmons and Allison Danner (2010) show that international human rights treaties affect state behavior by empowering new domestic actors. The international organizations themselves, therefore, are less important than the interactions they facilitate between or within states. Andrew Guzman and Jennifer Landsidle (2008, 17–18) argue that international organizations have a "negligible impact" because their collective principals so closely control them. Agents may help states prepare for meetings but do not decide who to invite, when to hold meetings, or what to include on the agenda. International organizations may help structure investments in specific assets but are basically passive conduits (Abbot and Snidal 1998; Epstein and O'Halloran 1999, 41; Martin 2006). If states can exploit private investment markets to raise capital, private satellite firms for imagery, and nongovernmental organizations for disaster response services, it seems reasonable to ask why the parties to the 1996 Comprehensive Test Ban Treaty could negotiate very precisely a monitoring system for nuclear testing but still saw a need to create even a highly limited agent.

Rational institutionalist conceptions of international organizations fall short of explaining the compelling effect that some have because the explanations rely on contracting language that assumes these political relationships are necessarily conditional in the short term. Delegation relationships, argue Hawkins and colleagues (2006b, 7), involve only "a conditional grant of authority . . . limited in time or scope and must be revocable by the principal." The legalization (Abbott et al. 2000) and rational design (Koremenos 2001) literatures argue that states are willing to cooperate because their obligations are limited by expiration and escape clauses. Barnett and Finnemore (2004, 22–25) argue that the authority of international organizations is "always authority on loan" and Lake (2009) sees the hierarchy between states, sometimes implemented through international organizations, as a consensual and revocable social contract. By implying a limited, revocable, and hierarchic relationship between states and international organizations in which states dominate and are free to withdraw, their accounts struggle to explain the persistence and growing effect on state behavior of some international organizations.

The conditionality of delegation could decline over time if states cannot terminate or adapt existing institutions to the current distribution of interests and capabilities as efficiently as rational institutionalists theorize. Daniel Carpenter (2001, 4) finds that US government bureaucracies acquire leverage because they "provide unique services, author new solutions to troubling national dilemmas, operate with newfound efficiency, or offer special protection to the public." This power is observable as the autonomy to "change the agendas and preferences of politicians and the organized public" (15). In his study of the emergent legitimacy of the US Food and Drug

Administration (FDA), Carpenter (2010, 15) writes, "Power exists not only in broad formal authority to direct the behavior of others (directive power) but also in appearances that are less obvious: the ability to define what sorts of problems, debates, and agendas structure human activity (gatekeeping power), and the ability to shape the content and structure of human cognition itself (conceptual power)" (15). The difficulty with many of these studies is that they discuss the observables of autonomy and its effects but rarely examine new demand for agents and cannot examine how agency evolves outside the highly hierarchic and legalized domestic environment. In Daniel Carpenter's studies, again as an example, it is unclear how reliant FDA authority is upon a domestic context where the authority of the US federal government to establish new bureaucracies is well established. In short, it still remains unclear how authority or legitimacy is constructed or maintained.

Historical institutionalists argue that policymakers evaluate the possible gains and costs of new strategies relative to the certainty of the existing institutional landscape (Fioretos 2011). The decision to create or reform institutions is a reaction to a particular constellation of beliefs about how and why institutions should structure, monitor, and enforce interactions within that issue area. The power of the IAEA to affect outcomes, they might suggest, is the result of choices by boundedly rational actors at different, and possibly chance, points in history. The IAEA, therefore, may not be a perfectly efficient outcome (we can imagine better alternatives) but still loses flexibility over time as the norms and rules of the Agency, the nonproliferation regime, and the international system are accepted as specific assets with known value to cooperation.

Others argue that the conditionality of delegation to an international organization may be reduced, and authority enhanced, by its legitimacy (Levi 1988; Bodansky 1999; Hurrell 2005). In its narrowest conception, according to Bodansky (2008), legitimacy is lawfulness: institutions possess rational-legal legitimacy if their creation and procedures accord with existing law. Thomas Franck (1990), for example, argues that states experience "compliance-pull" when an appropriate process creates rules with behavioral clarity, internal rationality, and a connection with existing rules. Hurd (2007, 7) argues that states internalize the belief an international organization "ought to be obeyed" and possesses "sovereign authority" when its outputs follow from accepted procedures and are fair but collectively favorable. Legitimacy may also derive from the quality of its policy outputs, and Hurd (2008b, 27) argues that states which accept outputs as "legitimate" tend to forgo subjecting specific decisions to comply with these outputs to a cost-benefit analysis.[9] The IAEA may acquire legitimacy, therefore, if its outputs are produced within the boundaries of international law, are produced by multilateral management of a professional, bureaucratized international organization, and are generally favorable.

Unfortunately, "legitimacy" is an incomplete explanation for the power international organizations may be exercising. Identifying legitimacy is often circular. In Bruce Cronin and Ian Hurd's (2008, 3) discussion of the UN Security Council, for example, its authority "depends on its ability to gain recognition as the body with the legitimate authority to take a particular action on a particular matter." Relying on the legitimacy of international organizations to explain their power to elicit compliance is also problematic when the preconditions for legitimacy are already present in the delegation story: institutional design, congruence with principal interests, and success in producing outcomes. It is not simply that an international organization acquires, as Barnett and Finnemore (2004) argue, technical legitimacy if its expertise is respected, rational-legal legitimacy if it acquires the "perception of procedural justice and neutral fairness" from applying its rules evenly, or moral legitimacy if its goals or processes accord with accepted norms of behavior. Legitimacy may also be a sociological effect of how well an international organization's goals and processes, from the collective principal on down, concord with norms of appropriate behavior. Legitimacy is largely an intervening variable such that adding "legitimacy" to the "delegation" metaphor to explain why an international organization "ought to be obeyed" provides us with little traction for understanding the source of its political authority.

Political scientists are therefore missing crucial aspects of the relationship between states and international organizations by characterizing their power as subsequent effects of hegemony, joint decision making, collective expectations, social environments, legalization, or delegation. The power with which some international organizations appear to now direct agendas, define issues, create and implement rules, and even judge and enforce compliance suggests that their effects are not captured by these explanations. However, the purpose of this study is not to reject realist arguments about power, constructivist explanations of constitutive norms, or rational institutionalist assumptions about the efficiency and conditionality of relational contracts. Rather, this study views each of the dominant paradigms as methodological bets on which sets of assumptions are generally useful to explaining our political world (Lake and Powell 1999; Frieden, Lake, and Schultz 2009). Their generality limits the explanatory power they hold when scholars descend from grand theorizing into the breach of problem-driven research. To understand the independent power an international organization can acquire over its state masters requires a new conceptualization of international organizations and their effects upon international politics.

THE THEORY OF INTERNATIONAL POLITICAL AUTHORITY

Why does the IAEA have the power to issue rules, make commands, and take actions on nuclear nonproliferation with which states feel pulled to comply? An agent is not strictly necessary to supply many of the services that international organizations could. And the IAEA does not have this power over other nuclear issues. I argue an international organization acquires authority if it repeatedly succeeds in overcoming the persistent barriers among its principals to their cooperating on an issue. For an agent to acquire authority, and to receive from states their accommodation and compliance with its rules and commands, states must want outcomes they cannot more directly produce *and* the agent must successfully supply these outcomes over time.

States demand international political authority when they encounter persistent barriers to cooperation. First, states demand international political authority when persistently faced with uncertainty over the possible effects of policy choices. Policy uncertainty can result from past underinvestment in understanding the issue area. It may increase because of changing technologies, new conceptions of the problem, or increased problem complexity (the issue becomes more integrated with other issues). Persistent nuclear policy uncertainty, for example, can result from future uncertainty in the technologies and economic organization of nuclear energy production, or external verification of those activities, as states encourage investment in new types of reactors. Persistent uncertainty can also exist if the political economy threatens to change, such as if nuclear production can diffuse through new pathways or to new actors. Including new or changing populations can affect policy effectiveness if there are domestic differences in their economic structure or political institutions. Mechanisms for verifying international compliance among liberal democracies, such as relying on a free press or free market to produce relevant information, may not carry over if cooperation is expanded to include states that lack these institutions.

To overcome policy uncertainty, states demand policy partiality: new or greater investments in specific assets helpful to identifying and achieving policy goals. An international organization whose management and staff are screened, selected, and rewarded for investing in policy expertise can generate new policy information (McCubbins, Noll, and Weingast 1987). The resulting expertise can enable the agent to recommend or implement policy partial to producing particular goals. International courts, for example, help states adjudicate among competing interpretations of international law through the expert and unbiased application of international law by judges (Alter 2008). Barnett and Finnemore (2004, 52) show that the IMF has become influential because its economists created new theories and techniques that enable its staff and others to effectively intervene in currency crises. World Bank professionals contribute not only objective expertise in development economics but also partiality in their interest in promoting economic development.[10] International organizations with policy partiality are motivated to supply the policy outcomes their principals are otherwise unable to supply themselves.

Successfully supplying policy partiality is more likely with continuous investment in the issue area. This includes policy expertise but also other specific assets employed by an international organization's management and staff, such as professional management, bureaucratic processes, and relationships with governments and epistemic communities (Adler 1992; Carpenter 2010, 45–47). These relationships create information multipliers, improving responsiveness to new technologies, better procedures, and potential employees. They also help the agent to transmit information about its successes to relevant external audiences. As with any entrepreneurial activity, there is a risk the agent will create specific assets inappropriate to the agency gains desired by its principals or redundant to the investments of others.

Second, states also demand authority when cooperation on one issue dimension is prevented by persistent differences in how they value outcomes on other issues. This barrier to cooperation can create persistent concern about motivated biases (Calvert 1985) and disagreement over specific cases (Brown 2011). For example, the United States may consistently support global nonproliferation efforts, but its other economic and security interests often prevent it from uniformly applying nonproliferation norms and rules (Zunes 2005). The need to insulate nuclear policy choices from the effects of persistent conflicts of interest creates demand for what Barnett and Finnemore (2004, 18) describe as an international organization's bureaucratic impersonality: rule-governed administration by trained and neutral officials. Recruitment procedures, oaths of support, acculturation, and personnel management can make international bureaucrats more successful at moderating among competing biases on other issue dimensions (Kahler 2001). The IAEA, for example, tries to control national biases by using multinational teams and by not placing individuals from nuclear weapon states in charge of safeguards monitoring. The leaders of international organizations must usually have the promise of maintaining a sufficiently wide coalition to be appointed in the first place. Supportive relationships with relevant stakeholder audiences can also supply behavioral information about national evolving interests (Adler 1992; Carpenter 2010).

Impersonality also works to insulate individual states from accountability for their agent's decisions in the short run. Reducing the agent's permeability to immediate formal influence by individual principals protects status quo policies until the collective principal organizes to redirect the agent. Even powerful states with extraordinary formal and informal influence are usually unable to unilaterally revise the delegation contract (Gould 2006b). Randall Stone (2011, 170–72), for example, discusses how Japan opposed but was unable to convince other IMF directors to modify the conditions imposed on IMF loans for Indonesia in 1997.[11] The international organization can therefore take the blame for policies that are in the collective interest but are also strongly opposed by domestic interest groups in some countries.

To summarize, uncertainty can impede cooperation: policy uncertainty creates demand for policy partial to achieving a particular goal while the individual incentives to be strategic—free-riding or pursuing divergent interests—creates demand for behavioral impersonality. While flexibility provisions can limit the effects of uncertainty, they also limit the gains from cooperation (Koremenos 2001). If a single rule or command provides a lasting solution, then there is no demand for political authority; no matter how powerful or "authoritative" the rule, the issuing agent can be discarded.[12] I argue that the demand for an international political authority is greater with more persistent demand to alleviate policy or behavioral uncertainty. Success is more likely with investment in useful specific assets: the expertise needed for policy partiality and a professional bureaucracy consciously attentive to building behavioral impersonality.

The demand for nuclear authority increases with new and more severe nuclear policy problems. The threat that a state perceives when another state acquires nuclear weapons is a highly subjective experience, but the collective international demand for cooperation on nuclear nonproliferation, disarmament, and nuclear security should increase if nuclear (or radiological) weapons increase in salience. The cost of uncoordinated action has been persistent since before the Baruch Plan failed but also appears to increase when existing stockpiles seem more likely to be used, new actors find acquiring nuclear arsenals easier, and acquisition by new actors makes use seem more likely. There is no simple linear relationship between the numbers of nuclear weapons or possessors and the threat of use: the identity of the particular proliferator matters, multiple thresholds exist, and both seem to change over time.

Similarly, the demand for nuclear safety cooperation will increase if the transnational risks of nuclear operations appear to worsen. Demand for nonproliferation and safety cooperation overlap with demand for cooperation on nuclear security to the extent threats are increasingly from nonstate actors seeking to misuse existing nuclear capabilities. And demand for cooperation on peaceful nuclear supply for medicine, agriculture, and science should increase if nuclear solutions become relatively more valuable but existing markets persistently fail to meet this demand. An international organization that successfully meets demand for agency gains over time—and demonstrates its success is a result of its autonomous choices—is more likely to acquire authority. This relationship is illustrated in the top right quadrant in figure 2.1.

Demand for political authority, however, is persistent demand for impersonality and policy partiality that more limited or temporary agents are unable to supply over time. If the collective principal successfully micro-manages its international organization, implying the need for limited if persistent agency gains, then we may observe an agent with no claim to authority. For example, because its principals could negotiate in detail its International Monitoring System, the Comprehensive Test Ban Treaty Organization appears to need indefinite but only minimal levels of impersonality and policy partiality. It likely belongs in the bottom left quadrant. A possible bottom-right example, where demand is extraordinary in partiality and impersonality but fleeting, is the UN Special Commission to disarm Iraq in the 1990s.

The top-left scenario—high demand and poor success in supply—is observed when states are trying to learn about the benefits of different strategies or because the agents they choose are failing to adequately satisfy the states they must to acquire a monopoly. If multiple agents can supply policy partiality or impersonality, states can compete to find the one that best satisfies their individual demand for agency gains. Mark Pollack and Gregory Shaffer (2009), for example, examine conflict in the 1990s between the United States and Europe over which institution should regulate genetically modified organisms. In addition to various unilateral actions on nuclear policy by individual states, a list by the Center for Nonproliferation Studies includes over thirty active multilateral nuclear nonproliferation institutions that effectively compete to affect nuclear policy outcomes.[13]

International organizations that are more successful over time should be rewarded with greater investment of resources and autonomy, ultimately achieving a greater monopoly over accommodation and compliance with their rules and commands. Monopolization can occur horizontally as international organizations and other transnational actors compete with each

Figure 2.1. Demand and Supply of Authority

other to supply political authority. Celeste Wallander (2000) argues that NATO "defeated" other European security institutions after the Cold War because it was easier to adapt even if its original purpose was further afield than the alternatives. The Comprehensive Test Ban Treaty Organization could perhaps move to the bottom-right quadrant if it applied its unique seismic monitoring expertise to become an authoritative source of advanced warnings of tsunamis. Its authority would be limited to initiating certain disaster responses, though, rather than over nuclear testing. Vertical monopolization also occurs, such as in the ongoing debate over whether UN states consented to the Security Council using its obligation to maintain international peace and security to extend beyond specific events to create a legislative source for international law (Rosand 2004; Joyner 2011–12).[14] Vertical transfers of autonomy and resources to international organizations, not only to the IAEA but also to international financial institutions and international courts, are central to debates over sovereignty (Krasner 1999). Agents can create new space for monopolizing political authority by using their partiality and impersonality to frame issues (offering new concepts, techniques, or measures), drive the agenda, and anticipate states' needs (Carpenter 2001, 15, 33–34).

The continuous nature of this competition means that authority over policy areas is always contested (Cronin and Hurd 2008). International financial institutions are widely accused of being compromised by the undue influence of a few wealthy states, especially the United States (Dreher and Jensen 2007; Urpelainen 2012). If previously authoritative agents recurrently fail to provide the policy partiality or impersonality their principals require, states will probably retract authority and experiment with new agents or strategies. Even successful international organizations must demonstrate that their ongoing agency is necessary to policy success; otherwise they can become highly circumscribed (limited delegation) or even dismissed (temporary delegation).

In summary, persistent international demand for agency gains is demand for international political authority. States that see cooperation impeded by persistent policy uncertainty demand an international authority to supply policy partiality. States that experience conflicts of interests on other issues preventing cooperation need the behavioral impersonality of an international authority. An international organization that successfully meets persistent demand for agency gains over time can become an international political authority: an actor with the power to issue rules and commands with which others feel pulled to comply.

INFERRING POLITICAL AUTHORITY

Political authority is a complex outcome that is difficult to directly observe because international organizations largely do not draw their authority from charisma, a coercive apparatus, or in grant from an extant authority. Functional and normative demand drives their creation but ad hoc processes negotiate and design them, often under incredible influence by great powers, leaving only temporary constitutional legitimacy. Their authority therefore derives primarily from *how* they serve states, but this poses an inference problem: authority is continuously contested, some commands are obviously illegitimate, and compliance is often problematic or coerced (Cronin and Hurd 2008, 17). However, international authority does have observable effects upon other actors that demonstrate the power to elicit accommodation and compliance.

First, political authority is empowered by the transfer of resources or autonomy to an agent. The absolute size of the agent's budget and staff, the extent of its responsibilities, or the principals' obligations are largely observable and important indicators of accommodation (Brown 2010). It is an empirical challenge to compare how "expert" are staff, to know with certainty how much states contribute indirectly or in kind, or how to compare to competing actors or alternative strategies. Why these change as states allocate resources or autonomy from among alternative uses is also suggestive for measuring authority because authority is a strategic bet. Conservative politicians in the United States were very concerned in 2002 that signing the Rome Statute of the International Criminal Court and Secretary of State Colin Powell's request of the Security Council to support military action against Iraq were too great a sacrifice of US sovereign powers. If an international organization increasingly monopolizes supply of policy within an issue area, then this should necessarily compromise or attenuate the independent ability of other actors to challenge its rules and commands.

Second, authority can be inferred from how states otherwise adjust their behavior to accommodate an agent's conceptualization, regulation, and implementation of norms and rules (Carpenter 2010). States often have the flexibility to increase their accommodation with greater political support, policymaker attention, voluntary payments, provision of cost-free experts, or in-kind contributions, including supporting conferences, personnel training, and materiel. Audiences signal declining respect for an agent's authority when they ignore its regulations of the issue area and resources and attention are instead given to other agents.

Accommodation is especially observed in how states comply with specific agent commands. Compliance occurs when states alter their behavior to comply with specific agent orders given directly to them. International organizations also confront a second-order compliance problem when their commands to one state require compliance by other relevant actors to be effective (Decker, Stiehler, and Strobel 2003). Security Council sanctions present such a problem because the United Nations needs individual members to implement sanctions on the collective behalf. Compliance is not a simple dichotomous choice, however. States can challenge parts of an agent's command but not its right to command, or they can revoke their consent to be commanded. For example, Iran has disputed whether it needs to report certain information but does not challenge the IAEA's general authority to expect information and report on compliance. States can appeal to alternative sources of authority, such as North Korea's failed attempt to solicit bilateral verification of the 1994 Agreed Framework or the US reliance on the Iraq Survey Group after 2003.

The power of the theory of political authority is its ability to explain how international organizations influence state behavior better than the three primary alternative theories of delegation, hegemonic influence, and coercive social norms. Delegation and political authority are both characterized by the transfer of resources, rights, or responsibilities. Delegation, however, implies that the agent's rules and commands result from effective multilateral control and that states comply because these outputs reflect their interests (Downs, Rocke, and Barsoom 1996). A highly circumscribed relationship should be observable in limited agent autonomy to affect bargaining, implementation, and enforcement.

In contrast, the theory of political authority expects successful agents to acquire greater autonomy. Autonomy for bargaining increases with the breadth and depth of policy areas for which the agent has competence to advise, propose, or even unilaterally set policy (Brown 2010). International organizations with greater implementation autonomy may design, offer, and alter or promote a greater variety of services. Greater monitoring autonomy, for example, includes greater flexibility to define the data to be collected; design and implement international organization access to a state's people, places, and information; and monopolize analysis of that data. Implementation autonomy may extend, implicitly or explicitly, to withholding services, issuing recommendations, or judging compliance. Reporting on compliance can be significant as a signal to enforcement by third parties. Erica Gould (2006b), for example, notes that private investors use IMF decisions as a signal. Political authority, therefore, qualitatively differs from delegation in the extent to which states have compromised their sovereignty (Krasner 1999, 27–33): the more states accept, accommodate, and comply with the autonomy of an international organization over national rules and commands, in either domestic or foreign policies, the more they accept its authority.

Political authority also has some effects similar to those caused by hegemonic influence if the international organization serves primarily as an extension of hegemonic coercion. The hegemonic or hierarchic control hypothesis has less power to explain outcomes, however, if the international organization is observed to resist or not comply with the rules and commands of its powerful states. The more the outputs of the international organization diverge from those the hegemon would prefer, and especially if the two enter into periods of open disagreement, the more this suggests the hierarchic relationship has been inverted in favor of the agent's authority.

International organizations may also lack agency in their effects if their rules and commands codify already existing and coercive norms of behavior. If the international social structure compels states to comply with norms of appropriate behavior, their nuclear policy choices should be observed being severely constrained by strong norms of nuclear nonproliferation, non-use, deterrence, or prestige. This requires, however, that international nuclear norms provide clear expectations and temporally precede international organization rules and commands. If international nuclear norm transmission and internalization follows international organization outputs, then norm compliance may instead be symptomatic of the pull of agent authority.

The hegemonic influence and nuclear norms hypotheses also imply effects that occur beyond a single international organization. Powerful states should be able to compel outcomes upon others not only within a single international organization or a single issue but also across issue areas. Renee de Nevers (2007) argues that this coercion may play a social role, too, introducing and then enforcing new norms of behavior. If actors are being socialized to the appropriateness of international bureaucratization, the reliance on international organizations should be evidenced by a general pattern of international institutional isomorphism. In short, if the appearance of international nuclear authority is an artifact of structural factors, normative or material, similar effects should be observed across the range of nuclear cooperation.

CONCLUSIONS

The demand for an international nuclear authority to supply unrealized collective action on international nuclear issues should increase with persistent conflicts of interest and persistent uncertainty about the effects of alternative nuclear policies. The central claim made in this book is that the IAEA has acquired authority over nuclear nonproliferation because of its ongoing investments in the specific assets needed to supply the policy partiality and behavioral impersonality in demand by the international community. Its nonproliferation authority is observed when audiences increasingly accommodate its rules and commands. This compliance with its nuclear authority is not expected to be complete but will be constantly contested, including especially by states asserting their sovereign authority to act in their own interests.

NOTES

1. This excludes Belarus, Kazakhstan, and Ukraine, which had nuclear weapons on their territories when they became independent of the Soviet Union.

2. One exception is the International Court of Justice Advisory Opinion, "Legality of the Threat or Use of Nuclear Weapons" (July 8, 1996). See Bello and Bekker (1997).

3. State interests may be materialist or normative in origins, and may be fixed, variable, or recursive, but interest similarity and interest uncertainty will affect the supply of cooperation in any form. See Koremenos, Lipson, and Snidal (2001).

4. See also: Ikenberry (2001). This contrasts with the view of a hegemon that coercively enforces order. See Kindleberger (1973) and Mearsheimer (2001).

5. See also Bradley and Kelley (2008b); Brown (2010); Koremenos (2008); Pollack (1997). On intrastate or domestic delegation, see Alesina and Tabellini (2007); Bendor, Glazer, and Hammond (2001); Dixit, Grossman, and Helpman (1997); Lupia and McCubbins (1994); Kiewiet and McCubbins (1991); McCubbins, Noll, and Weingast (1987); and McCubbins and Schwartz (1984).

6. Others argue delegation to an international legislature occurs whenever a group of actors agrees to accept decisions made according to less-than-consensus rules. See, for example, Bradley and Kelley (2008b) and McCubbins and Schwartz (1984).

7. The legalization literature describes state obligations as a critical component of institutionalizations. See Abbott et al. (2000).

8. On the problem of multiple principals, see Lyne, Nielson, and Tierney (2006).

9. Max Weber's (1978) original typology also describes tradition and charisma as sources of legitimacy. See also Gabel (1998) and Hooghe and Marks (2005).

10. Alternatively, the global availability of public health expertise may obviate need for the World Health Organization to offer substantial policy partiality for international public health issues, at least until transnational health crises worsen and states fail to resolve disputes amongst themselves over what health cooperation is necessary and when.

11. Stone (2011) also describes how the United States succeeded in blocking IMF enforcement of conditionality with Russia (1992–94).

12. Examples of rules exhibiting strong compliance pull without continuing political authority in the United States may include "drive on the right side of the road" or "dial 9-1-1 in an emergency."

13. "Inventory of International Nonproliferation Organizations & Regimes." James Martin Center for Nonproliferation Studies, updated May 10, 2013. http://cns.miis.edu/inventory/index.htm.

14. On the normative effect of Security Council decisions, see Johnstone (2008b).

3

The Birth of the IAEA, 1945–1961

SCIENTISTS INVOLVED in the secret US nuclear weapons program began advocating internationalization of atomic power before the first nuclear weapon was even tested. Their suggestion reflected an idealistic faith in internationalism and in scientific solutions to social problems. Joined by a few US government advisers, they hoped to remove nuclear science from the hands of sovereign governments. The momentum that built behind the idea that atomic power was dangerous compelled the great powers to create the United Nations Atomic Energy Commission (UNAEC) at the United Nations in 1945 to negotiate such international controls. An international approach did not succeed, however, until the creation of the IAEA in 1957.

This chapter analyzes whether demand for political authority drove the international community to create the IAEA and whether states then accommodated or otherwise complied with IAEA rules and commands across the areas of nuclear policy. It shows there was demand for an international agent in these early years of the Cold War, but this demand was conditional, limited, and influenced heavily by US interests. The initial proposals entertained at the UNAEC called for an agent that safeguarded against misuse largely by its total control, which was quite different from the limited agent states sought a few years later in the form of the IAEA. Although the Statute describes an agent with relatively grand ambitions and autonomy to act, the Secretariat was in fact given the resources only to support very narrow aspects of nuclear technology promotion, and its safeguards were limited to those that it could impose though its limited role in the nuclear market. The design and norms of the Board, representing so many of the developed member states, showed promise as an effective tool for multilateral control.

FROM "ABSOLUTE WEAPON" TO "ATOMS FOR PEACE"

The Second World War ended within days of the United States dropping a nuclear bomb on Hiroshima on August 6, 1945, and one on Nagasaki three days later. The United States decided to use the atomic bomb, essentially destroying each city with just one bomb each, to force Japan into surrendering without a land invasion but also to signal to the Soviet Union that a US atomic monopoly would be an important factor in the postwar settlement (Walker 2005).[1] This monopoly, though, was the product of a joint program with Canada and the United Kingdom. Bertrand Goldschmidt (1982, 65) describes the tensions that had formed quickly during the Manhattan Project over the future disposition of the result of their collaborations, forcing their political leaders to plan for the future within months of getting under way. By August 1943, still ten months before the first bomb could be tested, they had committed under the Quebec Agreement "not to communicate any information to third parties without mutual consent" (Roosevelt and Churchill 1943). This was the first international agreement to control nuclear technology.

Many involved in the Manhattan Project, fearful of the implications of atomic power, began to draw upon the arguments made by the popular movement for a "world solution" to the insecurity of the sovereign state system. World government was advocated during the 1940s by many who believed the sovereign state system made war inevitable, argues Lawrence Wittner (1993, 61). Niels Bohr, a Nobel Prize–winning physicist and adviser to the Manhattan Project, approached both UK prime minister Churchill and US president Roosevelt to ask them to broach with the Soviets controls before the atomic bomb was used. James Conant and Vannevar Bush, both senior government officials with some responsibility for administering the Manhattan Project and both members of the Interim Committee that recommended the atomic bomb should be used on Japan, also argued for discussing international controls before the US monopoly disappeared (Bernstein 1974, 1010).

Roosevelt and Churchill rejected opening negotiations with the Soviets over international controls and were determined to use the atomic bomb against Germany and for the seemingly inevitable postwar competition (Wittner 2009, 3). Gregg Herken (1980) argues that this decision was informed by the mistaken belief that a US monopoly could be maintained through its monopoly on uranium ore and an information embargo. US general Leslie Groves was convinced, for example, that even if the Soviets were not "far inferior," there was no threat because "there is no uranium in Russia" (Herken 1980, 56, 61). The decisions to use the bomb and to not broach discussions with the Soviets on international control were also reinforced by the sudden succession of Harry Truman to the presidency.

When the war did end, wrote Herb York (1987, 23–25), a physicist involved in the project, "everything we knew suggested that the bombs were the cause." Nuclear bombs were quickly termed by Bernard Brodie (1946, 29–30) to be "the absolute weapon," a weapon simultaneously of awesome destruction and indefensible "terror." The US military saw its monopoly useful to deter another Pearl Harbor–style surprise attack, punish aggression, and generally make the Soviets "more manageable" (US secretary of state James Byrnes, in Freedman 2003, 36–41). This value appeared far more credible in the short term than did disarmament and world government. Nuclear weapons might even make it possible for the United States to execute a surprise attack against an opponent otherwise hardened against strategic airpower. York (1987, 23–25) and many of his colleagues, however, still expressed "twinges of foreboding and sorrow" over a seemingly inevitable atomic arms race with the Soviets.

The United States and its allies moved quickly to impose new institutions of international governance that they hoped would prevent the beggar-thy-neighbor policies that helped precipitate the war. They replaced the failed League of Nations with a stronger United Nations and launched new international financial institutions. The United States, United Kingdom, and Canada also proposed creating a UN commission to make recommendations for international controls on peaceful uses and international verification of nuclear disarmament. Despite being short on specifics, the creation of the UNAEC was supported by the Soviets (Truman, Attlee, and King 1945). When the UNAEC was created in January 1946 by the first resolution of the UN General Assembly, most believed that the United States, as the world's only nuclear power, should be the first to offer specific proposals. Under Secretary of State Dean Acheson therefore directed a committee led by David Lilienthal to prepare a proposal covering verifiable disarmament and controls on future uses. The resulting Acheson–Lilienthal Report argued it was not enough to renounce atomic weapons possession or use or to rely on an international inspection system. It instead called for an "international authority" with the exclusive right to control and operate all nuclear activities (Fischer 1997, 19). Once such an authority was created, the United States could dismantle its nuclear weapons program.

President Truman's delegate to the UNAEC, Bernard Baruch, presented the result in a revised but clearly more ambitious form. At his own discretion, Baruch included broader disarmament goals, enforcement mechanisms, and a renunciation of the right of permanent UN Security Council members to veto the authority's activities (Goldschmidt 1977; Sims 1990, 97–106; Wittner 1993, 251–53). Baruch and most US officials appeared genuinely interested in negotiating an effective and comprehensive system of international controls on atomic power but also saw no reason to not bargain from a position of strength as long as there was no immediate threat to the US monopoly (Goldschmidt 1977; Herken 1980, 67–68; Williams and Cantelon 1984).

The "Baruch Plan" dominated the UNAEC's discussions and had broad support among the commission's members (Shils 1948). The majority produced multiple reports for the Security Council detailing a control agent that should at least conduct aerial on-site surveys but potentially should also be empowered to shut down facilities for inspections and even hold "management" of any "dangerous" nuclear activities (Shils 1948, 864; McKnight 1971, 15–17). The Soviets, meanwhile, publicly supported "strict and effective international control" but at the same time insisted "national controls" were sufficient and wanted to maintain their Security Council veto. The Soviets also insisted that an agreement be preceded by a ban and US disarmament (Frye 1961). The US position was hardening, believing the Soviets were obstructing international peace-building through repeated use of their Security Council veto, blocking an economic assistance plan for Europe in 1948, initiating a coup in Czechoslovakia, and blockading Allied-held Berlin. The United States, meanwhile, was supporting anti-Communist movements in Turkey and Greece and aiding the Kuomintang (Nationalists) against the Chinese Communist Party in China.

Prospects for international nuclear controls evaporated before the international community's collective eyes. Soviet responses were alternately contradictory, vague, and obstructionist; even US allies were skeptical about the chances of agreement (Shils 1948). The Soviets were at least hedging, if not outright disingenuous: they were also working hard on their own atomic bomb. US inflexibility in the UNAEC negotiations was reinforced by growing domestic support for a strategy of containment against the Soviet Union (Kennan 1947). The United Kingdom also wanted to keep open an independent nuclear option and secretly decided in 1947 to seek one. The UNAEC announced in 1948 it was stalemated by the "unabridged disagreement" between the majority and the Soviets (Shils 1948, 861). It stopped meeting entirely after the first Soviet nuclear test in 1949—a shock to the many who thought it would take them years longer—and was finally dissolved in 1952 by the UN General Assembly.

With its president uneasy with the idea of using nuclear weapons again, the United States continued to support arms control negotiations with the Soviets but also increasingly relied on its nuclear monopoly to deter Soviet aggression as the Cold War standoff threatened to spiral out of control. Then civil war on the Korean Peninsula drew the United States, the People's Republic of China, and the Soviet Union into worsening international tensions. The Korean War could trigger another world war but also presented the first opportunity since the Second World War for the use of nuclear weapons. The United States was increasingly determined to rely upon its growing nuclear arsenal and airpower superiority to deter Soviet aggression.

However, its threat to retaliate—massively and at times and places of its own choosing—was losing credibility with each passing day as the Soviet nuclear arsenal grew and its heavy bombers improved.[2]

In this increasingly desperate atmosphere, US president Dwight Eisenhower (1953) went before the UN General Assembly to give his now-famous "Atoms for Peace" speech. Although he discussed the dangers of nuclear war, he also called for a new international agency to provide all states with assistance developing peaceful nuclear technology in exchange for international safeguards against the misuse of that assistance for military purposes. Eisenhower hoped this agency would help divert scarce supplies of fissile materials away from being used for weapons and toward peaceful uses, although many states inferred this to mean that advanced states would make atomic energy freely available (Royden 2008, 58).

When it entered negotiations with the Soviet Union in March 1954, Bechhoefer (1959, 43) reports, the United States had prepared only an outline of the International Atomic Energy Agency's organization, financing, relationship to the United Nations, and its desirable roles. It hoped the IAEA would receive fissile materials to offer to others for peaceful uses and, in exchange, would receive the right with those states to dictate the design and operating conditions, health and safety regulations, and the disposition of by-product materials and wastes, as well as to verify the states' compliance with terms of sharing. Perhaps because Eisenhower's speech discussed the risk of nuclear war, the Soviets expected a proposal on arms control or disarmament and refused to negotiate.

The US proposal was not so far-fetched even though the movement for world disarmament had become a victim of repeated Cold War crises and the apparent triumph of realism over idealism (Wittner 1997, 12). Many analysts now hoped only for limited measures that might better rein in US–Soviet nuclear arms racing, offering at least short-term strategic stability, and might better respond to the threat from the horizontal proliferation of nuclear weapons to new countries (Brennan 1961a; Nacht 1981, 194–95). Among these, for example, a ban on nuclear testing drew increasing support from a wide range of groups after a US nuclear test in 1954 dropped massive amounts of fallout on the Bikini Atoll and on a Japanese fishing trawler also in the region, sickening hundreds (Goodby 2005).[3] A test ban might offer a practical and achievable means to address the continuously elevating risk of a nuclear world war and the popular perception of being bombarded by testing's environmental dangers.

The United States ignored the Soviet refusal of its Atoms for Peace plan and launched negotiations with several nuclear-active allied states, including Australia, Belgium, Canada, France, Portugal, South Africa, and the United Kingdom (McKnight 1971, 22). This meeting also nearly failed because even US allies were not happy about the structure proposed by the

United States (Patterson 1956, 8). The United States would not be dissuaded, Bechhoefer (1959, 52–53) argues. It aggressively pursued bilateral nuclear supply agreements, including research reactors fueled with highly enriched uranium, to spur interest in international commercial nuclear cooperation and to make clear their failure to agree would only mean unregulated nuclear commerce. The United States then drafted a statute, brought the proposal to the UN General Assembly for debate, and took it back to the allied negotiating states for more discussions.

The Soviets, although helping China with its nuclear weapons program, were concerned that this new agency would spur proliferation around the world out of the control of the nuclear weapon states (Royden 2008, 69–71). It decided to rejoin the talks in early 1956, bringing Czechoslovakia. India and Brazil also joined, and the "twelve-power conference" negotiated a draft agreement describing the basic organs of the future agency and how it would be managed. The draft Statute of the International Atomic Energy Agency left unanswered, however, how safeguards would work and still protect national sovereignty. Many of the negotiating states continued to argue against the need for an extensive inspection system.

A conference of eighty-one states met in September 1956 and largely approved the draft text. The conference may have succeeded because the twelve-power conference had agreed that no major amendments would be tolerated (Sole 1997, 20). Bechhoefer (1959, 58–59), though, points to strong US leadership and its coincidence with Soviet interests. Among the few changes, the negotiators agreed that safeguards would only be required on assistance provided by the IAEA, not as a condition of membership, and so were "voluntary" (McKnight 1971, 25). India was outspoken, among the many developing states, in expressing fear that international agreements like the IAEA could compromise their sovereignty and, echoing Soviet diplomacy, lead to the great powers reasserting control over developing states (Wittner 2009, 43). The Statute came into force as an international treaty on July 29, 1957, after more than eighteen states acceded.

The transition to stand up the Agency was not smooth, and it disappointed many in its early years. Under pressure from the US Congress, and contrary to the general expectation that a nuclear scientist from an advanced but non–nuclear weapon state would be chosen as the first director general, the US governor forced through the election of former US representative W. Sterling Cole (Quihillalt and Büchler 1997). As an American nonscientist with no international experience, Cole was resisted by the Secretariat and resented by many governors. Cole surprised many by criticizing US support for the European Atomic Energy Community (EURATOM) and the slow transfer to the IAEA of US bilateral safeguards, which bought him greater support among the members. It was his attempt to create the Safeguards Division, argue Pendley and colleagues (1975), that fractured a

Board torn over the Cold War. Pitted against pro-safeguards Western supplier states, the Soviets and their allies continued to oppose any international verification, even voluntary, for fear of legitimating the process.
Though joined by recipient states, Cole's opponents failed to block the
creation of the Safeguards Department and turned instead to block his
attempts to recruit safeguards staff and fund studying a safeguards system.
IAEA historian David Fischer (1997, 245) notes they succeeded in delaying
approval of the first safeguards agreement with Japan in 1959.

Still, it was clear Cole would not be reappointed when his term as director general came to a close in 1961. Quihillalt and Büchler (1997, 48) saw
"a certain stagnation in the Agency's program" when the Agency did not
jump into a meaningful role promoting peaceful nuclear energy. The Soviets
did not follow the US commitment of nuclear materials to create an international fissile material bank. The United States was not only not requiring
IAEA safeguards as a condition for their nuclear supply agreements, argues
Richard Hewlett (1985), it was also supporting EURATOM's role as an
alternative source of safeguards in Europe. IAEA safeguards simply could
not compete with the US bilateral safeguards system and, after making an
initial foray into nuclear safety after an accident at a facility in Vinča, Yugo-
slavia, the Board decided to remove health and safety monitoring from the
safeguards system (McKnight 1971, 49; Khan 1997).

As the IAEA was being stood up, the superpowers continued exploring
other arms control measures. Eisenhower had become convinced by 1957
that a test ban could be verifiable, and proposed an international scientific
conference on the technical feasibility of monitoring a test ban (Brown
2007). With participation by the major Western and Communist countries,
US negotiator James Goodby (2005) states that the 1958 conference recommended by consensus a "Geneva system" of fixed, passive monitoring stations and on-site inspections. Eisenhower felt encouraged to announce a test
moratorium, and the Soviets followed. They then formalized an agreement
in 1959 to demilitarize Antarctica under the Antarctic Treaty, which entered
into force in 1961 to also create the first nuclear weapons–free zone (or
NWFZ).

These small successes on nuclear testing created the political space
among the United Kingdom, United States, and Soviet Union for formal
negotiations toward a comprehensive test ban treaty (CTBT) to begin in
1959. While the Soviet Union continued to oppose on-site international verification, the United States favored only a "limited" test ban that allowed
underground testing (Goodby 2005, 387–87). The Soviets argued a limited
ban would be insufficient to stop France and China from testing and continued to demand a complete test ban linked to a broader complete and general
disarmament agreement. They only slowly began to concede on international verification and the need for on-site inspections. However, progress

on how many annual inspections would be allowed stalled when the Soviets in May 1960 shot down a US U-2 spy plane, followed by a failed US invasion of Cuba and the Soviet construction of the Berlin Wall. Negotiations stopped completely when the Soviets accused the "West" of breaking the moratorium after France tested its first nuclear weapon. International tensions then hit their greatest point when the United States detected Soviet missiles being placed into Cuba, the threat of nuclear war bringing a freeze to political talks.

EXPERIMENTATION TO CONTROL
THE "ABSOLUTE WEAPON"

Did demand for political authority motivate the international community to create the IAEA in 1957? Once it was created, did the IAEA's principals immediately begin to accommodate its mission with autonomy and resources? Did they comply with its rules and commands? Or, as the alternative arguments suggest, was the IAEA the result of demand for only limited delegation, a fulfillment of the expectations of a superpower, or a reflection of strengthening norms of international behavior?

US Imperialism

The received wisdom is that the creation of the IAEA was an extension of US dominion, or superpower condominium, over the system (Bechhoefer 1959, 58–59). The US plan offered by Baruch called for complete international control of atomic power, a sovereign abdication on nuclear issues potentially much greater than already attempted for international economic issues under the Bretton Woods institutions. Weapons use bans had been attempted in the recent past, including the Geneva Protocol (1928), which prohibited the use of chemical and biological weapons in warfare.

The US atomic bomb monopoly, however, presented a different bargaining problem when it came to timing individual states' contributions. The United States would have to endure a great risk if the international community decided that nuclear weapons must first be banned and the United States disarmed. Although the danger of a Soviet surprise attack seemed remote, US interests were quickly coalescing behind a strategy of containment for the Communist threat, and disarmament would remove a major source of its bargaining power.

Despite compelling most states to accept the United Nations and international financial institutions, the Baruch Plan foundered on being both too expansive in scope and too international in process. Edwin Firmage (1969) argues that the Soviets feared losing their Security Council veto over any institution numerically dominated by Western states and backed by a US nuclear monopoly. The United States held fast despite arguments by some, including Canadian representative to the UNAEC Andrew McNaughton, that the veto was irrelevant because any attempt to sanction a state over atomic power would already mean "absolute war" (Shils 1948, 859). Wittner (2009, 47) argues that states less aligned with the United States were worried about nuclear weapons but worried more that internationalization was thinly disguised imperialism. Even Soviet diplomat Andrei Gromyko (1947) expressed concern that an international nuclear agency could become powerful enough to threaten their sovereignty and economic independence. It did not help that strong opposition to disarmament by some government officials and military planners inside the United States and its allies, and the increasing attractiveness of containment, made failure seem a reasonable alternative.

While Winston Churchill (1946) said the United States was "at the pinnacle of world power," the end of the US atomic monopoly in 1949 gave the Soviets new leverage they would not easily abandon. Then, by the mid-1950s, US power was again ascendant with conventional military rebuilding after the Korean War and intense investment in its nuclear weapons arsenal, which more than doubled every two years during the decade (Freedman 2003). However, despite increasing absolute numbers, the American relative military and economic advantage was eroding even before the Soviets tested what the United States believed was a hydrogen bomb in 1953. Rhetorical support for complete and general disarmament also diminished as both sides adopted deterrence by nuclear retaliation as their first line of defense against the other. The risk that nuclear war could be precipitated by crises over peripheral interests and the need to counter Soviet overtures to Europe excited Eisenhower's interest in pursuing arms reductions and some kind of negotiated controls on atomic power. Both sides were aware that increasing numbers of countries had pretensions of power and modernity through peaceful nuclear programs, if not also overt considerations of nuclear weapons. However, their mutual reliance on nuclear deterrence agitated fear by each of revealing any nuclear knowledge that could give the other a crucial advantage.

These nuclear policy tensions worsened, argues Goldschmidt (1982, 242), as US unilateral control over the international nuclear market fell victim to its weakening monopoly on uranium supplies and continuing nuclear advancement by states capable of threatening the US commercial dominance. The Soviets were also watching the United States strengthen its ties with its European partners in the North Atlantic Treaty Organization (NATO). To better reassure its allies of its commitment to defend them after the 1956 Suez Crisis, NATO's command structure was consolidated, greater numbers of US nuclear weapons were deployed to Europe, and US control over those nuclear weapons was weakened. The Soviets may also have been aware the United States had restarted nuclear cooperation with the United Kingdom in 1958, transferring key nuclear materials and technologies (Mackby and Cornish 2008). As George Bunn (1992, 62–63) describes, the Soviet Union faced similar problems with its allies, leading it to create the Warsaw Pact alliance for Eastern Europe and make nuclear assistance more available.

For all its power, the United States was unable to impose upon the world, much less its allies, an international atomic organization. Allan McKnight (1971, 30–31) later complimented the Soviets for helping build consensus at the later IAEA negotiations, rather than their usual obstreperousness, but the Soviets had opposed nuclear internationalization outside of a broader program for complete and general disarmament and continued to oppose the need for international verification. Most countries of the world, and even US and Soviet allies, were stuck in the middle of this ideological and increasingly militarized competition. The idea of any new international agency invited practical skepticism if not some fear of it being used to impose control over them. Only through extensive negotiations over several years with distinctly different groups of states did the design and purpose of the IAEA elicit widespread support.

The support of the United States was certainly integral to the creation of the IAEA and remained necessary for its maintenance. The international community begrudgingly acknowledged the need to ensure continued US (congressional) support in acquiescing to an American director general. This assistance, particularly from its Atomic Energy Commission, argues Büchler (1997, 51), helped build bureaucratic processes and expertise for safeguards that developed with the Secretariat's implementation of the US voluntary offer to safeguard a small set of US facilities. However, the proposition that US hegemonic power coerced others to create the IAEA is difficult to support. A multilateral process led to internationalization of nuclear policy, and this effort succeeded even as other US efforts at internationalization did not. The Soviet Union successfully blocked the first US efforts to rebuild the global economy, obstructed action at the Security Council, and kept many of its allies from participating in the Marshall Fund and other international initiatives. Western states also opposed US attempts at further internationalization, including attempts to institutionalize the GATT (General Agreement on Tariffs and Trade) agreement on international trade beyond the negotiating rounds. In short, an interested hegemon strongly influenced the creation of this international agent, but it could not dictate its creation or its subsequent actions.

Norm Structure

At the forefront of nuclear norm entrepreneurship were many who shared York's fear of nuclear arms racing. US nuclear scientists involved in the Manhattan Project at its various locations came together to form the Federation of American Scientists in October 1945, as described in the first issue of their newsletter *The Bulletin of the Atomic Scientists of Chicago*, with the goal of identifying their collective opinion and responsibilities toward nuclear energy but also to educate the public about its dangers. *The Bulletin* quickly became known for its "Doomsday Clock," which evoked the scientists' belief of how close human civilization was to destroying itself. Although Ole Wæver (1999) argues that the normative elevation of (natural) scientific approaches was stronger in the United States than in European academic and policy traditions, the US weapons scientists believed that scientific analysis could help illuminate objective solutions to national and international problems.

Wittner (2009) describes another group of advocates of "complete and general disarmament" and of "one world" world government, holdovers from interwar idealism, argues Wæver (1999), who joined in the call for all nuclear technologies to be put under international controls. While the League of Nations had failed, they believed that internationalization on a grand scale, with better design and active participation by all the major powers, offered a credible strategy of self-denial to states whose sovereign pursuit of power had caused the two world wars. There was strong popular hope that the United Nations and its many specialized agencies would succeed at preventing the seeds of future international conflicts from being planted in the first place.

The norms of internationalization and nuclear danger were in increasing competition, though, with realist beliefs that human nature inspired a "lust of power," that politics was competition for power, and that the international system was inherently anarchical (Carr 1961; Morgenthau 1985). Peace could be secured, therefore, only through a strategy of balance of power, which in turn required embracing the power that only nuclear weapons could offer. Realist arguments also reinforced the importance of the principle of state sovereignty, ironically reified in the internationalist United Nations charter, to countries for which embracing international institutions could mean tacit suzerainty to Western powers. In the West, though, the advocacy of internationalization was tainted by its being most supported by individuals who were believed to be sympathetic to Communism (Wittner 2009, 34–46).

The norms of internationalization and nuclear danger were together not enough to propel adoption of the Baruch Plan or "complete and general disarmament" over individual concerns for sovereignty and security in the 1940s. By the time the IAEA was created in the 1950s, internationalization as a procedural norm had been undermined by stagnation at the UN Security Council and was too weak to compel states to accept international governance over issues such as international trade or human rights. The European experiment with political unification, after hesitant steps in the 1950s that included the US-supported creation of EURATOM, would also soon stall out in the 1960s.[4]

The 1940s behavioral norms included a belief that "complete and general disarmament" was appropriate while "arms racing" was dangerous. The belief that nuclear power was dangerous persisted through the 1960s, although the idealism of "disarmament" was increasingly tempered by the impracticality of its achievement. States substituted instead with incremental, short-term measures for strategic stability such that the idea of "arms control" was emerging by the late 1950s (Brennan 1961b; Schelling 1961). Opposition to nuclear testing also exploited this pressure on the superpowers to reduce the risk of an uncontrolled spasm into nuclear war through arms control. As dangerous as nuclear weapons were popularly perceived to be, nuclear weapons remained a valid security choice, if not a powerful source of prestige (Sagan 1996–97). As Maria Rublee (2009) describes, "nonproliferation" was still little more than a vaguely defined strategy to block the horizontal proliferation of nuclear weapons to others.

Eisenhower proposed the IAEA in the hope that states would realize that hitching a ride to a cooperative, peaceful atomic future offered better prospects for national development. The IAEA could possibly also contribute indirectly to "arms control" if its inspection system could provide a model for verification. However, there is little evidence that these anti–nuclear weapons norms slowed arms racing or convinced others to abstain. Further, support for the IAEA legitimated the right of states to access peaceful nuclear uses, which at least the Soviets feared would have dangerous effects.

Internationalization also did not automatically produce the technocratic organizations that many had expected. The individual principals measured the legitimacy of their international organizations in part by how closely their formal influence and representation in the staff matched their perceived power outside these new international organizations. Although intended to be apolitical bureaucracies staffed by objective issue experts, states immediately maneuvered to grab control of their top posts, believing that doing so would increase their informal influence (Sole 1997). This began at the IAEA, of course, with the appointment of its first director general. Inis Claude (1964) noted that even the most technical task of credentialing a member's representative became political by the late 1950s when it came to who would represent China at international institutions (Imber 1989, 8).

In short, there is little evidence the IAEA was created because of coercive norms of nuclear behavior or of procedural internationalism. Norms of nuclear behavior contributed to defining but also constraining the purpose of the IAEA. Norms of internationalism similarly contributed to defining the structure of the Agency's bureaucratic and executive agents but were also not sufficiently strong to protect them from politicization.

Limited Agency

Throughout the early negotiations at the UNAEC on internationalization of the atom, the United States was trying to maintain its nuclear weapons monopoly through hegemonic information embargo and uranium monopolization. The US strategy to control the spread of nuclear technologies slowed proliferation in the short run, and the emergence within a few years of new nuclear weapon states—the Soviet Union in 1949 and the United Kingdom in 1952—did not erode their concern about the acquisition of nuclear weapons by new countries. Even the numerical construction of the problem of acquisition by the fourth, fifth, or Nth country, argues York (1987, 117), reinforced the perception of a shared challenge.

Meanwhile, conflicts of political interest were developing along several dimensions. Most obvious was that the hardening ideological divide appeared increasingly to threaten another world war and raised the accompanying danger of a nuclear war. Despite the gains that promised to be within reach if this division could be overcome, the essential nature of the conflict over the appropriate role of individuals, government, and capital in national development magnified the technical uncertainty already adhering to any collective approach to nuclear power. The structure of the global economy was still at stake.

Among the most advanced nuclear states there was increasing competition because, blocked by the United States from collaborating, each was forced to find their own technical solution to the problem of commercially viable nuclear energy. Only the largest could reach the economies of scale in their national nuclear energy program for commercial viability without exports, which created a new coordination problem. The supplier states generally recognized the need to impose bilateral safeguards upon recipient states but were competing for exports and wanted to respect their sovereign rights. The US proposal for international safeguards and management of atomic power conformed to the appropriateness of internationalization but went far beyond the realm of practical experience technically and in the abrogation requested of sovereign powers. The resulting delay in identifying a common solution did not quite lead to a "race to the bottom" as a market evolved, but it did undermine the hegemonic US solution.

The current and future recipients of nuclear supply, though, felt threatened by these bilateral safeguards. Developed recipient states shared the perception of a global threat from US-Soviet arms racing but did not necessarily agree that horizontal proliferation was dangerous. Safeguards also threatened their ability to commercially benefit from innovating upon technologies they felt they had paid for. Developing states that hoped to become recipients felt threatened with indefinite subjugation by superpowers or former colonial powers through military interventions and increasing preconditions on international financial assistance (Gould 2006b; Brown 2010). Developing and developed states, argue Pendley and colleagues (1975, 10), shared the concern that supplier constraints limited their economic development, and intrusive nuclear safeguards compromised their sovereignty.[5]

It is not surprising, in retrospect, that cooperation across the range of nuclear policy areas was prevented in the early years of the Cold War by serious uncertainty about the future of nuclear power and stark differences of interest on nuclear weapons, nuclear safeguards, ideology, the security of national sovereignty, and the need for external assistance with economic development. By the early 1950s it appeared that effective markets for peaceful nuclear uses would not spontaneously develop. Solving this market failure might require, as with currency and trade, a centralized actor with the policy bias to foster investment and the behavioral impersonality to overcome national distributional conflicts.

To recipients and smaller suppliers, internationalism could supply the accelerated civilian nuclear technology research and development that many states could not realistically provide within their own sovereign boundaries. To the nuclear weapon states, internationalization of the atom offered a means to overcome the hold-up problems that were preventing the collective regulation of nuclear power necessary to avoid the dangers from nuclear proliferation and nuclear safety, much as David Mitrany (1948) argues states were already regulating international rail and air standards. The superpowers saw a test ban, for example, as useful to restraining their own arms racing and to preventing the emergence of new nuclear weapon states. Paul Boyer (1984) argues that international pressure to ban nuclear testing increased after widespread radioactive fallout from the 1954 US Castle Bravo test.[6]

In 1954, when Eisenhower launched the negotiations that created the IAEA, internationalization offered a basic functionalist solution to a specific transnational nuclear policy problem. The United States wanted to avoid beggar-thy-neighbor controls on supply and get itself out from under the incredible cost of bilateral safeguards. Lewis L. Strauss (US Senate 1957, 89) believed Eisenhower had also hoped that an IAEA safeguards system could lead to progress on a "working model" for a verifiable disarmament system. It might even be of direct use in verifying the fissile material treaty that Eisenhower proposed to the Soviets in 1956. Among others, there was an interest in extending the success of a few high-profile international nuclear technical conferences like the 1955 UN Conference on the Peaceful Uses of Atomic Energy (Goldschmidt 1982, 259). Many had arrived at the false belief that nuclear energy would soon be "too cheap to meter," and that advanced states, through internationalization and led by the United States, would make it freely available to all.[7] However, they also wished to see an agent limited to serving as a conduit for lending scarce fissile materials (diverted from the US and Soviet weapons programs), aggregating national investments in peaceful nuclear uses, and channeling nuclear power to recipients under safeguards against its misuse for weapons.

Three choices taken by the parties in the twelve-power negotiations on the IAEA Statute show their specific functionalist interest in creating a limited and conditional international organization. First, they decided that a Board, and not the General Conference, should have predominant oversight of the Agency and elect its director general. They consciously diminished the role of the General Conference to ensure that the organization was primarily responsive to those states whose contributions really made the Agency possible (Bechhoefer 1959, 49). When others later argued that growing nuclear states and developing states needed better representation in governance, they agreed to expand the Board to twenty-three governors and adopt a new formula that increased representation from the Middle East, Asia, and Eastern Europe. However, the motivation in the design of this executive agent was effective multilateral control over their implementing bureaucracy.

Second, they decided that effective control required the Board to have the legal autonomy to judge compliance by members with their obligations. While the Soviet Union had for years insisted on a primary role for the UN Security Council to maintain its veto in an institution where the West numerically dominated, it was now more optimistic about its ability to protect its interests in an international organization where most decisions could be made by simple majority. Further, if a member were to fail to respond to a Board judgment of noncompliance with appropriate remedial action, then the primary route by which the Board would respond would be to report the noncompliance to the UN Security Council. Board decisions to report noncompliance, curtail assistance, limit participation in the Agency, or call for the return of IAEA materials, however, would not be subject to a veto (US Senate 1957, 60). This choice reinforced strong multilateral control over the Agency but with greater accountability to a broader population of its principals, and also greater institutional constraints on both superpowers, than present elsewhere.

Third, the negotiators agreed that the Agency would be funded primarily through compulsory assessments where each member's share was roughly proportional to the size of its economy, as was used to finance the United Nations. However, as James Wadsworth, US deputy representative to the UN, summarized, nuclear weapons states feared the high costs if they had to bear the financial burden of effective inspections, advanced recipient states feared the intrusiveness and indirect costs of inspections, and neither wanted to be legally obligated to fund technical assistance at the levels the majority might desire if recipient states came to dominate the General Conference or Board (US Senate 1957, 136). They therefore agreed also that compulsory contributions to the general fund would only cover its administrative expenses, including the promotion of safety and other standards, and safeguards. Contrary to the wishes of developing states, technical assistance would be centrally administered, but most Agency programs for promoting peaceful uses would be funded by voluntary contributions. This approach ensured investment in nuclear policy bargaining and monitoring while insulating the largest donors against one source of budget uncertainty.

However, the principles that they agreed would inform the design of the Agency's future safeguards system were, as described in Article XII.A of the Statute of the IAEA (1957), less limited or conditional. First, the Agency would have the right to review the design of facilities using or storing safeguarded materials to determine whether safeguards could be effectively applied. Second, McKnight (1971, 35) states that the Agency would have access to any records for nuclear facility operations and the disposition of all safeguarded nuclear materials associated with them (beyond the initial uranium mining stage). Third, all states under safeguards would be required to report regularly on their inventory and use of safeguarded items. Fourth, states under safeguards would be required to submit to on-site inspections carried out by the Agency. These principles implied a conceptual shift from safeguards as a comprehensive control system to a more limited monitoring system that reduced policy uncertainty. Still, as Pendley and colleagues (1975, 594) argue, this consensus showed they were intending the most sovereignty-infringing monitoring system in history.

As much autonomy as inspectors could have in states under safeguards, the effect, they believed, would be limited because of strong multilateral control and the essentially voluntary nature of accepting safeguards: only recipients of IAEA supply would be forced to accept these intrusions on their sovereignty. Donald Sole (1997, 23–24), the first governor from South Africa, says most states did not object to IAEA health and safety measures being included in safeguards, for example, only to the inherent discrimination of safeguards imposed only upon recipients. "Our opposition would have been disarmed," Sole (1997, 23–24) writes, "had the nuclear powers agreed from the beginning to place their own peaceful nuclear facilities under Agency safeguards."

The Statute was an incredible international policy experiment. The parties were quite uncertain if the IAEA would become the promised vehicle for collective action on nuclear technology. It is worth quoting Sole at length: "We could not visualize materials being supplied to the Agency except on commercial terms; we doubted whether the Agency would be financed by its members to an extent enabling it to purchase materials . . . we did not believe that the Agency Secretariat would or should be qualified to act as a broker in the market for nuclear materials" (1997, 31). Instead, the goal for many was to lock in as best they could some voice as internationalization of the atom moved forward. Again Sole writes, "But we kept these reservations to ourselves. We had attained our primary objective—a seat on the Board of Governors—and it would have been folly to do or say anything that might prejudice our standing in this respect" (1997, 23–24).

There was doubt about the IAEA even in the United States. Secretary of State John Dulles tried to reassure Congress that US support was necessary to the IAEA's success, that IAEA safeguards would be more effective than relying on a system of (mostly US) bilateral safeguards, and that the IAEA would be responsive to US needs (US Senate 1957, 54–59). Dulles argued that the United States needed this international organization to take from it the burden of monitoring others, stating, "No one nation can, alone, indefinitely police the spread of nuclear power plants." He believed the IAEA would also accelerate development of peaceful nuclear technology, generate international health and safety codes, help collect scarce nuclear expertise, and increase nuclear transparency so others need not fear proliferation (US Senate 1957, 5). Although the United States expected to have significant influence, it also would benefit from more collective investments in nuclear policy and less policy uncertainty.

In short, the interactions prior to and during the negotiation of the IAEA Statute show international interest in pooling investment in peaceful nuclear uses, promoting its safe use, and implementing guarantees against its misuse for nuclear weapons. Internationalization of nuclear power appeared the best way to achieve these goals: an agency with little discretion from its principals could alleviate nuclear policy uncertainty while separating nuclear policy from their persistent, festering conflicts of interest. To many states only just emerging out of the legacy of war and colonialism, argues Goldschmidt (1982, 119), the IAEA's unequal obligations were discriminatory and neocolonial. However, even among stronger critics like Bechhoefer (1959), it was recognized that the consensus was sufficiently fragile that any attempts to force greater equity upon the great powers would break the larger agreement. They accepted the Statute because it offered the only opportunity to join the nuclear age that they were likely to see for a while.

After the Statute of the IAEA entered into force in 1957, the membership quickly grew from eighteen states at its entry-into-force to seventy-two by 1962 (figure 3.1). Even though more than half of the members were the nuclear weapon states and their closest allies (see figure 3.2), this also meant that almost two-thirds of all UN states were now members. This might suggest states were already beginning to strongly accommodate the IAEA's role as paying and participating members.

The Board, for example, was quickly proving it could become an effective mechanism for international nuclear policy management. When the first Board meetings seemed to become bogged down in ideological debates—the first year of the IAEA's existence coincided with the start of the space/missile race and new crises over the Taiwan Straits and Berlin—the governors agreed to make their meetings closed and confidential (Fischer 1997, 78). It

Figure 3.1.   Number of Members and Management Autonomy of the Board, 1957–2012

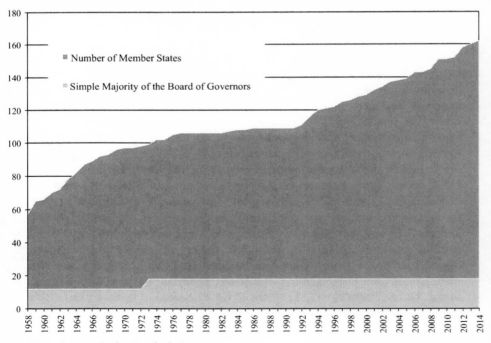

Data Source: Author's calculation.

Figure 3.2.   Number of Member States by Region

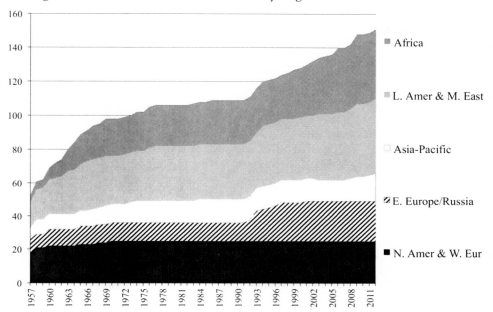

Data Sources: IAEA, *The Annual Report* (Vienna: IAEA, 1958–2012); IAEA, GC(02)/
INF/11: *Report to the General Assembly of the United Nations Covering the Period up
to 31 October 1957* (Vienna: IAEA, 1957); IAEA, *Election of Members to the Board of
Governors* (Vienna: IAEA, 1958–2012); IAEA, GC(17)/INF/145/Rev.2: *Delegations*
(Vienna: IAEA, 1973); and IAEA, GC(19)/INF/157/Rev. 2: *Delegations* (Vienna: IAEA,
1975); IAEA, *General Conference Plenary Record*: 49th (2005) Regular Session, 50th
(2006) Regular Session, 51st (2007) Regular Session, 52nd (2008) Regular Session, 53rd
(2009) Regular Session, 55th (2011) Regular Session, and 56th (2012) Regular Session
(Vienna: IAEA, 2006, 2008, 2009, 2011, 2012).

likely helped that most governors at the time were not professional diplomats but began participating in the negotiations as technical experts and
were capable of dealing substantively with technical issues. These rules
reduced the benefit of political grandstanding by individual governors but
also reduced, some complained, transparency into its decisions. Still, these
features on balance positioned the Board to provide useful policy direction
to the Secretariat even as they increased its autonomy from its collective
principal, the General Conference. These features also locked in the need
for future governors to have some technical expertise and gave an advantage
to the personal relationships and institutional memory of individual
governors.

The Board only tolerated Cole at first. He ensured US political and economic support, but the Soviets resented him because he was American. The Europeans feared that Cole's desire to invest in laboratories and safeguards would create the expensive Agency they had hoped to avoid (Fischer 1997, 74–75). Although Cole proved himself to not be a US pawn, Royden (2008, 83) and Barton (1997, 41) describe Cole and his small staff as suffering onerous reporting conditions for a Board that met 156 times in the first two years. (To compare, the Board in 2011 met only 6 times over twenty-five days, despite facing major crises with Iranian noncompliance and Japan's Fukushima Daiichi meltdowns.) The Board carefully reviewed each of his appointments for management and inspector positions to guard against the Agency becoming a Western tool to suppress nuclear advancement of developing states.

It was clear in the first years that the Board held tight formal control over a Secretariat with little discretion. While much of its senior managers and professional staff had carried over from the negotiations, individuals with strong nuclear policy and technology experience, the aggregate numbers point to less accommodation of the Agency than an observer would have expected even in 1956: the budget was small and the staff remained few in number (figure 1.2). In truth, the substantial variation across the different nuclear issues suggests that states were accommodating what they saw as real value being created or likely at this early stage.

Peaceful Uses

The IAEA was more limited as a conduit for nuclear assistance than recipient states had expected when Eisenhower gave the "Atoms for Peace" speech because the nuclear landscape in 1962 was quite different. The first commercial-scale power reactors had begun operating in the late 1950s and early 1960s, but Canada, France, the United States, the United Kingdom, and the Soviet Union were all experimenting with different approaches.[8] Of most use to the most advanced nuclear states, therefore, were its large international technical conferences on nuclear power. Uranium ore was much less scarce, and a commercial fuel market was emerging beyond the United States. Commercial nuclear reactor construction was also finally under way but was also proving less economical than anticipated, especially as oil prices and international transport fees dropped (Goldschmidt 1982, 264). Since the IAEA's services were not needed to solve these major market problems, it did not build or operate major nuclear facilities or provide nuclear fuel.

Developing states became disappointed because IAEA technical assistance, as described in the 1960 Annual Report (27), became limited to the "provision of experts, equipment and supplies, fellowships, exchange professors, training courses and the use of the Agency's two mobile radioisotope laboratories." The Agency's role was still smaller because its assistance was also often offered in conjunction with the larger and better established UN Development Program or Food and Agriculture Organization. It still required safeguards as a condition of assistance, eroding recipients' sovereignty. This erosion, though, was less than originally anticipated by the negotiating states because they had hoped IAEA assistance would be the primary means of getting states under safeguards against misuse. Squeezing the IAEA out of its intended intervention into the nuclear market contributed, argue Quihillalt and Büchler (1997, 48), to broader "stagnation in the Agency's program."

Developed and developing states did not miss the fact that assistance proved so limited despite the earlier grandiose promises. Recipient states began to argue that advanced states must be actively withholding the technologies necessary for their development. A representative of a developing but US-friendly state was paraphrased by Bechhoefer (1959, 41) as stating, "My country has limitless supplies of uranium located in its hills. We need power. Why do we not have atomic power? Because the United States is holding out on us." The United States was using its dominance in uranium enrichment to discourage regional enrichment programs, and to encourage purchasing US research reactors.[9] The United States was also hesitant to support IAEA technical assistance if this support could go to Communist states. However, it was still true that full-scale nuclear reactors for electricity production were proving more costly to safely build than expected.

To summarize, the scale of initial investments necessary to make nuclear power viable quickly proved larger than expected but also promised incredible gains to whichever of the advanced nuclear states could solve its straightforward engineering problems. For their part, potential recipient states bought into the Agency and its safeguards obligations to alleviate great policy uncertainty on peaceful nuclear uses created by limited expertise and perceived supplier reticence. They wanted the development assistance and technical guidance that they not only believed was promised to them but that they also began to see as within their rights as states in good standing. The nuclear supplier states, though, no longer saw the need for substantial international intervention to facilitate commercial nuclear cooperation. The Agency could invest in the specific assets necessary to promote limited peaceful uses but was not accommodated with the resources needed to subsidize nuclear energy into commercial viability. In short, the IAEA initially acquired such a limited promotion role that there was little space to acquire authority over the supply of peaceful uses.

Disarmament

Cold War tensions and the threat of nuclear conflict continued to escalate after the birth of the IAEA. The Soviet arsenal was thirty times larger by 1962 than it had been in 1953, although in absolute numbers it still paled in comparison to US arsenal, which increased tenfold over the same period. The United States and Soviet Union leap frogged each other for advantage as they advanced their bomber and then missile capabilities. Although uncertain about the size of this advantage at any point in time, US analysts alternated between alerting others to "windows of vulnerability" to a Soviet first strike and calling for the United States to execute its own disabling surprise attack (Freedman 2003, 149–55). Dissuaded from complete and general disarmament but seeking to retard this dangerous spiral and potentially also block other potential proliferators, the United States and Soviet Union proposed to each other a number of limited measures. They considered fissile material limits, for example, but pursued a test ban as the most feasible. The United States had hoped that the IAEA safeguards system could provide a model for international arms control verification but in 1958 rejected a role for the IAEA in verifying a test ban to keep it focused on peaceful uses (Fischer 1997, 81).

When test ban talks failed in 1961, the greatest cause was increasing international tensions. The United States and Soviet Union were also too far apart over the breadth of the ban and the design of a verification system, particularly over on-site inspections, to negotiate who would verify it. The IAEA had barely launched item- or facility-specific safeguards and certainly had not invested in specific assets useful to verifying disarmament, leaving little reason to imagine it had the technical aptitude or behavioral impersonality for a high-stakes disarmament mission. The real problem, of course, was that neither political leaders nor militaries in the nuclear weapon states wanted nuclear disarmament, much less its international verification, and therefore did not demand disarmament authority.

Nonproliferation

The United States and Soviet Union had for years tried to prevent the proliferation of nuclear weapons to new states. However, to send strong and reassuring signals to their allies, they were simultaneously providing assistance that could (or would) be helpful to nuclear weapons programs (Fuhrmann 2009a). This tension was part of the reason the United States had wanted international safeguards, which the USSR had consistently opposed, arguing that a state's promise to not misuse assistance should be enough to obviate a need for verification (Pendley et al. 1975, 604). This contributed to clear tension between the selective "right" to proliferate nuclear weapons and the obligation to accept safeguards against misuse when the Board began debating whether and how to approach international safeguards.

The weak Board consensus on safeguards was first challenged when India, with the support of Egypt, Indonesia, and the USSR, fought Director General Cole's attempts to create the Safeguards Division (Fischer 1997, 246). The West supported Cole, but the exposure to safeguards obligations would clearly be asymmetric. Close US allies like the United Kingdom and France were unlikely to become recipients of IAEA supply and come under safeguards even before a US-EURATOM "Agreement for Cooperation" kept safeguards on Western Europe out of the Agency. Approving the department was a straightforward decision, though, that the Board could make.

It was more contentious for the governors when Japan came to the IAEA in 1958 to request safeguards because they would have to actually design a verification system (Pendley et al. 1975, 602). Those opposed to safeguards argued that national commitments should be sufficient assurance while pro-safeguards states insisted that reassuring the international community of non-diversion required at least on-site inspections if not operational control. Their disagreement on even the basic principles of safeguards, argue Pendley and colleagues (1975, 600), "is evidenced by the constant abrasiveness of the debate and the frequency with which roll-call votes were demanded in this non-public forum."

They approved an ad hoc agreement for Japan in January 1959 but recognized that they needed to depoliticize not only the implementation of safeguards but also their initial negotiation and design. To create behavioral impersonality, the Board agreed to give the Secretariat the autonomy to negotiate future individual agreements. It was still more than twenty-eight Board meetings, however, before they agreed on the text that became published as Information Circular #26, or INFCIRC/26, a model agreement for smaller power reactors (Pendley et al., 1975). The most important IAEA documents have been released as "Information Circulars" and are referred to using their numerical designation, as in INFCIRC/26. As mentioned earlier, though, one compromise was to exclude from safeguards any monitoring over nuclear safety even though one reason for its inclusion was the safety of the international inspectors themselves.

Carlos Büchler (1997, 48), an Argentine who retired as a division director in the Safeguards Department, later stated, "The ensuing safeguards activities of the Agency . . . were as a rule only grudgingly accepted by the recipient States." India and others only accepted safeguards when the United States made clear they would not otherwise access US civilian nuclear technology (Fischer 2007). The Department of Safeguards was also heavily reliant for training on the United States, among the only countries with any significant experience to this point in actually implementing nuclear safeguards. And, when started, the implementation of safeguards was viewed, Büchler (1997, 48–49) writes, as "amateurish" and "regarded by the rest of the staff . . . as a disruptive element and responsible for delaying action by the Board on the truly important functions of the Agency."

Negotiations to close gaps in what David Fischer (2007) described as the "spider web" of safeguards were no more successful when excluding the anti-control states from discussions. The United States tried bringing together the pro-safeguards states to meet in 1960, and again in 1965, Goldschmidt (1982, 286) writes, but they would not agree to require safeguards as a condition of bilateral supply. France, for example, was emerging as an important nuclear supplier and had joined the ranks of the nuclear weapon states with its own test in 1960, but it vigorously opposed any constraints on French military or economic independence.

The United States was a major force in the expansion of international safeguards but could only advance the IAEA's role on safeguards, write Pendley and colleagues (1975, 604), if it could first build a consensus on the Board among "the seventeen pro-control nations," if not also of the "six who presented themselves as being irrevocably anti-control." As a result, the willingness of the IAEA Board to issue rules and commands on safeguards developed very slowly. The safeguards it approved compromised the "access at all times to all places and data and to any person" standard written into the Statute but still led to greater infringements of national sovereignty than previously volunteered by states. As limited an agent as the IAEA initially was for international verification, the design of its Board and Secretariat offered greater behavioral impersonality in its application than its bilateral alternatives.

CONCLUSIONS

The internationalization of atomic power was formally proposed in 1946 as an extension of the legitimacy of the United Nations to solve international problems. It turned out to be a bridge too far when the United States and the Soviet Union could not even agree whether disarmament or control should come first. As long as some US policymakers believed a US monopoly could be maintained for years without cooperation of the Soviets or even US allies, there was not yet an identifiable common index of want toward which the behavioral impersonality or policy expertise of an external agent could be applied.

Internationalization gained traction when Eisenhower's "Atoms for Peace" speech stimulated hope that collective action could deliver the promises of the atomic age without its dangers. Although the Soviets disagreed, the US argued that an "International Atomic Energy Agency" could divert others from pursuing the "absolute weapon." It might, somehow, also alleviate the increasingly tense standoff between the three nuclear weapon states. The creation of the IAEA was a response to high demand for international cooperation on peaceful nuclear uses and nuclear nonproliferation. However, in the mid-1950s this was primarily perceived to be a problem of how to pool national efforts. Still lacking a consensus on norms of appropriate nuclear behavior in the mid-1950s, states in the negotiation of the IAEA largely wanted only a limited agent that could pool their national resources.

When the IAEA was born, developing norms at the Board of informed governors, closed meetings, and consensus decision making helped it emerge as a multilateral forum for nuclear governance. The effect of these strengths was limited by the weak consensus on norms of appropriate nuclear behavior, which left many members wondering why some states did not have to submit to limits on their programs. The Board's distance from the General Conference was still quite small, with one-third benefiting from representation at the Board, and these were all (if not more than) the population of advanced nuclear states. As more developing states joined the Agency from Latin America, the Middle East, and Africa (figure 3.2), its failure to promote nuclear development became more obvious. The budget and the number of staff increased but at levels that showed the members were unwilling to provide the resources needed to accommodate an investment in nuclear policy bias or impersonality beyond limited peaceful uses and limited safeguards. The agency that emerged was so closely controlled by its collective principals but divided about its purpose that even the United States could not drive through missions it wanted to see.

NOTES

1. On the decision, see Truman (1945).

2. Russia might have had more than one hundred nuclear weapons by 1953; see data from Natural Resources Defense Council, "Archive of Nuclear Data," accessed February 26, 2014, http://www.nrdc.org/nuclear/nudb/datainx.asp.

3. The Marshall Islands have commemorated the event annually as Nuclear Remembrance Day, held each year on March 1.

4. In addition to EURATOM, several European institutions were created in the 1950s, including the European Coal and Steel Community and the European Economic Community.

5. On juridical sovereignty, see Jackson (1987) and Krasner (1999).

6. On the early test ban negotiations, see also Brown (2007); Goodby (2005); Goldschmidt (1977); Loeb (1991); McBride (1967); and York (1987).

7. This phrase is widely attributed first to a September 16, 1954, speech by Lewis L. Strauss, chairman of the US Atomic Energy Commission, 1953–58, to the National Association of Science Writers.

8. "Outline History of Nuclear Energy," WNA, March 2014, http://www.world
-nuclear.org/info/Current-and-Future-Generation/Outline-History-of-Nuclear-Energy/.

9. The push to accept US research reactors reflected the assumption that the United
States maintained greater political control if these reactors were reliant on continued US
supplies of highly enriched uranium.

The Adolescence of the Agency, 1962–1985

C HANGES INSIDE AND OUTSIDE the Agency began to occur after 1962 that increased demand for it to contribute to nuclear policy coopera-tion. The preconditions for authority developed at the Agency's Board and Secretariat over a twenty-five-year period as historical events coincided with the IAEA's investment in delivering services in safeguards, safety, and development assistance. Sigvard Eklund was elected as the IAEA's second director general, the Nuclear Non-Proliferation Treaty (NPT) was negotiated and brought into force, and accidents occurred in 1979 at Three Mile Island and in 1986 at Chernobyl. At the close of this period the Agency remained a limited agent that accommodated its princi-pals' interests more than it demanded accommodation of its rules and com-mands. However, by 1986 it also was better positioned to supply policy partiality and impersonality should external events cause its principals' demand to increase.

NUCLEAR DEVELOPMENT AND NUCLEAR INSTABILITY

The Soviet Union was quite upset when the Board decided to recommend to the General Conference that a European with a scientific background, not a Russian, be approved as director general. The Soviets had expected they would next "control" the Secretariat after accepting a turn at American control. Their representative announced he would have no contact with Eklund and stormed out of the Board meeting, followed by his delegation and that of several other countries (Quihillalt and Büchler 1997, 60–61). Similar confrontations occurred outside the Agency in Berlin, Czechoslovakia, and elsewhere. A "delicate balance of terror" had emerged as the United States and the Soviet Union raced to ever-larger deterrent arsenals and preemptive strike capabilities (Kaplan 1983).[1] Uncertainty caused repeated crises as they tried to get the measure of each other's capabilities and interests (Powell 1990). As close as the world came to nuclear war in the 1962 Cuban missile crisis, for example, the United States had not known Soviet nuclear weapons were present, operational, and within Cuban reach to seize.

The realization that continuous nuclear brinksmanship risked an accidental nuclear war increased pressure on the superpowers for arms control. They purchased strategic stability first with restraint against pushing below the nuclear threshold in regional crises. Restraint benefited the superpowers at the expense of their allies' interests, undermining the credibility of their alliance commitments. Restraint therefore also created incentives for their allies to provide for themselves the nuclear security that their patrons might withhold if asked, for example, to "trade Boston for Bonn" (Posen and Van Evera 1983, 8).

The superpowers were uncertain about who was pursuing nuclear weapons. The Soviets worried about West Germany and China (Burr and Richelson 2000). The United States worried first about India, Japan, Sweden, Canada, Italy, or West Germany, believing China and Israel were still years away.[2] In fact, four states had already begun programs by 1963, and another fifteen potentially had a nuclear weapons program within reach if they took the political decision to try (Jo and Gartzke 2007). They feared horizontal proliferation would cause regional conflicts with small nuclear powers to be transformed into a global conflagration (Trachtenberg 1989), 320).[3]

The most public change after the Cuban crisis was a new effort by the Soviet Union, the United Kingdom, and the United States to negotiate a test ban. After test ban negotiations had undergone stops and starts for year, they finally succeeded in 1963 in concluding the Limited Test Ban Treaty (LTBT). Although "limited" because it did not ban underground tests, with sixty-two states quickly acceding, it promised to solve most of the environmental problems of nuclear testing and was at least a step toward reining in the US–Soviet arms race (Brennan 1961a; Williams and Cantelon 1984). Some feared potential proliferators were unlikely to sign, and France and China did reject it as an indirect attack on their strategic independence (York 1987; Goodby 2005, 397). Others feared proliferators could still develop nuclear weapons without testing or with small, undetectable tests (Brennan and Halperin 1961).

A quieter development was the Soviet decision to abandon its opposition to international verification. Seeking better guarantees of Germany's nuclear restraint than it believed would come from the European Atomic Energy Community (EURATOM), the Soviets finally endorsed the idea of imposing the Agency's monitoring system on others. This reversal was most significant because it also effectively ended the East–West rivalry at the IAEA (Goodby 2005, 403). The Soviet shift was presaged in part by the joint decision in 1961 to create the Eighteen Nation Disarmament Committee (ENDC) as a dedicated forum at the United Nations, and by its slowly increased willingness to consider some verification of a test ban.

After the LTBT entered into force, the United States broached a nonproliferation treaty as another way to address horizontal proliferation (McKnight 1971, 67). A nonproliferation treaty had been proposed earlier, and most scholars look to the 1961 "Irish Resolution."[4] The idea gained traction because commercial expansion of nuclear power meant by the mid-1960s the major powers were again racing to stop unrestrained—and unsafeguarded—nuclear supply. The United States had begun promoting "light" or natural water reactors (LWR), but with US control of the enriched uranium fuel market for these reactors slipping since the 1950s, its political control over proliferation was loosened (Goldschmidt 1982, 181, 266). Canada, France, Germany, and the Soviet Union were also offering reactors and fuel-cycle facilities (McKnight 1971, xiv; Goldschmidt 1977; 1982, 331–42).

After the fights over IAEA safeguards just a few years before, both the United States and the Soviet Union knew a nonproliferation treaty must have the support of the developed and allied states that faced real risks to renouncing nuclear weapons and accepting intrusive inspections (Ølgaard 1969). Some states were hopeful that a nonproliferation treaty could help stop neighbors or rivals from acquiring nuclear weapons. Opposition was particularly strong from developing states, which had organized in 1964 into the Group of 77 (G-77) to rally the Global South against inequality that they argued was being cemented by the international political and economic system.

After years of superpower negotiation, months of talks at the ENDC, and more debate at the UN General Assembly, the NPT was opened for signature on June 12, 1968. The ten articles of the NPT consecrated principles of behavior that are now recognized as the bedrock of the nonproliferation regime: verified nonproliferation by non–nuclear weapon states (NNWS, or any state that had not tested prior to 1968), "the inalienable right" to peaceful uses, and progress on complete and general disarmament.[5] The text has not been amended in over forty years and is now almost universally acceded and adhered to. However, holding review conferences every five years has proved important because amending the NPT is virtually impossible.[6] Review conferences have served to clarify the evolving meaning of commitments to "disarmament" and "comprehensive safeguards," and whether verifiable nonproliferation is a precondition for the right of peaceful uses.

The NPT specifically delegates the implementation of "comprehensive safeguards" on NNWS obligations to nonproliferation to the IAEA. Within eighteen months of the NPT entering into force, the Board had legalized the intrusive international imposition of safeguards in the Comprehensive Safeguards Agreement (CSA) system under INFCIRC/153. The Secretariat immediately began negotiating INFCIRC/153-style agreements with NPT states that provide the IAEA's right to judge a state's compliance with the IAEA's responsibility and obligation to "verify that there has been no diversion of nuclear material required to be safeguarded" (IAEA 1972a, para. 20).[7] The CSA includes provisions for the timely detection of diversion of significant quantities of nuclear materials using materials accountancy, containment, and surveillance of all nuclear materials (Scheinman 1987, 163–65). The NPT directs the IAEA to inform the UN Security Council of safeguards violations, but many expected retaliation by other states in the form of reciprocal withdrawal from the treaty (Hirdman 1972, 101–5). An informal committee was also established in 1971 under Claude Zangger to help NPT states by harmonizing NPT state approaches to nuclear export controls. Importantly, the Zangger Committee, as it became known, also began negotiating a "trigger list" of nuclear materials and technologies that NPT states should require to be safeguarded as a condition of supply (Potter 1985).

The rate of nuclear power plant construction, and especially the increase in commercial power-generating capacity, was slower than had been expected during the NPT's negotiation (see figure 4.1). Reactor construction costs were climbing, reaching over $400 million by the mid-1970s, and US guarantees for fuel supplies were less reliable (Scheinman 1987, 178–80). Solving energy insecurity therefore also created demand for others to enter the uranium market and offer enrichment and reprocessing technologies to sweeten their reactor supply deals (McKnight 1971, xiv; Goldschmidt 1977; 1982, 181–266, 331–42). These changes would make it easier for states to walk up to the proliferation threshold and eliminate the timely warning of diversion that Comprehensive Safeguards assumed (Burr 2005).

Nuclear power did become more cost effective as oil prices climbed in the early 1970s with Middle East instability and then quadrupled after the Iranian revolution in 1979. States concerned that persistent energy insecurity would further undermine economic growth expanded their investments in nuclear power (Cohen 1990, chap. 9). So-called petrodollars, the extraordinary income from inflated petroleum prices, began to flow and was used

Figure 4.1.   Size of Nuclear Power Industry, 1954–2013

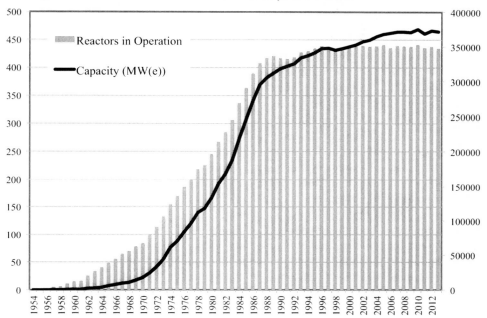

Data Source: IAEA, *Nuclear Power Reactors in the World.* Reference Data Series No. 2 (Vienna: IAEA, 2014), 20.

by many to finance nuclear energy programs (Greenwood and Haffa 1981). This expansion includes countries like Iran, which began major investments in nuclear power by contracting with German and French suppliers for four reactors and an apparent investment of $1 billion in Eurodif, a French uranium enrichment consortium. Unfortunately, the costs also continued to climb because of parts shortages, problems scaling up from demonstration plants, and increasingly stringent health and safety standards (Goldschmidt 1982, 331–32). There was also continuing uncertainty over the long-term costs, including waste treatment and storage. By the mid-1980s, when the flow of petrodollars dried up and precipitated a global debt crisis among developing states, the price tag for a single reactor was over $2 billion. (Iran's program was also interrupted by its revolution and then the destructive war with Iraq.)

Growth was slower than expected for a political reason: on May 18, 1974, India conducted what it called a peaceful nuclear explosion. By mating civilian nuclear activities with a secret weapons development program, India forced supplier states to confront the previously hypothetical "threshold state" problem (Statement of Sen. Stuart Symington, in US Senate 1977,

2–5). The United States and Canada especially, but also others, put new pressure on states to accede to the NPT and to accept IAEA safeguards.[8] They also pressed other suppliers to withhold sensitive fuel-cycle technologies.

All the major nuclear supplier states, after failing to do so in the 1960s, finally came together to discuss coordinating their supply standards (US Senate 1977). The meeting, described first as the London Club and later called the Nuclear Suppliers Group (NSG), included Western and Communist suppliers and was the first nonproliferation institution to include France (Tate 1990, 407). The group produced, by consensus, a trigger list of nuclear technologies and materials for which recipients would be required by their suppliers to apply IAEA safeguards, give assurances of non-use for nuclear explosives, ensure adequate physical security, and demand the same requirements if retransferred to a third party (US Senate 1977, 271, 309; Thorne 1997). They divided over allowing new states to import reprocessing, enrichment, or heavy-water production facilities (Schmidt 1994). Outside the London Club, there was opposition to this new discriminatory arrangement that was a direct challenge to the Zangger Committee, which did not produce its own trigger list until September 1974 (IAEA 1972b).

Unsatisfied with either consensus, the US Congress demanded that all US supply contracts be retroactively and unilaterally renegotiated to require a CSA and the right to refuse recipient country reprocessing.[9] President Jimmy Carter then moved to kill US investment in spent-fuel reprocessing and breeder reactor technologies. US allies were upset by this high-handedness, which also threatened development programs that the United States had been encouraging (Greenwood and Haffa 1981; Martinez 2002, 272). Carter tried to reassure states that more enrichment and reprocessing capacity was not necessary because there was still a several-year oversupply of uranium (Goldschmidt 1982, 413). Finally, Carter convened the International Fuel Cycle Evaluation (INFCE) meetings, hoping for a new international consensus on a more proliferation-resistant nuclear fuel cycle. However, the INFCE process failed to support Carter's preferred policy of eliminating reprocessing (Gummett 1981).

Nuclear energy investment was then interrupted when a minor failure triggered the first major nuclear reactor accident. The 1979 accident at the US Three Mile Island nuclear power facility drew international attention to not only the risk of environmental radiation but also the incredible cost ($1 billion) to clean up the site (Peterson 1989).[10] New nuclear investment slowed, many reactors planned and initiated in the 1970s were cancelled, and within several years fewer new facilities were coming on line. Energy insecurity was real, though, and continued to drive states toward nuclear power. While the number of reactors brought into operation was roughly equal to the number being retired, the new facilities were larger and total electricity generating capacity increased.[11]

Another wedge between the G-77 and others developed on nuclear issues when US satellites detected what might be an atmospheric nuclear test over the Atlantic Ocean to the southwest of South Africa (Power 1986, 485). The weak international response to the test, G-77 states argued, was indicative of "Northern" indifference to "Southern" complaints about a discriminatory economic system, superpower military interventions in the third world, and continued political support for South Africa and Israel. The test reminded them of the continuing US–Soviet failure to conclude a comprehensive test ban or another SALT (Strategic Arms Limitations Talks) agreement on nuclear delivery systems (York 1987, 290–308). Progress on both had stopped after Soviet forces were again discovered in Cuba, the Soviets invaded Afghanistan, and US conservatives argued that Carter's engagement was handing the Soviets a dangerous strategic advantage (Posen and Van Evera 1983, 37–39; Caldwell 1991, 279–85).

Developing states increasingly politicized meetings with their criticisms of Israel and South Africa (Hecht 2006). Their schism widened when Eklund announced he would retire in 1982, and the G-77, which included most of the threshold states of proliferation concern at the time, organized to support a developing state candidate (Le Guelte 1997, 89; Loosch 1997, 74–75). Beyond the G-77's consensus to support nuclear assistance, however, they did not exploit their Board or General Conference majority well (Jönsson and Bolin 1988, 311; Potter and Mukhatzhanova 2012). When a squadron of Israeli jets crossed deep into Iraq and bombed Iraq's Tuwaitha nuclear facility, for example, this reignited concerns about horizontal proliferation, the effectiveness of IAEA safeguards, and the balance between nuclear regulation and promotion (Gummett 1981; Imber 1989, 74–95). The attack reinforced the North–South conflict to some extent, but it broke the consensus over Eklund's replacement because many G-77 states feared proliferation even among their own ranks (Scheinman 1987, 270). The same 1981 IAEA General Conference that voted to suspend technical assistance to Israel and tabled a resolution for the September 1982 meeting to suspend Israel's participation and other rights of membership in the IAEA, if it did not open all its nuclear facilities to IAEA inspection, also decided to confirm Hans Blix as the next director general (Imber 1989, 74).

The new US president, Ronald Reagan, was critical of the compromises implied by Carter's international approach. After stating in January 1980, during his campaign for election, "I just don't think it's any of our business" if countries wanted to develop nuclear weapons (Smith 1981), Reagan's administration began differentiating between legitimate and illegitimate proliferators (Scheinman 1983, 363). This decision was met with fresh accusations of a discriminatory regime by countries like India and Argentina (Smith 1981).

When the resolution on Israel did come before the 1982 General Conference, the United States convinced a majority to reject it but then failed by one vote to stop the General Conference from denying credentials to Israel's delegation (Kennedy 1997, 118; Kirk 1997, 95–99). After threatening "serious consequences" if this happened, the United States delegation felt forced to literally pack and leave the IAEA, withdrawing incredible diplomatic support, a quarter of the regular budget, and incalculable contributions in training, safeguards research and development, cost-free experts, and other assistance (Stoiber 1983, 374). The United States returned five months later after Blix issued his formal assurance of Israel's full participation at the IAEA.

Reagan also initially abandoned arms control in the early years of his administration in favor of "prevailing" in a nuclear war (Grey 1983, 389–91; Posen and Van Evera 1983). The Soviets responded with a renewed emphasis on conventional forces (Kaplan 1983, chap. 26; Freedman 2003, 378–406). The increased tensions paradoxically reopened both superpowers to arms control, including the Strategic Arms Reduction Talks (START), rebalancing their strategic forces but with an emphasis on verification, and then the Intermediate-Range Nuclear Forces (INF) talks, which removed an entire class of missiles from both their arsenals. Reagan expressed hope that, with proper verification, the United States and Soviet Union could create peace through the international legalization of nuclear parity. However, these negotiations were not launched until late 1986, months after an accident at the Chernobyl nuclear power plant unfolded to become the worst nuclear disaster ever.

AGENCY ADOLESCENCE

The IAEA in 1962 was highly limited and under the tight multilateral control of advanced states but also dependent on the United States. The IAEA grew, expanding its assistance but especially its safeguards, and by 1985 had 108 members. To compare, as in figure 1.1, the United Nations in 1985 had 159 members and the NPT had 131 states. The IAEA staff was nearly 1,600 persons, and its regular budget was $106.8 million, a seventeenfold resource increase from the early 1960s (IAEA 1985 Annual Report). Adjusted for inflation, this was a real increase of 480 percent but was still insufficient to meet the IAEA's needs. Between industry expansion and the NPT, for example, the number of annual safeguards inspections increased from 18 in 1965 to over 1,100 in 1985, a sixtyfold increase.

These numbers suggest increasing accommodation of the IAEA's supply of nuclear cooperation. Did this occur because of persistent demand for its policy partiality and impersonality? Did the IAEA issue rules and commands over a greater range of nuclear policy, and did states acknowledge its authority to do so with accommodation and compliance? The rest of this chapter analyzes whether this accommodation and compliance was a result of the coercive effects of superpower influence or international norms, effective multilateral control, or the pull of IAEA authority.

Superpower Dominion?

The US and Soviet views of proliferation were converging after the Cuban crisis in 1962. They shared a mutual interest in improving bilateral strategic stability and in suppressing horizontal proliferation, especially by China. This facilitated first the limited test ban and then, with Soviet support for international monitoring, a verified nonproliferation treaty. However, despite what Imber (1989, 73) describes as an "atomic condominium," neither could impose their nuclear policy interests upon the other or even their more independent allies. The quality of the US nuclear arsenal improved throughout the period, but the total number of US warheads dropped after 1966, as did the relative size of its economy and military.[12] These declines worsened with the failure in Vietnam and economic recession, encouraging others to exploit the resulting loosening yoke of American hierarchy. Superpower attempts to coerce their allies only worsened the proliferation problem, leading to, for the United States, independent British (1952) and French (1961) nuclear arsenals and France's partial withdrawal from NATO. The United States then had to work quite hard to stop proliferation by South Korea, Taiwan, and others. For the Soviet Union, it contributed directly to China's nuclear program and the Sino-Soviet split.

The United States and Soviet Union certainly dominated the NPT negotiations (Goldschmidt 1981). Long before subjecting their proposals to international negotiation, they agreed in bilateral talks that the focus on nonproliferation would not interfere with accessing peaceful uses (Article IV), including peaceful nuclear explosions (Article V). Neither, however, broached verification in the bilateral negotiations. Also, it was not until the UN negotiations that IAEA verification triumphed over the alternatives. The resulting NPT, discussed more fully later, was not imposed by superpower dominion, and superpower support for NPT accession or Agency safeguards did not translate into submission by the NPT's intended targets. Many likely proliferators were slow to accede, and key states like France and China remained "holdouts" for years. Even the US threat to leave the Agency in 1981, and repeated in 1982 (and similar to threats it made elsewhere), was insufficient to protect an ally from sanction, and the United States was forced to return within months after recognizing it could not do without the IAEA in its current form (Stoiber 1983, 374; Scheinman 1987, 21). The United States was also unable to convince the nuclear suppliers to require comprehensive safeguards as a requirement for supply, despite years of pressing them (Miller 1981).

In short, the superpowers were a necessary ingredient to the expansion of the IAEA in the period, but their interests were by themselves insufficient to explain the international demand for Agency services, or its supply, that we observe during the period.

Nonproliferation Norms?

This period saw great evolution in the structure of international procedural and outcome norms. International organizations had been seen as appropriate mechanisms for international political and technical collaborations in the 1940s and 1950s (Suschny 1997, 213). Greater Soviet obstructionism at the UN Security Council and other UN-related bodies undermined their legitimacy both by calling into question their ideological orientation and by preventing them from being functionally effective. This problem, though, diminished at the IAEA after 1962 with the Western-Socialist consensus on the dangers of proliferation.

Nuclear norms were also contentious. The antinuclear movement continued to build against nuclear deterrence as brinksmanship threatened the accidental spasm into nuclear world war. Nuclear testing expelled mounting environmental radiation but reinforced the credibility of deterrence, which in turn appeared to be preventing a more deliberate path to limited nuclear war. "Atoms for Peace" had promoted a norm of guaranteed access to "peaceful uses" of nuclear technology and advocated a conditional, though contested, norm of accepting safeguards against its misuse (Bunn 1992).

Tannenwald (2007) argues that the taboo against nuclear use was strengthening, but Pierre Goldschmidt (1982, 183) states that there was still no moral condemnation of proliferation. Regional acquisition of nuclear weapons was expensive and could increase insecurity by forcing a competitor to address their greater insecurity. Proliferation might also make one a strategic target in the event of a superpower conflict. Proliferation was not "bad," and nonproliferation in the mid-1960s was instead a rational response.

Nuclear norms became less contested and conditional in the mid-1960s as the negotiation of the NPT and domestic accessions that followed reinforced beliefs about the dangers of proliferation. The NPT, as Rublee (2009, 42) argues, was "the main source of formal normative transmissions . . . that designated nuclear weapons acquisition as unacceptable." NPT accession socialized actors that it was in their own self-interest to not contribute to global instability by spreading nuclear weapons, but its slow pace is evidence that the nonproliferation norm was just emerging. The number of NPT states is shown in figure 1.1 relative to the total population of UN and IAEA members because so many new states were being created with decolonization.

This pace only hinted at the reticence of key target states. Germany, Italy, and Japan, which did not accede until 1975, had largely commercial concerns. Other developed states, though, could not reject the possible usefulness of nuclear weapons if superpower security guarantees weakened—and the US experience in Vietnam had worsened doubts about security commitments. India, France, and others argued that the NPT was discriminatory, interfered selectively with national development, and was too weak on disarmament (Barnaby 1969a; Rublee 2009, 66–67). They saw "nonproliferation" as another way for nuclear weapons states to maintain their strategic privilege, and they refused to accede (Scheinman 1987, 269).

For developing states, nonproliferation was an ongoing concession to the great powers. They wanted compensation with continuing security benefits, nuclear disarmament, and support for peaceful nuclear uses (Pastinen 1977). Without compensation, they were unwilling to forgo the "politicization" that undermined the effectiveness of functionally organized UN system bodies (Jönsson and Bolin 1988).[13] Perceived politicization rested on Western assumptions that the technocratic goals of international organizations could be separated from politics, which socialist and developing states disputed as also political in purpose (Imber 1989, 13, 24–26). For example, IMF members who believed they had a "right" to borrow criticized the increasingly demanding changes to their domestic economies, or "conditionality," to which they were forced to commit (Peet 2003, 65–71). As Lisa Martin (2006, 157) shows, the IMF executive board by the late 1970s then had to reassert control from its staff over conditionality. These conflicts contributed to the G-77 narrative that developing states were being politically and economically disenfranchised by the international system, a narrative supported by social science theories of "dependency" (Dos Santos 1991; Portes 1998). The conflict over sovereignty and economic development norms spread to the IAEA as competition between nuclear access and accountability.

The terms of this debate were to be clouded, however, when India called its 1974 test a "peaceful nuclear explosion." India also undermined the proliferation norm by arguing that nuclear weapons could not be proscribed for some as long as they were legal for others. "Nonproliferation" was still increasingly coercive, and many target states acceded to the NPT in the next few years. Even holdouts abided while refusing to be legally bound. France, for example, promised to obey the spirit of the NPT and joined the London Club consensus. Also, only three of the NPT holdout states conducted nuclear weapons tests during this period, and of these only China's test violated the purpose of the LTBT.

The UN Security Council had for decades failed to serve its collective security purpose, and by the 1980s the norm of internationalization encountered greater conflict between the Western, socialist, and developing states. As much as the IAEA safeguards system had to expand to implement the NPT, states were also too willing to subordinate safeguards to "national sovereignty" and "economic development." The safeguards budget was held hostage by developing state demands for greater assistance. Developing states also sidelined reforms of international financial institutions. Developed states had confronted into the 1970s development economists' arguments that cheap capital spurred development (Lipset 1981; Rostow 1960). Even as this strategy appeared to fail, donor states seeking greater accountability were drowned out by the easy availability of petrodollars. Developing states then grabbed on to new models of "bureaucratic authoritarianism" (O'Donnell 1973) and "developmental states" (Johnson 1982) that argued for active government intervention in the economy and justified continued access to developed state lending while excluding their imports or direct investment. Developed states, though, found the lack of financial accountability increasingly problematic even before conservative forces were elected to power in the United States, the United Kingdom, and other developed states. Their support for international organizations only decreased when they could not impose greater financial discipline or make recipients more accountable.

In short, the normative environment provides little traction in explaining expanding reliance on the IAEA for safeguards, safety, or assistance by the states that had to consent to its expansion at the Agency. For these donor states, accommodation of the IAEA increased despite weakening appropriateness of internationalization. Nuclear norms of nonproliferation and non-testing were emerging, joining the strong norm of non-use, but any strengthening appears to follow the success of the IAEA in undermining the alternatives.

Demand and Supply of Agency

Despite the IAEA's creation, the continuing uncertainty in the 1960s over the future of nuclear energy and the risk if more states acquired nuclear weapons presented persistent demand for nuclear policy partiality and impersonality. The strength of framing nuclear acquisition as the "Nth country problem" was its focus on the threat that *any* proliferation could destabilize Cold War crises. Many states shared this superpower concern with proliferation by China and others but were still conflicted. Foreswearing nuclear weapons perpetuated the need for US or Soviet security guarantees (Koremenos 2001, 305–7), and few could if their regional rivals could still acquire and threaten to use nuclear weapons with impunity. And twice as many states were pursuing nuclear weapons by the 1970s, enabled by advanced states' exports of peaceful but dual-use nuclear technologies (Fuhrmann 2009a, 2009b; Kroenig 2009a, 2009b) and even by IAEA assistance (Brown and Kaplow 2014). France had acquired nuclear weapons largely on its own in 1961, but assistance had helped China (1964) and Israel (1967).

Demand for commitments to verifiable nonproliferation was already strong when global energy insecurity delivered the long-anticipated commercial demand for nuclear power. That India's nuclear test occurred almost simultaneously also proved that the risk of diversion from legitimate peaceful uses was real and unmitigated for states outside the NPT. It pointed to need for a more coordinated approach to restraint among the nuclear suppliers, states that had so far failed to manage the trade-offs between economic and security interests.

In response to the greater international demand to prevent vertical and horizontal proliferation, the capacity of the Agency's Board and Secretariat to act increased. The many new states joining with nuclear assistance and NPT verification at stake loosened collective multilateral control by the General Conference, the Agency's primary collective principal. Fewer than 17 percent of its members could form a majority at the Board in 1962, and by 1972 it was fewer than 12 percent. Many developed states, though, found common cause with developing states on the burdens of expanded safeguards and supply constraints (Fischer 1997, 90–93). They agreed together to reverse the erosion of principal control, and in 1972 the General Conference approved, and two-thirds of the members ratified, a statute amendment expanding the Board to thirty-four governors. The General Conference now elected twenty-two governors, and the outgoing Board chose the remaining twelve (Scheinman 1985, 39). The share of members represented at the Board temporarily increased to 16.5 percent, still less than before 1962.

Just as the Zangger Committee was weakened by its broad membership, the coordination role of the Board was undermined when its expansion in 1972 gave a majority to the developing states members that were increasingly the target of nonproliferation policies (Aler 1997). Developing states saw no reason not to use the IAEA to challenge the broader structure of the international system. They accused London Club controls of being discriminatory violations of the IAEA and NPT norms of access to peaceful nuclear technology. They also finally deprived South Africa of its Board seat in 1977 over apartheid after it had successfully defended for decades using technical criteria for Agency activities (Hecht 2006).[14]

Although undermined, the Board still provided a forum for multilateral coordination on nuclear policy through the early 1970s. The Board's

"Vienna Spirit" of confidential debates and consensus decision making, even with its increased heterogeneity, allowed the multiple crosscutting interest cleavages to form temporary coalitions behind policy decisions (Loosch 1997, 65–66). These norms of procedure and of excluding "political" issues reinforced the Board's functional capacity to serve multiple constituencies. It helped that G-77 states were often too different to consistently act as a concerted majority except on nuclear development assistance (Loosch 1997, 85; Potter and Mukhatzhanova 2012). Most G-77 states outside the Middle East, for example, placed low importance on the Arab–Israel conflict, including its nuclear dimensions (Scheinman 1985, 39). As a result, the Board could extend its and the Secretariat's formal autonomy from its collective principal when it had a consensus to do so.

G-77 numerical strength at the IAEA grew and became their rationale in demanding that the next director general be from a developing state when the 1981 campaign to replace Eklund began. Their campaign pitted nonproliferation against development goals and suppliers against recipients (Khan 1997, 306). It became a battle over Agency priorities until the G-77 split over Israel's attack created room for Swedish diplomat Hans Blix to become the Board's candidate. To get elected, Blix promised to tackle not only Western criticisms over administrative inefficiencies and post-Iraq (1981) questions of safeguards effectiveness but also G-77 demands for greater technical assistance (Scheinman 1987, xi). Western and Communist developed states successfully aligned to oppose any major policy changes desired by developing states, including any real expansion of Technical Cooperation. The Board, for example, blocked a resolution establishing quotas for hiring staff from third world countries. However, it had to promise to consider a third world representative when Blix's (first) term expired in 1985 (Miller 1981).

The IAEA had previously received little international attention because of its reputation as a technical agency relatively unaffected by political conflicts (Imber 1989, 70). As is clear in figure 4.2, this inattention ended when Israel's attack in 1981 and the US temporary withdrawal in 1982 opened up popular debate of the Agency's role and effectiveness. Western officials still worried the IAEA would collapse under politicization (Miller 1981) even before the United States withdrew. More questions would arise three years later, when China joined the Agency and the Board again expanded, now to thirty-five members (the amendment entered into force in 1989).

Despite resisting many developing state demands, the United States, the Soviet Union, and the other "Geneva Group" developed states that funded most international activities were unable to impose fiscal discipline. They finally agreed in 1984 to hold hostage the budget of the Agency, as well as budgets across the UN system, by imposing a "zero growth" budget policy. A majority of the 15.45 percent of members that controlled the Board by

Figure 4.2. Media Salience of IAEA

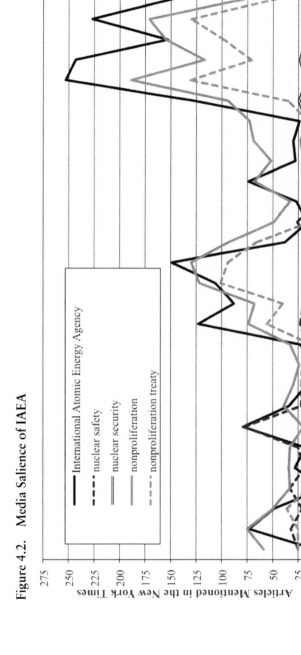

Data Source: Author's calculation using count of LexisNexis Academic results for search strings of listed terms (January 1980–December 2011).

1985 wanted fiscal discipline but lacked the required two-thirds majority of the General Conference that had to approve a budget that the developed pro-safeguards that states wanted to propose.

The Board's success in managing these international cleavages relied increasingly on the Secretariat. When Eklund took office in 1962, he created impersonality by institutionalizing national control over specific leadership positions. Just as the director general was intended to be a scientist from a developed non–nuclear weapon state, now the heads of the departments of Safeguards would always be from a developed non–nuclear weapon state, Nuclear Energy from Russia, Administration from the United States, and Technical Assistance from a developing state. Eklund reassured developing states early on by appointing their qualified candidates to senior posts and reforming the Technical Assistance program to deliver more significant projects. He focused on serving the members by growing the Secretariat's technical competence in the least controversial missions of safeguards techniques, safety standards, and technical development assistance (Khan 1997, 301).

Eklund and his senior staff also served the Board by directly consulting with governors in advance of their meetings (Quihillalt and Büchler 1997, 61). Many governors flew to Vienna for each Board meeting, and few states had permanent IAEA missions, which made the "Vienna Spirit" important to meetings going smoothly. Eklund's, and later Blix's, consultations with the Secretariat's constituencies was so successful that, by the mid-1980s, developing states were concerned that the director general was "precooking" decisions before their formal consideration by the Board (Scheinman 1987, 291).

Agency staffing also became contentious as international organizations generally became more politicized. Members expected their nationals to be appointed in proportion to their budget contributions to ensure a fair distribution of the international spoils. The NPT made geographic diversity even more important to preventing political capture by major donor states because many developing states expected that the inspectors would be nuclear weapons state experts (Koremenos 2001). Eklund acknowledged the normative goal of overall proportionality in appointments, and members under safeguards were entitled to block particular inspectors from being assigned to their facilities. Members felt free to lobby on specific vacancies, and Eklund adopted a norm of allowing members to reject candidates from their country considered by the Agency for specific positions. Although Eklund tried to block national preferences from affecting recruitment below the most senior levels, patronage or political hiring was not fully eradicated. The primary qualifications of at least one inspector from a developing state in the 1980s, for example, reportedly included experience as a grocery store manager and familial ties to senior officials of his nation's government.[15] In short, the director general early on confronted the need to balance the policy impersonality of geographic diversity with recruiting for policy bias.

Norms were clearly not irrelevant to creating policy impersonality and partiality in the Secretariat. Early in their efficiency drive in the 1970s, Western states sought to reduce patronage hiring and reliance on midlevel bureaucrats by shifting to a "permanent" civil service of long-term professional staff (Jönsson and Bolin 1988, 313–15). The Soviets instead demanded extendable contracts to maintain political control over their people and were supported by G-77 states that wanted to ensure that their people returned home with their new skills. As Christer Jönsson and Staffan Bolin (1988, 314) show, the IAEA was an extreme outlier among international organizations: more than 80 percent of Agency staff was on fixed-term contracts in 1975 when the UN average was about 34 percent.

Eklund also built an international bureaucracy with policy partiality by recruiting staff that favored the international promotion and regulation of peaceful nuclear technology. Daniel Carpenter (2010, 42) argues that individuals are often predisposed to the mission of the organizations where they take employment, but even former IAEA staff critical of aspects of the Agency expressed in interviews a strong affinity for it and its mission. Kaoru Naito, a nuclear engineer from Japan who helped develop safeguards approaches and eventually served as a deputy director general, described working at the IAEA as having "some magic power" to pull people into the Agency's mission (Hooper and Shea 2007, 4). Staff members were encouraged to maintain personal and professional contacts to keep their governments informed. Agency employment also encouraged an "internationalist professional perspective" because it took many experts off career tracks back home (Brewer 1978, 223). This was possible only because working relationships with its various constituencies enabled good candidates to emerge, and the Agency salaries were highly competitive with those outside the United States.

In short, the Board and the Secretariat acquired increasing accommodation after 1962 from its collective principal because of persistent demand for its policy partiality and impersonality. Eklund built broad if shallow support for the Secretariat, and for himself through three successive reelections, by combining professionalism and internationalism in the supply of peaceful uses of nuclear science. The strongest inferences about the relationship between persistent demand for agency gains, and state accommodation of IAEA supply, however, are from issue-specific analyses.

Peaceful Uses

With construction costs rising and little consensus over which technologies to pursue, many middle-income and developing states were disappointed that the Agency abstained from supplying large-scale projects (Goldschmidt 1982, 264). The Agency relied heavily on more established UN agencies to jointly apply nuclear techniques to medicine, agriculture, and water resources (Aler 1997, 152; Suschny 1997, 213). The IAEA itself spent little and funded only small projects lasting less than one year and providing a single instrument, training course, or fellowship (Fischer 1997). Eklund instead invested in research laboratories and safety standards, and he coordinated scientific and policy meetings, training programs, and technical publications. These investments allowed the IAEA to fill a unique assistance niche, if primarily for middle-income and advanced states.

Discord over IAEA priorities grew as the NPT seemed likely to enter into force. Developing states wanted any expanded regulatory functions to be balanced with more assistance, and wanted that assistance to be moved into the regular budget (Le Guelte 1997, 81; Loosch 1997). The Board agreed as early as 1969 to some budget parity between "promotion" (technical assistance in nuclear areas) and "regulation" (safeguards). Still, voluntary contributions for promotion increased from $1.3 million in 1965 to only $2.5 million in 1972, and safeguards spending, with the NPT in force, overtook Technical Assistance for the first time (figure 4.3). However, developed states still refused to accept a normative or legal requirement to support nuclear assistance (US Senate 1969). In the long run, this probably raised the price of technical assistance and restricted the growth of safeguards spending relative to what developed states preferred (Khan 1997, 303; Le Guelte 1997, 81).

To mollify developing states, the Board agreed to freeze safeguards assessments for developing states (Findlay 2012a) and increased Technical Assistance spending to over $36 million by 1985, a more than fourfold increase in real terms (inflation adjusted). The Board also offered longer-term institution- and capacity-building programs by moving Technical Assistance to a Secretariat-administered two-year planning and review cycle. The Board gave up its primary review responsibility, it said, because it lacked the time and necessary information to effectively assess project appropriateness (Wojcik 1997, 262). Engaging the Secretariat in direct reviews of assistance increased the Board's reliance on the Secretariat's policy bias and impersonality but also increased the Secretariat's autonomy by making the process more opaque to the Board.

The regulation/promotion debate also continued outside the Agency. Energy insecurity after the first oil shock stimulated interest in nuclear reactors but also in indigenous enrichment and in "closing" the fuel cycle by reprocessing used or "spent" fuel for plutonium. Many suppliers initially supported these investments despite US fears that this could stimulate weapons proliferation. When India's 1974 test showed the dangers of "sensitive" fuel-cycle technologies contributing to nuclear weapons even in developing

Figure 4.3.   Voluntary Contributions and Safeguards in Regular Budget

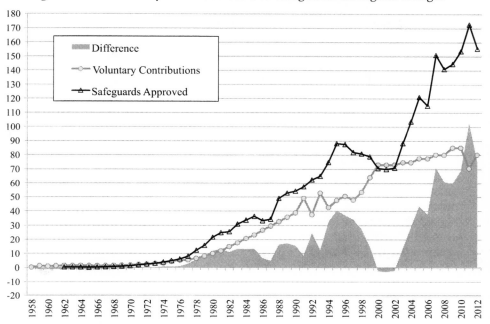

Data Source: Author's calculations.
Note: This graph reports only the regular budget for Safeguards and the target for
Voluntary Contributions for Technical Cooperation specified in the Annual Reports and
the Agency's Accounts documents. Both are adjusted for inflation to 2003 US dollars,
and neither includes extrabudgetary spending.

states without comprehensive safeguards, intelligence agencies began looking around more carefully, and others were also probably seeking to acquire
enrichment or reprocessing to support a nuclear weapons program (CIA
2005). The most direct solution was to coerce states into the NPT, although
this met with varying success. The United States, for example, succeeded in
convincing South Korea to accede in 1975 but failed with Brazil, which did
not accede until 1998.

Suppliers also worked indirectly to limit access. Participants in the London Club meetings finally agreed that suppliers should require IAEA safeguards as a condition of supply. France and West Germany blocked a
consensus to limit exports of fuel-cycle facilities to recipients under Comprehensive Safeguards, although none of them would thereafter do so. They
also convinced the IAEA Department of Technical Assistance and Publications to stop supplying "sensitive" fuel-cycle technologies and to commit to

include the Safeguards Department when reviewing projects before their submission to the Board for approval (Khan 1997, 307). Other international organizations were also convinced to defer to the Agency, requiring its partnership and even leadership in projects with nuclear components, extending an IAEA monopoly over international (but not national) nuclear assistance.

However, the regulation/promotion conflict was well established at the Agency, and the Secretariat was already insulated from significant new supply constraints. Safeguards inspectors would rarely (if ever) actually be consulted in assistance reviews, and the London Club had been formed because suppliers thought the Zangger Committee too weak. The G-77 further countered with demands that the Board establish a Committee on Assurances of Supply (CAS) with equal representation of the G-77 "South" and the developed "North," the first time a political caucus was the basis for official political or administrative units (Loosch 1997, 81). Developed states argued the CAS was unnecessary because the fuel market had never been politically interrupted and supply was expected to indefinitely exceed demand (Kislyak 1985, 214; Le Guelte 1997, 87).

The CAS also helped the Secretariat expand its involvement in broader nuclear industry trends (Le Guelte 1997). As more states brought on line more, larger, and more diverse nuclear facilities, IAEA Annual Reports made a point by the mid-1970s of tracking who was building which reactor types where. They also noted who had stopped, whether fuel supplies appeared sufficient, and how members planned to cope with spent fuel. IAEA independent expertise was valuable to many recipients in identifying these trends and making their own plans.

The United States and Canada, despite losing at the London Club, continued to push for exports for new fuel-cycle services to be under multinational management and to require a CSA for any new nuclear supply (US Senate 1977, 309). Multilateralization, they argued, could allay fears of fuel supplies being interrupted for political reasons but still prevent recipient states from acquiring sensitive capabilities (Goldschmidt 1977, 84; Scheinman 1981, 97; Khan 1997, 307). Largely unsuccessful, President Carter launched his INFCE initiative to identify proliferation-resistant alternatives to plutonium and enriched uranium fuel cycles (Gummett 1981). INFCE failed, but the seriousness with which the participants contemplated nuclear fuel-cycle options showed the continuing technical and economic uncertainty facing the nuclear energy industry.

"Peaceful nuclear explosives" received little attention outside of India's test. Almost every application threatened the same environmental radiation as the atmospheric or underwater nuclear tests that most agreed had to be stopped. Developing states, already placing a different value on protecting the environment relative to promoting economic development, held out hope that uses could be found that balanced the environmental costs. It was an accomplishment for antinuclear and nonproliferation advocates that the 1975 NPT Review Conference named the IAEA as the appropriate conduit for exploiting "peaceful nuclear explosives." This responsibility was added in recognition of its ability to make the "right" choice to not provide such devices, though the responsible office in the Secretariat would close in 1982 (Jönsson and Bolin 1988).

When petrodollars dried up in the early 1980s and triggered debt crises, developing states accelerated their demands for greater IAEA development assistance. They also wished to free it from developed state control over how it might be used. Similar conflicts also unfolded at a number of international financial institutions, which impeded donors from reforming international development programs to become more effective or accountable under the prevailing sovereignty norms. This encouraged the reactionary "zero growth" policy that donors imposed after 1984.

In summary, the expansion of the nuclear industry increased the potential distributional effects of regulation to recipient states that also remained collectively uncertain about the merits of various nuclear technologies relative to each other and to non-nuclear alternatives. The IAEA did not do much to assist advanced supplier states, but its information and expertise was helping middle-income and developing states make informed choices. The role was small, but states and their other international agents were clearly accommodating its promotion of peaceful nuclear uses. To meet the G-77 demand for impersonality in promotion, the director general and his staff acquired a greater intermediary role in managing competing interests inside the IAEA. Developing states continued to complain throughout the period, though, that the IAEA was neglecting its "primary mission" of promotion (Barkenbus 1987, 484).

Safety and Security

The Agency was the only international agent authorized to promote nuclear safety during this period. Under Eklund, the IAEA built its technical expertise in safety by drafting Basic Safety Standards, first published in 1962, and issuing guidelines on the safe handling and transport of radioactive materials. In 1972 it issued a new booklet written by a working group meeting of experts titled "Recommendations for the Physical Protection of Nuclear Materials" (Findlay 2010). "Standards" publications are not internationally negotiated and have no legally binding effects but require Board approval. For example, the foreword by Sterling Cole of Safety Series No. 4, "Safe Operation of Critical Assemblies and Research Reactors" (1961) clearly states that the standards are "in no sense intended to be mandatory; they should be regarded as a guide." In 1974 the Board then approved creating a standing advisory group, composed of nominally independent member state experts, to develop and report to the director general on "nuclear safety standards" (Gonzalez 2002, 283–84). They approved a revision to the 1972 recommendations that were published as INFCIRC/225 in December 1975, revised for the fifth time in January 2011 as "IAEA Nuclear Security Series No. 13" (INFCIRC/225/Rev.5).

The Secretariat's investment in nuclear safety, Enzo Iansiti (1976, 37) argues, was little more than an "exchange of information" and "increased mutual knowledge of the safety practices used in different Member States." The Secretariat offered voluntary "safety inspections" to consult with interested states, but only a few agreements were negotiated (IAEA 1960). And inspections were only ever carried out at the request of states and were never uninvited (Washington 1999, 197). This downgraded role was further acknowledged in 1976 by explicitly renaming the inspections "safety missions" (IAEA 1976b).

The 1979 accident at Three Mile Island proved expensive and increased interest in nuclear safety, but, without any apparent transnational effects, there was no interest in internationalizing safety regulation. The Board negotiated but did not conclude a binding international safety agreement and did not return health and safety monitoring responsibilities to the Secretariat. The Secretariat initiated its own nonbinding measures (Gonzalez 2002), including redrafting its Nuclear Safety Standards for nuclear power plants and creating an incident reporting system and the operational safety review team system (van Gorkom 1997, 175; Findlay 2010). The Secretariat was increasingly invited to conduct "safety missions" in the 1980s, but Wojcik (1997, 254) argues that its reliance on ad hoc contributions by national and industry experts created a highly uneven experience for states.

The highest profile "international" response was the nuclear industry's decision to organize the Institute of Nuclear Power Operations (INPO). Headquartered in the United States, this attempt at transnational cooperation was a private industry organization. The INPO was intended to promote industry-wide information sharing and conduct safety reviews, but the results of its reviews are confidential and not shared with governments or the public. Barkenbus (1987) argues that the willingness of plant operators to ignore INPO's recommendations led it to consider in 1986 a public ranking of low- and high-safety operators but also notes that "the threat of public disclosure" has compelled operators to comply at least partially.

Nuclear security begins to emerge as a distinct issue by the mid-1970s. While the Secretariat had already begun issuing its recommendations on nuclear security in the document that became INFCIRC/225 (discussed earlier), the final declaration of the 1975 NPT Review Conference and a 1975 General Conference resolution raised concerns about nuclear transport

safety, and the London Club also agreed to make physical protection a criterion in supply contracts (Pastinen 1977, 35). Eklund used the issue's attention to facilitate international negotiation of a US-drafted Convention on
the Physical Protection of Nuclear Materials (Vez Carmona 2005, 33).
Whereas most arms-related treaties began bilaterally (US–Soviet) or were
negotiated within a UN body such as the ENDC, this convention was negotiated under the IAEA's auspices, and the IAEA is the official depository
actor (IAEA 1980). Concluded in 1979, it obligates state signatories, but
not the Agency, to prevent, detect, and punish offenses related to the civilian
transnational transportation of nuclear materials (IAEA 2006, 1). There
was little international interest in supplying collective nuclear security, however, and the convention did not enter into force until 1987, after the Chernobyl accident.

In short, nuclear safety and security remained sovereign prerogatives
amid weak demand for international solutions. For decades, the IAEA supply of nuclear safety meant limited information sharing and training for
prevention and response (Le Guelte 1997, 88). Its safety standards were
helpful, but most states continued to rely on supplier expertise and national
regulators to identify and solve specific safety problems. Even in the United
States, the reaction to Three Mile Island was not new government intervention but the creation of the INPO, a nongovernmental organization. As Barkenbus (1987, 484) summarizes, nuclear safety was "not high on the
Agency's priority agenda."

Nonproliferation

In 1962 there were still many more states under bilateral safeguards than
under IAEA safeguards. The IAEA did not have its own stable of qualified
inspectors, so the first inspections were largely carried out under an appren-
ticeship program with US experts by seconded national inspectors (Büchler
1997, 51). The safeguards system also faced competition from EURATOM,
which the United States was supporting to help build a European identity
(Goldschmidt 1982, 383–86).

When the Soviet Union decided to support IAEA safeguards, a committee of Board states began renegotiating INFCIRC/66 to allow for more varied types of facilities. The safeguards system was also originally designed to
safeguard IAEA supply and had been stretched to apply to state-to-state
supply. The system was now expanded to explicitly accommodate state-to-
state nuclear supply agreements. Paragraphs 53 and 54 of INFCIRC/66/
Rev.2 also included the right to "special inspections" if the Agency determined that regular safeguards inspections were inadequate to resolve verification questions. This was a potentially extraordinary compromise of state
sovereignty even if limited to specific materials or facilities.

The Secretariat was then responsible for devising the actual inspection system, building on the existing national safeguards systems. Once the system was designed, the Secretariat began negotiating with individual states the public treaties outlining the system as well as the subsidiary legal agreements needed to implement safeguards. The attachments detail for each facility or item the strategic points for inspector access, inspection procedures, and the expected rate of inspections. They are also confidential even from the Board to protect commercial secrets and state sovereignty, requiring the Board to accept Secretariat discretion in their implementation. To enforce impersonality in the safeguards system, the Secretariat identifies inspectors as candidates for similar facilities within one of three regional operations directorates but excludes nationals of the target country. Each safeguarded state can reject any individual inspector without reason, usually those from countries hostile to the target.

The United States broached with the Soviet Union the nonproliferation treaty when it appeared that the "voluntary" system had been undermined by changes in the political economy of nuclear supply that were unexpected when the IAEA entered into force. Negotiations were largely bilateral at first, but both consulted with their allies extensively, knowing they needed to incorporate their demands. When the negotiations became international, the United States and the Soviet Union rejected a ban on nuclear weapons and refused to promise to neither make threats with nor use nuclear weapons against non–nuclear weapon states (Pendley et al. 1975, 609). They did agree to include language encouraging all parties to "pursue negotiations" on ending arms races and on disarmament (Article VI 1970), though there is no indication they expected they would actually be accountable. China and France argued that these obligations were discriminatory, and they joined India in rejecting the NPT.

There was clear interest among non–nuclear weapon states for a nonproliferation treaty and its international verification but also apprehension. When the UN General Assembly opened debate on the text approved at the ENDC, Bertrand Goldschmidt (1981, 75) describes "an atmosphere of bitterness, disappointment and resentment, reflecting the need of the countries in question to vent their feelings, if not to rebel, against the great powers, which had been exerting constant pressure on them all through the latter stages of the negotiations." Developed states already worried they would pay most of the overhead costs of supporting the Secretariat's safeguards budget and the direct local expenses of verification inspections (Ølgaard 1969). When the United States and the Soviet Union ruled out safeguards on nuclear weapon states, they now also feared a permanent economic disadvantage from greater disruptions, greater risk of technological secrets being compromised, and the loss of spin-off military technologies for civilian uses (see Prawitz 1969, 123; Hafele 1974, 148). George Quester

(1970) argues that developing states also feared the NPT would reduce support for promoting peaceful uses and economic development.

To reduce uncertainty about its effects, the negotiating states included the right under Article X to withdraw and a potential expiration date at twenty-five years (Koremenos 2001). These features, and allowing both peaceful explosions and unsafeguarded military uses (primarily nuclear-powered navies), caused many to hesitate (McKnight 1971, 69–70; Scheinman 1985, 25–31). It was reassuring to have the United States and the United Kingdom agree to open their commercial nuclear facilities to safeguards under "voluntary offer" agreements to help balance the burden others were being asked to accept. The Soviets refused (US Senate 1968, 11; Goldschmidt 1981, 80).

The compromise on safeguards provided little guidance about the safeguards that all NPT non–nuclear weapon states would be required to conclude within eighteen months of accession. The obligation that becomes an important focal point of the entire nonproliferation regime is described in just three sentences in Article III:

> Each Non-nuclear-weapon State Party to the Treaty undertakes to accept safeguards, as set forth in an agreement to be negotiated and concluded with the International Atomic Energy Agency in accordance with the Statute of the International Atomic Energy Agency and the Agency's safeguards system, for the exclusive purpose of verification of the fulfillment of its obligations assumed under this Treaty with a view to preventing diversion of nuclear energy from peaceful uses to nuclear weapons or other nuclear explosive devices. Procedures for the safeguards required by this Article shall be followed with respect to source or special fissionable material whether it is being produced, processed or used in any principal nuclear facility or is outside any such facility. The safeguards required by this Article shall be applied on all source or special fissionable material in all peaceful nuclear activities within the territory of such State, under its jurisdiction, or carried out under its control anywhere.

A major point of contention was the European demand for a special role for EURATOM or another European agency. Because the few nuclear facilities outside Europe were under bilateral safeguards, NPT verification could have exploited existing bilateral safeguards and European nuclear agencies, including EURATOM, the Organisation for Economic Co-operation and Development's European Nuclear Energy Agency, or the Western European Union's Armaments Control Agency (Rosen 1967, 173; Barnaby 1969b). The Soviets argued that "self-inspection" would not ensure European compliance (Bunn 1967; Firmage 1969, 717).[16] A compromise was reached when the United States suggested that EURATOM could be incorporated by allowing IAEA safeguards to be negotiated "either individually or together" (Article III.4).

Delegating to the IAEA was ultimately a gamble because it was not clear in 1968 that the Secretariat could supply an effective global verification system or that the Board could be an impersonal arbiter of asymmetric political commitments (Scheinman 1985, 29). The Secretariat had only inspected 23 facilities in seven countries in 1964, while the US Atomic Energy Commission had inspected 121 facilities in twenty-one countries (US Senate 1968, 168). The Secretariat might be too accommodating of target states in its early application of safeguards, consulting and compromising on its implementation, and limiting itself to reviewing paper records. Although contradicted by senior US government officials, US Rep. Craig Hosmer argued that the "IAEA's knowledge, skills and techniques in the art of inspection are rudimentary and its research towards improvements is essentially nil" (US Senate 1968, 168). Others argued that the IAEA appeared prepared to supply a technically rigorous, intrusive, and impartial NPT safeguards system (US Senate 1968, 93, 99–101).

There was also concern about foisting a more political role on the Board. Scientists or engineers, not diplomats, represented the Agency's most active states but, Georges Le Guelte (1997, 81) argues, it was "a mere fiction" to describe the Board as making decisions on a "purely scientific or technical basis." With the NPT in force, it might be no longer feasible to hope conflicts can be simply settled outside the IAEA. Others worried enforcement would divide the Board and ultimately fall to individual states (Pendley et al. 1975, 609).

When the NPT opened for signature in 1968, most states appeared to be reassured by the political commitments of NPT accession and IAEA safeguards (Bragin, Carlson, and Leslie 2001, 103; Matthews, Rockwood, and Hooper 2009, 8). These states were less concerned about the details of the NPT's implementation even though most nuclear industry expansion was occurring in advanced non–nuclear weapon states that were also the most likely proliferators (Pendley et al. 1975, 613). They found common cause with a group of Board members, primarily developed non–nuclear weapon states, who opposed defining "comprehensive safeguards" until they knew to whom they would be applied.

Only after its entry into force did the Board create a temporary Safeguards Committee to negotiate the CSA system described in INFCIRC/153. This committee was open to all members, and as many as fifty participated, pitting strong-safeguards advocates like the United States, Soviet Union, and Canada against defenders of looser safeguards. Japan, West Germany, and Italy were among those explicitly delaying their accession until it was clear they could negotiate NPT safeguards that would not be too intrusive, disruptive, or costly (International Energy Associates 1984, ii; Le Guelte 1997). In between, but still pro-safeguards, were Belgium, Hungary, and—perhaps most surprising—India.

The "comprehensive safeguards" system built on the recent consensus behind INFCIRC/66, but, highlighting the gap between the different collective principals, several compromises were still necessary to address IAEA members' concerns about the risk from NPT safeguards (International Energy Associates 1984, 10; Kratzer, Hooper, and Wulf 2005). First, the Statute offered the Secretariat "any time, any place" access to information, people, and facilities, but the CSA would limit "regular" verification of non-diversion to strategic points in declared facilities once the correctness of a state's declaration was verified through "ad hoc" inspections (Jensen 1974; IAEA 1998, 13; Rockwood 2002). Some believed that the risk of undeclared activities, and the chance of inspectors revealing them, to be quite small relative to the risk of states achieving threshold status and then diverting (International Energy Associates 1984). The United States and others suspected it was wrong to focus only on the diversion problem (US Senate 1968, 219; Hooper and Shea 2007, 10) but would accept a norm of materials accounting as long as INFCIRC/153 was legally more inclusive (International Energy Associates 1984; Rockwood 2002). The consensus that emerged would dominate for two decades: "comprehensive safeguards" only required proving non-diversion of materials from declared facilities. Jacques Baute argues that the Secretariat was explicitly told to not disruptively search for undeclared nuclear activities (International Energy Associates 1984, 27, 82; Matthews, Rockwood, and Hooper 2009, 8). The Board also explicitly excluded safety reviews or advanced reviews of planned facilities (Pendley et al. 1975, 614).

Second, the Safeguards Committee kept the provision from INFCIRC/66 for "special inspections" but agreed that inspections should not become routine (International Energy Associates 1984, ix, 78). Japan, India, and others argued that inspections were never intended to catch cheaters in the act, only to allow "timely" detection before states could benefit from misuse (International Energy Associates 1984, 76–77). The many objections created doubt that the Board would support even rare "special inspections." In an early test in 1976, for example, inspectors arrived at a safeguarded Japanese facility after midnight and requested access only to see the Board rebuke the Secretariat when Japan complained.[17]

Third, the committee left undefined key terms like "significant quantities," which were potentially different for different nuclear materials, and "timeliness," which might depend on the effectiveness of a state's accounting and the accuracy of Agency measurements. The Board asked the Standing Advisory Group on Safeguards Implementation to objectively define these for application in the field (Hooper and Shea 2007, 6). Finally, INFCIRC/153 still relied on confidential subsidiary agreements, precluding the Board from judging the day-to-day implementation of safeguards except through periodic reports summarizing its activities and judgments.[18] The

United States believed that these confidentiality provisions gave the Secretariat the discretion to choose to *not* report suspicions of noncompliance (US Senate 1968, 168; International Energy Associates 1984, 59).

Some compromises were technically necessary because, argues British safeguards inspector Roger Howsley, few national regulators or facility operators were ready for accurate accounts of nuclear materials or inspectors (Hooper and Shea 2007, 10). Kaoru Naito says, further, that facilities before the 1980s were not designed with safeguards in mind, so operators all too often triggered safeguard alarms accidentally by turning off the wrong lights or blocking IAEA cameras with their equipment (Hooper and Shea 2007, 12). IAEA inspectors therefore had to cooperate with operators, which improved Agency access and could enable inspectors to notice changes that might signal diversion.

Other compromises were politically necessary to limit the intrusiveness of safeguards. Through the 1980s inspectors were discouraged from asking questions or looking beyond the strategic points (Bragin, Carlson, and Leslie 2001, 103). They were to stay strictly within the confines of INFCIRC/ 153, published as a little pamphlet with a blue cover. They were so defensive in their application of safeguards, one former inspector said, "They wanted us to have the mentality of not looking at programs except with blinders. States would get upset if we challenged their good faith. Some states would sit there with their blue books when we arrived and wait for us to ask a question that we shouldn't."[19]

The members primarily limited the effects of safeguards by limiting its resources. Whereas the IAEA served its 72 members with a total budget of $7.94 million and 683 staff in 1965 (see figure 1.2), by 1972 the IAEA, with just 17 more members, had 1,044 staff and the total budget was $16.5 million (IAEA Annual Reports, 1965 and 1971). In those seven years, the safeguards budget increased from $235,000 to $2.45 million and the number of safeguards inspections from 18 in 1965 to 234. Safeguards were incredibly labor intensive, even with materials accountancy, and the Agency never had the resources that it believed it needed to fully implement its responsibilities once the NPT entered into force.

To save inspection costs, the Secretariat proposed that CSA implementation might be suspended in NPT states that declared they had no significant nuclear activities (Leslie, Carlson, and Berriman 2007). The Board agreed and allowed these states to sign a Small Quantities Protocol.[20] The Secretariat also began to automate safeguards as much as possible to reduce the on-site inspection burden. Seals with unique codes and melt or scarring patterns could verify that a door had not been opened since the inspector's last visit and cameras could continuously monitor whether or how often materials had moved through an area, though neither could guarantee the absence of other means of access. Automation also helped because the equipment that inspectors could physically carry was limited and would often perform poorly in the field, leaving neither the inspector nor the inspected with confidence in the results (Hooper and Shea 2007, 12–13). The Agency, with help from member states, was continuously working on new systems and technologies to reduce the cost and increase the effectiveness of safeguards. However, the problem with these new approaches, as described then by Brookhaven National Laboratory scientist William Higinbotham, was getting them adopted when the Agency's budget was tight and many of its members were suspicious.

For all its initial compromises, the Secretariat's implementation of the NPT would require a new collective principal—the NPT states—to actively and continuously accommodate its supply of intrusive information about state behavior. The Board translated three sentences in the NPT into a structure, but the policy information was largely defined by the Secretariat and then embedded by it into bilateral treaties approved by the Board. It was a collaborative process but also one that required substantial investment in policy partiality by the Secretariat and a willingness by the Board and states to accommodate its rules. As Hans Blix (1985, 6) later stated, this was "the first instance in history of sovereign States inviting an impartial international organization to audit their accounts and carry out inventories and other inspections on their own territory." Even critics described the Agency's safeguards "as an impressive accomplishment—the only case in today's world where quarreling nations have agreed to on-site inspections of sensitive facilities" (Boffey 1981). States, including even some nuclear weapon states, voluntarily accepted this regulation of aspects of their nuclear behavior by an international agent, an accommodation observed in their daily acceptance of intrusive verification activities in their sensitive nuclear facilities.

India's influence as a non-NPT signatory over the negotiation of INFC-IRC/153 had been an early sign of problems from the discontinuity between NPT and IAEA membership. The conflict between their collective principals expanded when India conducted its nuclear test in 1974, signaling a greater risk of horizontal proliferation than suspected as NPT states began their first Review Conference.[21] Trying to plug holes in the NPT, their consensus final declaration asked the IAEA to recommend approaches to internationalizing fuel-cycle services. Echoing the US and Canadian position at the London Club, they agreed also to ask supplier states to require non-NPT states to accept comprehensive safeguards as a supply condition (Gallini 1985). Although the London Club refused to require a CSA, the United States announced it would unilaterally revise its supply agreements to require one. These proposals expanded demand for IAEA services but were national initiatives, proposed and negotiated outside the IAEA.

The IAEA continued to struggle with supplying the growing safeguards demand within the restraints of regulation-promotion parity. The financial difficulties were bad enough that State Department official George S. Vest had to reassure the US Congress that it still believed the Agency "is the only one around that is acceptable to the large bunch of countries that we would like to have inspected; therefore our objective is to try to do what we can to beef it up" (US Senate 1977, 319). Larger donor states like Canada and the United States in 1976, and Japan in 1981, officially launched domestic programs to research and develop approaches to help the Secretariat improve its safeguards procedures, concepts, and technologies.[22] These investments were significant additions, with the US Support Program, for example, starting at one-third the level of its regular budget assessment (IAEA 1976a, 34; Losquadro 2007, 7). Pro-safeguards states also began redirecting their voluntary contributions. In adapting domestic expenditures to support the Agency's autonomy to implement its safeguards responsibilities, individual principals were aiding the Secretariat's ability to supply nuclear policy. These strategies were welcomed by the Secretariat but also required approval by the same Board that could not agree to raise the regular budget to provide these funds more directly.

Developed states might have believed the proliferation threat had shifted to the developing world, but the G-77 complained that nuclear weapon states were not fulfilling their Article VI commitments on disarmament and that suppliers were violating the Article IV commitments to peaceful uses. The widening gulf was first hinted at in the failure of the 1980 Review Conference to achieve a consensus final declaration (US Senate 1980; Gallini 1985, 20; Power 1986, 477). More indicative of the gulf was the international discord that followed Israel's attack on Iraq's Osirak reactor facility. Israel, an IAEA member but not an NPT state, accused the IAEA safeguards system of failing to detect Iraqi undeclared activities (IAEA 1998, 18). The IAEA's negotiator of Osirak's facility-level safeguards agreement, Roger Richter, resigned just before testifying to the US Congress that he believed the Secretariat had not negotiated the access necessary to verify non-diversion (US House of Representatives 1981). Director General Eklund and external experts argued that safeguards were sufficient to detect an Iraqi diversion in time for the international community to act (Eklund 1981; Feldman 1982).

Israel escaped with only international admonishment by the IAEA and the UN Security Council. UN Security Council Resolution #487 (June 19, 1981), passed by consensus, called upon Israel "to place its nuclear facilities under IAEA safeguards." The Security Council also noted the "the Agency has testified" that safeguards were applied satisfactorily in Iraq and that Iraq and all other states have "the inalienable right" to nuclear programs for peaceful purposes. Israel's attack remained a major point of criticism at the Board and General Conference until the Chernobyl accident in 1986 drew away their collective attention.

As this period came to a close, states continued to complain about discrimination inherent to the IAEA and NPT, not to mention the use of the London Club to bypass the IAEA. However, they remained individually interested in accepting the security advantages of safeguards. The number of states under any safeguards grew from twenty-one in 1965 to ninety-six by 1985 (IAEA 1985 Annual Report). With Russia also concluding a voluntary offer agreement in 1985, following the United Kingdom (1978), United States (1980), and France (1981), four of the five nuclear weapon states had made some nuclear activities under their control eligible for a CSA (Carlson 2011). The quantity of safeguarded materials also increased, from 3.1 tons of plutonium and enriched uranium in 1975 to 24,722 tons in 1985 (IAEA 1985 Annual Report, 61). This quantitative expansion reflected international accommodation of the Agency's supply of international nonproliferation by multiple collective principals: the General Conference and the parties to the NPT and Treaty of Tlatelolco. The negotiation and implementation of CSAs facilitated the internalization of the norm of nonproliferation while acculturating states to accommodating the Agency's investments in nonproliferation policy bias and impersonality. The success of these choices was implied in the absence of cases of undetected diversion of materials under comprehensive safeguards or of the misuse of safeguards information for commercial gain. Although NPT commitments gave the Secretariat extensive and intrusive access and made the Board the judge of states' compliance, the practical effect of international accommodation of the Agency was balanced, argues George Quester (1970, 168–74), by the intrinsic checks of its noninspection duties, financial constraints, the distribution of voting power guaranteeing formal influence to non–nuclear weapon states, and the need for states to consent to Agency safeguards agreements.

Disarmament

The Agency did not contribute in this period to disarmament or arms control negotiations or implementation. The NPT, for example, did not include verification of the Article VI disarmament commitment. Outside the nonproliferation regime, the US–Soviet SALT agreements were verified only by "national technical means." The superpowers decided this was sufficient to judge each other's compliance, but the treaties were also designed with this constraint in mind. The superpowers also concluded the 1974 Threshold Test Ban Treaty (TTBT), capping the size of underground nuclear tests still permitted under the LTBT. However, Herb York (1987) argues that the

TTBT and a comprehensive test ban foundered on continuing Soviet resistance to US and UK demands for effective verification. Despite concluding at least nine US–Soviet arms control treaties during the 1970s, others continued to criticize their failure to make substantial progress on disarmament. As long as the norm of "progress on disarmament" only applied to them, there was no demand to internationalize the process.

CONCLUSIONS

The promise of peaceful nuclear technology remained futuristic in 1962. The scale required and the persistent uncertainty over what technologies exactly should be pursued held up international investment in peaceful uses beyond technical conferences. Demand for collective solutions to this uncertainty over the possible effects of nuclear energy choices came also from the persistent and increasing risk that some states might misuse peaceful uses to acquire and use nuclear weapons. This risk only worsened as Cold War conflicts threatened to spiral out of control into a global nuclear war. Multilateral approaches became more necessary as nuclear technology and nuclear weapons spread to new states but were often subordinated by US–Soviet negotiations preceding, or substituting for, international involvement. Superpower confluence on nuclear proliferation after 1962 did spur greater international cooperation, including at the IAEA, even as their declining relative power and their loss of imperial legitimacy weakened the ability of either to coerce their close allies or developing states into compliance. The possibility of their using their nuclear condominium to protect their superpower status, though, only worsened the perception, including by some of their allies, of political bias in who could and could not acquire nuclear capabilities.

Increased internationalization of nuclear policy did not follow internalization of new nuclear or procedural norms. Many felt the strengthening simultaneously of norms of non-use and of nuclear deterrence alongside growing dissatisfaction with internationalization. A norm of nonproliferation was also not fully articulated until the NPT negotiations and, even then, persistent uncertainty about the global effects of proliferation meant particularly insecure states could legitimately seek nuclear weapons. Contestation over norms of appropriate nuclear behavior continued even as national acculturation to the practice of IAEA comprehensive safeguards and successful safeguards implementation helped harden the international norm of nonproliferation.

Accommodation with the IAEA supply of nuclear policy is observable most generally in the delegation to it by the international community of greater resources and policy roles. Throughout this period many more states joined the IAEA to acquire its benefits but also to gain greater voice as more states committed to accepting its safeguards under the NPT and the Treaty of Tlatelolco. The resources increased not because of greater membership, especially as the greater diversity of members made contributions to the Agency more politically sensitive, but because of the objectively measurable increase in demand for the Agency's outputs. The public was also paying increasing attention to the IAEA's role. Meanwhile, as the membership grew, the Board acquired increasing autonomy as fewer members were represented but also because of its continued success in balancing the needs of its members.

However, this success was not uniform across the nuclear issue areas. First, demand for agency bias and impersonality was weakest for disarmament. Arms control became focused on the US–Soviet relationship and increasingly excluded others as participants or targets as "complete and general disarmament" became impractical. The distributional effects of cheating were simply too great for either state, and, in the absence of superpower progress, most other states questioned the need to start.

Second, Eklund's choice to focus the Agency's efforts first on assistance and later safeguards diminished attention to the possible nuclear safety and security missions. Middle-income and later developing states did want help building national safety institutions and accommodated the Agency's investment in developing and promoting safety standards and training. The worst safety failure at Three Mile Island did not present a transnational problem and therefore did not increase demand for international safety regulation. Safety regulation and verification could safely continue as a purely national problem for which national regulators and industry vendors appeared best positioned to help.

Third, the international community accommodated the Agency's increasing monopolization of authority as the only legitimate supplier, or coordinator, of international nuclear assistance. Elkund focused the Agency's role on supplying small projects, nuclear training, and international technical conferences, largely benefiting middle-income states. The Agency then began adding medical and agricultural applications useful for developing states. When nonproliferation began to noticeably interfere with the "inalienable right" to peaceful uses, first with the NPT and then when supplier states formed the London Club, developing and middle-income states rallied behind greater Agency authority over peaceful uses. Reviews of Technical Assistance were placed into the hands of staff to make reviews more technically effective but also to strengthen the separation from the Secretariat's regulatory mission and Board politics.

Finally, the desire of many to extend nonproliferation toward a larger and more diverse array of states created demand for economies of scale but also persistent demand for new policy bias and greater impersonality in the

supply of nonproliferation. While some argued that the political commitments made in new agreements was enough, the Agency designed and began
to successfully implement safeguards that were probabilistically effective yet
unlikely to be disruptive or discriminatory. States collectively accommodated the Agency's rules and commands with ever-greater transfers of
resources and responsibilities for nonproliferation. Individual states signaled their accommodation in their accessions to, and apparent compliance
with, safeguards. Major powers also signaled their accommodation of IAEA
authority over nonproliferation. They accepted "voluntary offer" safeguards and devoted more resources to the regular budget, voluntary contributions, and national support programs. Their support made it possible for
the Agency to build the safeguards program and engage with policy and
technical professionals in these states. Nonproliferation experimentation
occurred outside the IAEA, but the most significant of these—the NPT,
nuclear weapon–free zones, and the London Club—were still implemented
largely by the IAEA.

In short, the Agency had demonstrated initial success as a limited agent
and received increasing accommodation of its missions, but when this
period closed in 1985, it did not have the power to issue rules and commands with which states felt pulled to comply. After 1962 it expanded its
supply of assistance and safety through active collaboration with its principals and investments in skilled personnel, training, scientific laboratories,
and a culture of international professionalism. These investments enabled
the Secretariat to extend its limited policy bias and impersonality to safeguards, which increased demand for the Agency as exogenous events
worsened the risks of uncoordinated nuclear and security policies. Despite
representing a decreasing share of the membership, the Vienna Spirit of
closed meetings and consensus decisions helped the Board build compromise as dynamic coalitions formed to support relatively exclusive policies in
nonproliferation, nuclear access, and economic development. The separate
successes of the Board and Secretariat elicited increasing accommodation
by states, which in turn acculturated states to the practice and norms of
nonproliferation and access to peaceful uses. However, it was not yet an
international nuclear authority.

NOTES

1. On the "delicate balance of terror," see Wohlstetter (1959).
2. See Document 8, National Intelligence Estimate Number 4–63, "Likelihood and
Consequences of a Proliferation of Nuclear Weapons Systems," June 28, 1963, in Burr
(2005).
3. On the "spasm" into nuclear war, see Kahn (1960).

4. "Nonproliferation" had been a component of the EURATOM proposal in 1955 (Goldschmidt 1982) and a 1960 Irish proposal to the UN General Assembly (Barnaby 1969c).

5. Treaty on the Non-Proliferation of Nuclear Weapons. Washington, DC: US Department of State. Treaties and Other International Acts Series.

6. The NPT actually called only for one review after five years and an extension conference at twenty-five years. On this and the amendment process, see the Article VIII.2 in the NPT (ibid.).

7. INFCIRC/155, for example, extended comprehensive safeguards over Finland's nuclear program and was approved in October 1971.

8. Even then, President Richard Nixon turned to offer reactors to Israel and Egypt, neither of which were NPT states, in the name of Middle East politics; see Scheinman (1987).

9. On the 1976 Symington Amendment to the Arms Control Export Act and the 1978 Nuclear Nonproliferation Act (NPAA), see Brown (1982) and Saleem (2001).

10. In August 2013 it was reported that completing the decommissioning of the site would require $918 million and would begin in 2034; see "$918M: The Cost to Dismantle Three Mile Island," NBC 10 Philadelphia, August 29, 2013, http://www.nbcphiladelphia.com/news/local/Three-Mile-Island-221665871.html.

11. "Outline History of Nuclear Energy," World Nuclear Association, March 2014, http://www.world-nuclear.org/info/Current-and-Future-Generation/Outline-History-of-Nuclear-Energy/.

12. These measures draw upon the Correlates of War data set by Singer (1987).

13. Scheinman (1987) also discusses earlier US politicization when it rejected admission for some Soviet allies.

14. South Africa's seat was also protected for many years by skewing the definition of "nuclear advancement" to include uranium ore producers.

15. Interview with IAEA Safeguards Operations Director, La Jolla, CA, August 2008.

16. On the possibility of using "public records" and national technical means, see Rosen (1967).

17. Lawrence Scheinman interview with author, Washington, DC, 2005.

18. Annual Safeguards Implementation Reports would provide some information; see Scheinman (1985). IAEA officials indicated these reports contained some facility-specific information but were rarely, if ever, actually requested or read by Members (interview with retired IAEA official).

19. Interview of IAEA officials, Vienna, Austria (group interview), 2005.

20. The number of states with Small Quantities Protocols in force accounts, in IAEA Annual Reports, for almost all the NPT parties counted as without CSAs in force.

21. "The Final Document of the Review Conference of the Parties to the Treaty on the Non-Proliferation of Nuclear Weapons." Geneva, 1975, p. 1.

22. The Brookhaven National Laboratory International Safeguards Project Office states that the US Support Program to IAEA Safeguards formally began in 1976; see "The US Support Program to IAEA Safeguards," International Safeguards Project Office, http://www.bnl.gov/ispo/ussp/. Jim Tape states the US support program began in 1966; see Hooper and Shea (2007).

5

The IAEA Challenged, 1986–1998

BEGINNING IN 1986 with the meltdown of Soviet nuclear power reactors in Chernobyl, Ukraine, and continuing through the early years of the post–Cold War era, the IAEA encountered several new and simultaneous opportunities to supply nuclear authority. With Hans Blix at the helm, the IAEA would choose to embrace challenges to its structure and mission that could have diminished its role in the norms, rules, and institutions of international nuclear cooperation. Variation in the IAEA's authority over each nuclear issue area continues to be the contingent result of many factors. As this chapter shows, the Agency began to assert political authority with its power to issue rules and make commands with which others must comply. The Agency supply of nuclear policy grew in all the issue areas, but demand was less persistent for the policy partiality and impersonality of a nuclear authority over nuclear safety or peaceful uses than for nonproliferation and disarmament.

NUCLEAR NONSAFETY, DISARMAMENT, AND NONPROLIFERATION CHALLENGES

US–Soviet relations had continued to deteriorate after the Soviet invasion of Afghanistan and Ronald Reagan's election as president. The US nuclear stockpile had declined by about eight thousand warheads from its peak in 1966, but Soviet warhead counts continued to steadily increase. Reagan began massive investments in strategic systems to regain what he saw as lost security. The popular fear of global nuclear war was again pervasive by the time Mikhail Gorbachev became Soviet premier in 1985 and launched the domestic political and economic reforms that would eventually dissolve the Soviet Union.

Reagan (1983) had famously referred to the Soviet Union as "an evil empire" just a couple years previously, and the United States remained uncertain about the credibility of Soviet interests when Gorbachev first proposed that the two superpowers should eliminate half, and later all, of their nuclear weapons. Bilateral relations began their thaw through a series of superpower summits, and the United States and the Soviet Union quickly negotiated and brought into force a series of bilateral arms control treaties, including the Intermediate Nuclear Forces Treaty, the Threshold Test Ban Treaty, and, to close the loophole in the Nuclear Non-Proliferation Treaty (NPT) by banning "peaceful" nuclear explosions, the Peaceful Nuclear Explosive Treaty (York 1987; Medalia 1998). Other bilateral and multilateral arms control agreements were also in the works, including the eventual Chemical Weapons Convention and the Strategic Arms Reduction Treaty or START. Despite these advances, the United States was criticized by developing states because it was believed to have reduced pressure on Pakistan to strengthen it against Soviet intervention in Afghanistan, ignored potential proliferation activities in Iraq to support it against Iran, and hidden the possibility of a South African nuclear weapons program (Rathjens 1995; Zunes 2005).

Just a few months after the first of those historic summits, in April 1986, reactor operators began to shut down for routine maintenance the relatively new Chernobyl 4 reactor in eastern Ukraine, then still a Soviet republic. Several fuel assemblies overheated and caused two explosions, killing two plant workers immediately but also precipitating a full reactor meltdown that killed another twenty-eight. This was the first nuclear power plant accident to cause a major environmental release of radiation: over 5 million people were exposed to more than a minimal dose of radiation, and 134 suffered acute radiation sickness; 335,000 people were resettled.[1] No one had expected an accident of this magnitude to occur in a country that had pioneered nuclear energy (Khan 1997).

The Soviets initially reacted with opacity. Only after Sweden detected radioactive fallout two days later did the Soviet Union inform the IAEA of the accident. People across Europe became anxious, if not panicked, but received little reassurance from the Soviet Union or their own governments (Milne 1987, 54). International requests for information about the accident were ignored. Finally, on May 4 the Soviet Union invited the Agency for consultations. Blix flew to Moscow the next day with two of his senior advisors (one Russian and one American), becoming the first from outside the Soviet Union to see Chernobyl. He reported to the world a calming message that, as they flew over, they saw "people working in the fields, livestock in the pastures and cars driving in the streets" (Mayr 2006). Blix did not even officially report to the Board on his visit until specifically asked to by West Germany.

Blix soon learned he had been deceived. Although the Board had kept the Agency's mandate in the area of nuclear safety limited after Three Mile Island, Blix pressed the Board to immediately adopt "a comprehensive program on safety" (van Gorkom 1997, 173). The Board created a new standing advisory group to study the accident, which returned shortly with a report on its causes and proposed two international safety conventions (IAEA 1992a). The Board endorsed both conventions, which states quickly ratified, and they entered into force in 1987. The Board did not, however, significantly expand IAEA spending on nuclear safety or create a Board-level committee.

Relations between the United States and the Soviet Union continued to warm, but the tearing down of the Berlin Wall in 1989 marked the real end of the Cold War. Many expected a peace dividend, including the destruction of the nuclear weapons so central to Cold War insecurity. However, the 1990 NPT Review Conference was challenged, for the West, by NPT holdouts, cheaters, and an emerging gray nuclear market (US House of Representatives 1990, 40). The failure to reach consensus on a final declaration, though, was blamed on the US–Soviet failure to reduce their total warhead numbers, end modernization programs, or complete a comprehensive test ban treaty (Aler 1997, 155). The United States and many others now looked worriedly toward the 1995 Review Conference, at which under Article X a majority of the parties would "decide whether the Treaty shall continue in force."

The rapid collapse of the Soviet Union between August and December 1991 took even Soviet specialists by surprise (Kolodziej 1992; Waltz 1993; Mearsheimer 1994). The exit of its constituent republics further discredited communism, triggering what Samuel Huntington (1991) termed the "third wave of democracy." It also created incredible uncertainty about the future of the international system. Many prominent political scientists questioned whether the NATO alliance, or any of the Cold War's major institutions, would survive without the primary motivation for cooperation (Mearsheimer 1994). The ultimate decision by Russia to accept all the Soviet Union's legal and economic commitments turned a Western victory for democracy and free markets into a victory also for Western-dominated international institutions (Freedman 2003, 444).

The end of the Cold War also exposed critical structural weaknesses. Superpower competition, with support by their major allies, had kept a tight leash on regional animosities and certain civil conflicts. Although fewer conflicts were internationalized by the Cold War, civil violence worsened, fomented by cheap small arms. Threats to the post–Cold War peace and prosperity drove an expansion of NATO in Eastern Europe. Many former

Soviet republics joined Russia's Commonwealth of Independent States. Many of its Central Asian ex-republics also joined China's Shanghai Cooperative Council.

The Soviet disintegration had also meant new states with stockpiles of nuclear, biological, and chemical weapons as well as production and delivery system capabilities. These states threatened the nonproliferation regime if they kept these capabilities, but they could also leak them to insecure states, terrorists, or transnational organized criminals. The West put intense pressure on these states by making disarmament necessary for membership in international institutions. Belarus, Kazakhstan, and Ukraine eventually "returned" their nuclear warheads to Russia, verifiably dismantled the military dimensions of their nuclear capabilities, and by 1994 accepted the NPT and IAEA safeguards. The United States also launched the Cooperative Threat Reduction program with over $400 million in its first year to support Russia, and later several other Soviet successor states, in securing and redirecting weapons capabilities to peaceful uses. The program soon grew into a $1 billion per year initiative to dismantle or otherwise secure from misuse former Soviet "weapons of mass destruction" facilities and personnel. Meanwhile, the United States followed Russia's 1991 nuclear testing moratorium with its own moratorium in 1992.

Even as some embraced disarmament and the nonproliferation regime, Iraq was found to have circumvented its NPT safeguards for some years, South Africa sought to accede to the NPT after being suspected of having a nuclear weapons program, and then purposeful proliferation was detected in North Korea. Michael Wilson (1997, 132), then Australia's governor, later wrote that the Agency, "after more than thirty years of operating effectively in decent obscurity, temporarily found itself the object of international public and media attention." Because these nuclear policy–relevant events began in series but unfolded in parallel, I now diverge from a straight chronological retelling to tackle them individually.

∞

Iraq's 1990 invasion of Kuwait encapsulated many of the new global risks facing the West. As President Bill Clinton would describe in 1994, "Regional instabilities, the end of the cold war, and the growing threat of proliferation of nuclear weapons have created new and compelling circumstances to encourage progress in disarmament" (Holum 1994). After decades of dysfunction, the UN Security Council rallied to condemn the invasion (Resolution #660) and then authorize military retaliation (Resolution #678). As the US-led coalition gathered—supported by Russia, despite its interests in Iraq—many feared the steps Saddam Hussein might take to preserve the Bathist regime. Though it was especially concerned about chemical weapons (Miller, Engelberg, and Broad 2001), the United States also had for years suspected that Iraq had been rebuilding its nuclear capabilities and might even have a secret nuclear weapons program. This information was not shared with the IAEA, which had reported for years that "comprehensive safeguards" had verified the non-diversion of declared nuclear materials within Iraq. But, as Jeffrey Richelson (2004, doc. #4, March 20, 1990) shows, the only direct nuclear threat was the possibility of diverting highly enriched uranium from safeguards for a single crude device.

The cease-fire offered in April 1991 by the Security Council (Resolution #687) reflected their collective concern with regional proliferation. They demanded that Iraq verifiably destroy any nuclear, biological, and chemical capabilities and any missiles with 150 km or greater range. For disarmament of Iraq's chemical and biological weapons and missile capabilities, the Security Council experimented by creating a single-use organization: the UN Special Commission (UNSCOM).[2] Although some on the Security Council suspected the IAEA was not up to the task, the resolution requested that the IAEA assist UNSCOM with destroying any Iraqi offensive nuclear capabilities. Inspectors had a tough task ahead of them to convince their newest collective principal, the Security Council, to trust the Agency's ability to deliver in Iraq.

Formally subordinate to UNSCOM, the first IAEA inspections under Resolution #687 occurred in May 1991. It was not until July, however, that IAEA inspectors uncovered evidence that it had failed for years to catch multiple routes for uranium enrichment or an active experimental program for designing weapons components (IAEA 2002; Butler et al. 2004, 44–45). Although it had raised some questions about Iraq's declaration back in April, it was clear these activities had occurred literally within sight of safeguarded activities, as illustrated in maps of Iraq's Tuwaitha facility used in IAEA briefings in subsequent years.[3] The IAEA was roundly criticized for failing to detect Iraq's advanced nuclear weapons program. These criticisms were, as Wilson (1997, 131) argued, "a self-serving attempt to divert attention from misjudgments in policies or practice of industrialized suppliers." States had to also be responsible because some supplied the dual-use equipment and others had not shared their suspicions about Iraq's program.

The Agency, though, "was candid about the flaws in the system" and argued it needed additional legal authorities (ElBaradei 2011, 26). Comprehensive Safeguards Agreements (CSA), after all, were designed to limit the Secretariat's information about national fuel-cycle activities. The Secretariat had been specifically directed only to verify the non-diversion of declared nuclear materials and to ignore the risk of undeclared materials and activities. Although Blix continued to oppose turning the Agency into a confrontational inspectorate, experts within the Secretariat had already begun preparing the Secretariat to pursue reforms (Rockwood 2002), and Blix was ready to ask for greater authority for safeguards (Rosenthal et al. 2010, 15). After an initial round of negotiations within the Agency, the Board authorized the Secretariat to conduct a full review of the CSA system, called the 93+2 Program because it began in 1993 was expected complete its work in advance of the 1995 NPT Review Conference.

The realization that Iraq had successfully exploited dual-use trade for its weapons programs resulted in the London Club being reconvened in 1991 for the first time in over a decade. Now called the Nuclear Suppliers Group (NSG), it became an important forum for coordinating nonproliferation efforts. The United States again pressed the NSG to expand its controls on dual-use technologies and by 1992 had achieved consensus on a memorandum of understanding and a set of dual-use guidelines (Thorne 1997). The NSG then agreed the next year to require comprehensive safeguards as a condition for nuclear exports, something several members had resisted for decades.

When Hussein Kamal defected in 1995, he opened avenues to explore Iraq's biological weapons program but also raised new doubts about its nuclear program. Still, Blix would declare in his 1996 report to the UN secretary-general that, despite Iraqi obstruction, all of Iraq's highly enriched uranium and plutonium were removed and its entire nuclear weapon infrastructure destroyed. Blix's final report in October 1997 would summarize that the Agency had blown up dozens of buildings; melted, cut up, or removed from the country thousands of pieces of equipment for enrichment and weaponization; and removed tens of kilograms of fissile material (IAEA 1997b). After initially resisting the Agency being given such a prominent role, the United States now resisted its departure to maintain support for the less successful UNSCOM. It was unclear, though, what work remained for either when they were expelled in 1998, an expulsion that was relatively unchallenged by a now divided Security Council (Ekéus 2012).

∞

South Africa was seeking international recognition of its transition from apartheid when, among other steps, it signed the NPT in 1991 and tried to regain rights lost at the IAEA. It had become increasingly isolated by the 1970s by sanctions, consumer boycotts, and diplomatic ostracism. At the Agency, it had lost its Board seat in 1977, been denied the right to participate in the 1979 General Conference (much as Israel had been in 1982; see chapter 4), and then, in a rare roll call vote in June 1987, the Board suspended its rights and privileges of membership (Pabian 1995). These rebukes seemed particularly strong after South Africa had long defended the technical orientation of the Agency to exclude "political" issues (Hecht 2006).

Before IAEA inspectors arrived in November 1991 to verify the correctness of South Africa's declaration, the Board included a new directive from the General Conference to verify also its completeness (Hooper and Shea 2007, 9). The Agency had traditionally verified only that declarations correctly accounted for all materials declared by states; inspectors were now to verify that its declaration did not omit materials or activities it was obligated to declare. The request from the General Conference was intended as a rebuke from developing states concerned about Western indifference to the possible secret weapons program (Albright 1994; Liberman 2001, 51), although Purkitt and Burgess (2002) argue that US pressure had actually been quite instrumental in compelling South Africa's disarmament. Already aware it had missed much in Iraq, the Secretariat embraced "completeness" as an opportunity to prove it could uncover the entire history of South Africa's program.[4]

Within the year, inspectors began leaking that there were inconsistencies with the declaration (Albright 1994, von Baeckmann, Dillon, and Perricos 1995). Pressed by the Agency and others, President F. W. de Klerk publicly declared in March 1993 that South Africa had actually built six gun-type bombs and had experimented with implosion and other advanced designs before dismantling its weapons program (Richelson 2006). De Klerk invited the IAEA to verify its disarmament, promising it full access to its facilities, materials, record, and personnel. Verifying South Africa's disarmament, as with Iraq, would go far beyond routine safeguards.

While the Agency noted it was not completely free from uncertainty, it reported in 1994 that "the results of extensive inspection and assessment, and the transparency and openness shown," allowed it to conclude that South Africa's nuclear weapons program was completely dismantled (von Baeckmann, Dillon, and Perricos 1995, 7). It had also accomplished this without direct external help, having rejected US assistance out of concern for its "institutional impartiality and integrity" (Richelson 2006, doc. 34). South Africa was summarily invited to resume its participation in all IAEA activities in 1994 and, upon the Board's recommendation to the General Conference, was reelected to the Board in 1995 (Kennedy 1997, 125).

∞

North Korea's nuclear energy program began in the 1950s and added in the 1960s a small Soviet-supplied research reactor (under INFCIRC/66 safeguards, at Soviet insistence). The Soviets also trained hundreds of North Korean nuclear scientists, engineers, and technicians. By 1983 the United States had begun to worry about North Korea's nuclear weapons potential and pressed the Soviets to convince North Korea to sign the NPT in 1985. North Korea then began operating a new 30-MW reactor and mining uranium ore, the latter with Agency assistance, but delayed signing its NPT-mandated CSA. Even with IAEA paperwork errors and North Korea's technically limited ability to conduct international negotiations, the United States became increasingly suspicious after years of delay (Wampler 2003).[5]

The United States was initially receptive to North Korea's expressed insecurities and offered, in exchange for its signing its CSA, to begin negotiations on normalization and for trade and other economic relations. By 1988, though, the United States was demanding that North Korea accept safeguards on all its nuclear activities (Reiss 1995, 235). The United States still continued to encourage North Korea, unilaterally withdrawing all its nuclear weapons from the Korean Peninsula (more than it did for Europe, where tactical or nonstrategic nuclear weapons continue to be deployed) and suspending several major military exercises in the region.

North Korea had first rejected the Secretariat's proposed text for allowing, it argued, a more intrusive than usual inspection regime. It then tried repeatedly to insert conditions relating to the US security role in the region.[6] In September 1990, for example, North Korea stated it would "immediately" sign a CSA "if favorable circumstances allowing full implementation of the NPT were to be created on the Korean Peninsula" (IAEA 1990b, 16–17). North Korea was demanding denuclearization of the Korean Peninsula as a precondition to a CSA: an end to foreign nuclear weapons in South Korea and to "nuclear war training" by United States and South Korean military forces (Wilson 1997, 134). The IAEA rejected these as unrelated to the technical goals of safeguards.

By 1992, argues Mitchell Reiss (1995, 241), a senior US diplomat working on North Korea in the 1990s, the United States believed it had been sufficiently generous without success. It began to diplomatically withdraw to allow the IAEA and South Korea to take the political lead. As the IAEA continued its negotiations, Japan joined the effort, offering talks on normalization, trade relations, and even compensation for its colonial past. South Korea was the most successful, convincing North Korea in January 1992 to sign the North–South Denuclearization Agreement, a bilaterally verifiable nuclear weapons–free zone for the Korean Peninsula.[7]

North Korea finally signed its CSA in April 1992, and the IAEA began ad hoc inspections to verify its declaration within days, less than a year after the first inspections in Iraq. Much of its subsequent behavior raises questions about why it bothered. It is likely that North Korea was unable to resist the combined Japanese, South Korean, and US positive overtures once reinforced by Russian and Chinese threats to withhold their dwindling aid and to extend greater recognition to South Korea (Reiss 1995, 234–37). It is also possible North Korea underestimated the technical capacity of the IAEA to fully uncover its program. As suspicious as were North Korea's neighbors, they hoped engagement would succeed.

Within weeks, inspectors expressed concern about the correctness and completeness of North Korea's declaration. A sample of plutonium metal that North Korea had reported was from several small-scale reprocessing experiments was instead determined by the Secretariat to be too homoge-nous to be from separate reprocessing events; either North Korea was only providing the sample from one event or it had engaged in activities beyond what had been declared (Kratzer, Hooper, and Wulf 2005).[8] The IAEA was already suspicious when the United States decided to share intelligence with Blix pointing to a suspected reprocessing facility and other undeclared activ-ities within the Yongbyon complex. Agency inspectors simply asked to visit the suspected sites. North Korea refused, and Blix then formally asked the Board to support a "special inspection," a rarely exploited safeguards provi-sion designed to allow the Agency to access suspected undeclared or diverted nuclear materials. When the Board agreed, North Korea renounced the NPT under its Article X right to do so with ninety days' notice.

A triangular game unfolded over the coming months. The Secretariat was demanding access and asserting North Korea's continuing obligation to comply until its NPT withdrawal was complete. Blix increasingly forced the issue, threatening to use his autonomy to report—or not, if North Korea would cooperate—that North Korea was no longer in compliance with its CSA. The United States and its Asian allies were pushing and pulling at North Korea, with the United States accepting bilateral negotiations only after strong international pressure. North Korea would occasionally accede to international demands, including suspending its NPT withdrawal, but just as suddenly would inexplicably turn truculent. Meanwhile, it continued to enjoy the full benefits of IAEA membership, including technical assistance projects on uranium prospecting and mining that had been approved by the Board (GAO 1997, 16).

Diplomacy beyond this triangle was minimal. A small group of Board governors did meet with increasing frequency, sometimes even daily, as the issue grew urgent in 1993. They reviewed the Agency's position, made rec-ommendations to Blix and the Board, and pressed North Korea at Board meetings, but they had little agreement about how to solve the problem (Wilson 1997, 136). Notably absent except to block action at the Security Council were Russia, well into a major economic collapse, and China, which was avoiding major diplomatic activity. Their excision also reflected North Korea's choice to singularly focus on the United States.

The Board decided in June 1994 that it would terminate North Korea's Technical Cooperation projects for its safeguards noncompliance (Aloise 2011). Their economic value was not immense, but the projects would be difficult to replace, as Iran later also found (see chapter 6). The perceived insult prompted North Korea to leave the Agency. It was North Korea's NPT commitment—not IAEA membership—that was the legal foundation for its CSA. The Agency continued to press, and war seemed imminent as the United States again pushed for Security Council sanctions, again opposed by China. North Korea threatened to treat UN sanctions as the opening volley of a real war. South Korea reacted by activating its military reserve forces, and the United States began reinforcing the more than thirty thousand US troops still stationed in South Korea. Gen. Gary E. Luck, commander of the US forces in Korea, voiced concern that taking these steps to deter North Korea could also provoke it.

Into this powder keg stepped former US president Jimmy Carter. During a personal visit to Pyongyang, Carter negotiated North Korea's agreement to the outlines of a bargain that could end the crisis. Under the Agreed Framework, North Korea promised to remain in the NPT, implement its CSA, and freeze and eventually dismantle most of its nuclear activities. In exchange, the United States and others would have to agree to deliver supplies of heavy fuel oil until two light-water reactors were built for North Korea. Although war was averted, North Korea quickly tempered any enthusiasm by declaring it had merely stopped the clock on its NPT withdrawal, enabling it to hold "unique status" as an NPT state only one day from effecting a withdrawal.

∞

Meanwhile, the commonality of international interests on nonproliferation that held the Board together was fracturing at the 1995 NPT Review Conference. The parties did eventually agree to indefinitely extend the NPT, making permanent an international commitment to nuclear nonproliferation, disarmament, and noninterference with peaceful nuclear uses (Essis 2005). Overcoming the desire of some for only a limited extension required a hard push by the United States, including its promise to quickly conclude the Comprehensive Test Ban Treaty (CTBT), negotiate further arms reductions with Russia, and offer negative security assurances to non–nuclear weapons states. The parties also committed to make progress on a Middle East peace process and WMDFZ, or weapons of mass destruction–free zone (Essis 2005). Their failure to otherwise agree on a final declaration showed a deepening division.

NPT extension fit the Clinton administration's broadly internationalist approach to new security threats. The United States had continued to expand the Cooperative Threat Reduction program to over $500 million a year by 1998. It restarted talks on the CTBT and advanced the Chemical Weapons Convention, opening both for signature in 1996. It again proposed talks on a Fissile Material Cut-off Treaty. These measures encouraged US–Russian disarmament but were also intended to prevent proliferation by unsafeguarded states (Holum 1994).

Successful extension also enabled the IAEA to conclude the first stage of the 93+2 Program. In the month following the NPT Review Conference, the Board approved the Secretariat's proposal for reinforcing CSAs to provide better assurances of the absence of undeclared activities. The Board also approved further study of additional measures that the Secretariat wished states would accept but that were beyond its perceived authority to require. These measures became the foundation for the Model Additional Protocol (INFCIRC/540) approved by the Board in 1998. Designed as a "voluntary" annex to any safeguards agreement, states acceding to an Additional Protocol (AP) must provide greater information about and access to every part of their nuclear fuel cycle, including any locations where the Secretariat believes the undeclared nuclear activities may be occurring.

International politics had already entered a new era of American hegemony imposed through international institutions. Regional insecurity was engaged by US affirmation of its alliances, by extension of NATO in various forms throughout Eastern Europe, and by UN-sanctioned military interventions in civil conflicts around the world. The IMF and World Bank assistance encouraged economic development but was conditional upon embracing globalization and neoliberal economics. Western economic and military interventions, including no-fly zones over Iraq that continued after UN and IAEA inspectors were expelled, threatened the sovereignty of less stable regional powers. They also became potential threats to Russia and China, both experiencing unrest inside and near their borders. The United States found it increasingly difficult but also less necessary to assemble truly international coalitions behind these interventions and resorted more often to unilateral action (Voeten 2004).

TEMPERING AGENCY AUTHORITY

Does demand for a nuclear authority increase after 1986 with changes in the threats from noncooperative nuclear policy, the distribution of interests on nuclear and other issues, and the strength of the technical consensus on how to achieve collective nuclear goals? How does the Agency evolve in response to challenges to the existing nuclear policy architecture? Is the pull felt by states to accommodate and comply created by the control of the collective principals or influential individual principals, acting inside and outside the Agency, or the coercive effect of international procedural norms and nuclear norms?

United States Hegemony?

By the mid-1980s, both the United States and the Soviet Union were willing to negotiate bilateral arms control treaties and contemplate nuclear disarmament. Economic growth in Japan and Germany had brought home the cost to the US public of its informal empire, though there had been little substantial change in the distribution of material power until the sudden disintegration of the Soviet Union. If the distribution of power in the system had caused the Cold War, and not the ideological divide, the collapse of the Soviet Union ended it (Waltz 1993). But the early post–Cold War era found a still formidable Russia, economic powerhouses in Japan and West Germany, and a successful European Union experiment. Even if the United States was a solitary superpower in 1991, it was potentially in economic decline and would need to coexist with others in a multipolar world.

Unable or unwilling to impose its preferred nuclear policy outcomes on others, the United States turned to multilateral compromise and reliance on international organizations. While a focus on the distribution of power suggests multilateralism was necessary for bargaining among the several major powers, internationalization may instead have dominated because more similar preferences over outcomes made accommodation less costly (Voeten 2004). This convergence could eliminate most Western need for nuclear weapons and allowed the Security Council to finally function as it was intended. The East–West conflict over nonproliferation and within the IAEA had effectively ended in the 1960s, but the risk of nuclear policy cooperation now diminished further with convergence on other issue dimensions: the Soviets were moving toward a more open political system under glasnost and perestroika, and many developing states in Asia and Latin America were joining Japan and Europe to enjoy resurgent economic growth of a world economy on the cusp of a new era of globalization (Boughton 2001).

At the same time, the US military's performance in the 1991 Gulf War and other interventions showed the success of a dramatic "revolution in military affairs." The apparent contenders for great power status were not even in the running: Russia's and Japan's separate economic contractions continued, Germany was bogged down by reunification, and China was unwilling to assert itself. Whereas in the early post–Cold War period the United States had arguably been restrained by multipolarity or using multilateralism to restrain the rise of challengers, by the mid-1990s US unipolarity was clear (Layne 2006).

Eastern European states did distance themselves from Russia even as Western European and nonaligned states found themselves clashing more often with the United States (Voeten 2000, 2011). The inability to get Security Council sanctions against North Korea during 1993 and 1994, the ability of Iraq to also resist and then expel international inspectors without serious consequences, and economic instability under globalization all highlighted increasing alignment by the international community if not with each other then at least against US policy. The United States was dominant but unable to impose its interests on others.

Norms

The United States and others held starkly different views on nuclear weapons and international institutions in the 1980s. Fears of a nuclear holocaust were pandemic, with the Reagan administration promising that the United States would prevail in any nuclear war. Europeans felt at greater risk from new nuclear weapon deployments in their countries (Freedman 2003, 382–86). Social protest movements resurfaced, demanding a ban on the bomb and an end to nuclear testing (Wittner 2009). Fears of a "nuclear winter" enveloping the Earth after a nuclear war were then fueled by the environmental dangers of nuclear power after Chernobyl. When Gorbachev proposed eliminating nuclear weapons from the US and Soviet arsenals, there was great popular support for nuclear disarmament. Within the US defense community, however, the voices that advocated massive reductions followed not the norm of non-use but its inherent irrationality when any nuclear use would result in mutually assured destruction (Freedman 2003, 390, 405).

The Reagan administration still rejected the internationalist approaches it believed responsible in the 1970s for eroding US military power relative to the Soviet Union and its economic power by exploitative Japanese and European trade practices. The functional benefit to the United States of coordinating interests and investments and of accepting constraints on its freedom of action had also, Imber (1989) shows, been undermined by Soviet and developing state politicization. US and Soviet allies had accepted international derogations of their sovereignty as the increasing price of economic, social, and political security (Krasner 1999). They saw the value of internationalization reduced when it also helped the G-77 to organize their opposition to the international system. Tension continued to increase throughout the 1980s over the norm of internationalization as "politicization" by developing states threatened the supply for developed states of international solutions to global problems.

The end of the Cold War was a victory for Western norms of democracy, free markets, and internationalization. Earning membership in international institutions could signal legitimacy for regimes seeking recognition by the West. With the Security Council finally working as it was originally intended, its consent could signal that actions preferred by powerful states were legitimate and served collective interests (Finnemore 1996; Thompson 2006). Internationalization also deepened on issues, from the conversion of the General Agreement on Tariffs and Trade (GATT) into the World Trade Organization in 1996 to the advancement of the European experiment with the European Union and the euro currency.

Internalization of the norms of nonproliferation and disarmament also occurred as post-Soviet successor states publicly debated their conflicting strategic interests but chose disarmament and accession to the NPT. For example, Ukraine's wish to hedge against Russian irredentism forced a difficult choice between keeping an indigenous nuclear deterrent or relying on uncertain Western security guarantees (Sagan 1996–97). The domestic debate in Ukraine was fierce, essentially forcing anti-Russian and pro-Western groups into opposition with each other (Dunn 1993). Gaining international support for their sovereignty and subsequent foreign aid also helped.

Other states, particularly in the G-77, reacted to increased insecurity from intervention by pursuing nuclear weapons. Norms of nuclear non-use and nonproliferation were strong, but for them were trumped by norms of sovereignty and national survival. The greater the value of nuclear weapons for countries like Iraq and North Korea, the greater the apparent need also for the United States to continue to rely on nuclear weapons (see, for example, the 1994 Nuclear Posture Review). This refreshed accusations of inherent discrimination in the nonproliferation regime by countries like India and now also South Africa.

In short, a new if short-lived consensus arose at the IAEA, the UN Security Council, and other international organizations. It remains unclear if internationalization was deemed more "appropriate." The procedural norm of internationalization may have acquired coercive effect in the 1990s or, after several decades of functioning poorly, the international community finally experienced the convergence of interests necessary for functionalist internationalization to be effective. Changes in the structure of nuclear norms and their effect upon IAEA political authority would vary by issue.

Demand for Nuclear Authority

The easing of the Western–Communist ideological divide after the mid-1980s diminished the distributional effects of cooperation. A greater IAEA supply of nuclear policy could result from greater demand for political authority, a growing belief that multilateralism was more appropriate, or the greater utility for international coordination given the multipolar reality. Demand for international political authority on nuclear issues increased in the 1990s as the threat from international noncooperation increased but also because of persistent barriers to cooperation from policy uncertainty as nuclear technology diffused and many new and diverse states became relevant. Increasing conflict between the West, but especially the United States, and others over a wide range of international issues contributed to conflicts over nuclear policy and created persistent demand for policy impersonality.

AGENCY AUTONOMY

The greater popular awareness of the IAEA and nuclear safety after the Chernobyl accident quickly evaporated afterward (figure 4.3). Governments, though, continued to slowly expand their economic support of the Agency. Despite the imposition of "zero growth" in 1985, the budget had grown to $178.6 million in 1990 (plus $39 million in "voluntary contributions" and another $22 million in "extrabudgetary contributions"), up from $106.8 million in 1986 (IAEA 1987 Annual Report, 1987; IAEA 1990 Annual Report, 1991). The staffing of the Secretariat also increased from 1,630 to 2,175 in the same period.

This growth superficially reflects the functional demand of a larger Agency. The membership had also grown from a small club of mostly advanced nuclear states in the 1960s to include more from every region of the world (112 in 1990, see figure 3.2). However, the Agency now supported the expansion of nuclear technology in over 120 countries through equipment grants, training, fellowships, and local programs ranging from agricultural uses of radioisotopes to uranium ore prospecting (IAEA 1990a; IAEA 1990 Annual Report, 1991). The Agency was now implementing nuclear safeguards in 104 states (and Taiwan, China) and 86 were under the NPT. It was also conducting more inspections (2,188 in 1990, up slightly from 1,980 in 1985) to safeguard a larger nuclear industry (see the comparison line in figure 4.1) in more countries. This misses other important nuances. The Board remained fixed at thirty-five governors after China was welcomed so that the share of states comprising a Board majority dropped to 16.4 percent of 109 members by 1990 (see figure 3.1).

After 1990, however, this small and relatively obscure Agency "found itself the object of international public and media attention" (Wilson 1997, 132). Mentioned in only 10 *New York Times* articles in 1989, conflict over Iraq, South Africa, and North Korea meant reports grew to 24 in 1990, and then 124 in 1991 (figure 4.2). To implement stronger safeguards and ad hoc disarmament, the Secretariat added 120 staff by 1995 and the budget grew to $258.5 million, an inflation-adjusted increase from 1986 of over 70 percent (IAEA 1995 Annual Report, 1996). The Board did reduce the Agency's resources as intensive verification in South Africa and Iraq ended: by 1998 the budget dropped to $225.9 million, safeguards spending to $111.75 million from approximately $123.4 million, and the staff to 2,133 (IAEA 1998 Annual Report, 1999). The share of states representing a Board majority in 1998 fell further to 14.6 percent of 126 members (figure 3.1). The Board approved an amendment to the Statute in 1998 to expand the Board again, but it still lacks enough support to enter into force (IAEA 1996, 2011a).

Supplying multilateral cooperation was certainly easier in the early 1990s. The risk of global nuclear war had entirely disappeared, and it was difficult to contemplate any reason why the United States would use its nuclear arsenal. The US Congress funded the Cooperative Threat Reduction program to enhance nuclear security in former Soviet states and was willing to join the Russians in observing a nuclear test moratorium. There also appeared less risk of nuclear use outside the established nuclear weapon states once Iraq had been contained. The only serious continuing case of proliferation was North Korea, but blackmail for economic and security concessions appeared the primary goal of its nuclear weapons program.

After the mid-1990s, international interests began to conflict more often, including on nuclear issues. This was powerfully apparent in the different approaches preferred by America's coalition partners, not to mention Russia and China, in Iraq on sovereignty, the humanitarian costs of sanctions, and loss of foreign investment opportunities. The economic consensus was further challenged when globalization seemed to increase regional economic instability for many middle-income states. Polarization of the international community worsened as the G-77 as a political actor returned from obsolescence to join Russia and China in opposing the Western liberal economic agenda.

The observed expansion of the IAEA in the late 1980s and early 1990s could have reflected increased exploitation of international institutions under multilateral control more than increased demand for nuclear authority. However, policy uncertainty on nuclear issues appeared to steadily increase throughout the period as technical uncertainty increased. There was greater policy uncertainty when considering how international nuclear supply could *not* contribute to undeclared or unsafe nuclear activities. Cooperation was also being applied (or coerced) upon a more diverse population of states than during the Cold War, elevating the need for impersonality. With increasing political conflict, states also recognized that verifiable nonproliferation and disarmament could become almost impossibly difficult. To examine how the specific choices of actors inside and outside the Agency affect the demand and supply of nuclear authority, the remainder of this section examines the effects of these challenges, and the structure of the external power and normative environment upon the specific nuclear issue areas.

Safety and Security

When informed of the Chernobyl accident, Blix quickly offered that the IAEA could assist by collecting relevant expertise and serving as a conduit to collect and share information. A few days later, the Soviet Union invited the Agency to visit, and only it, which led to Blix's misleading report on the accident's severity. The Secretariat's major contribution was hosting a technical conference of six hundred member-designated experts several weeks later, at which Blix was able to convince the Soviet Union to report publicly. While many remained skeptical of the Soviet report, news reports at the time argued the IAEA had exceeded others' expectations by using the conference to build bridges on international safety (Patterson 1987, 52).

The Board, argues Lodewijk van Gorkom (1997, 172), "acted with less expediency." It created the International Nuclear Safety Advisory Group to report on the accident and then drafted two international safety conventions (Gonzalez 2002, 277). The first, the Convention on the Early Notification of a Nuclear Accident, would enter into force in October 1986, just six months after Chernobyl. This convention obligates states to quickly notify the IAEA of any nuclear accidents that may lead to the transboundary release of radiation, including details about the accident and whatever is known about the environmental effects of the release (IAEA 1986b). The IAEA is then responsible for notifying anyone who could be affected and sharing with them information it receives about the event. The convention also names the IAEA as the depository, not a state party.

The second, the Convention on Assistance in the Case of a Nuclear Accident or Radiological Emergency, would enter into force in February 1987 (IAEA 1986b). It directs the Agency to prepare, in advance of accidents, expert lists, assistance materials and equipment, emergency response training programs, radiation monitoring programs, feasibility studies, and more safety standards (Findlay 2012a, 122–23). In the event of an accident, the IAEA is also to provide assistance and transmit requests for assistance to other parties who should be prepared to assist and, if needed, "coordinate assistance on the international level." Importantly, the provision of Agency assistance would require the specific request of the party experiencing the emergency.

The Board also helped bring into force the Convention on the Physical Protection of Nuclear Materials in 1987 (IAEA 1980). Despite languishing since being negotiated in 1979, it became the only international legal structure obligating its parties to ensure the protection of nuclear materials during transnational transport. However, as with the other conventions, as (Findlay 2012a, 131) points out, there were no provisions to enforce states' obligations.

The Board's inspiration for international action quickly evaporated. One journalist half joked that the Board's attention to nuclear safety "had a half-life almost as short as that of Iodine-131" (Patterson 1987, 50) (half of the atoms in a given sample of Iodine-131 decays or decomposes within eight days). Although Three Mile Island and the normalization of oil prices since the 1970s had slowed nuclear investments, there was not a substantial reversal of nuclear power programs or desire to enhance international safety regulations. Instead, national nuclear industry representatives and government bureaucracies had closed ranks in opposition to international coordination, placing greater attention on safety, plant operations, and maintenance but defending exclusive national controls (IAEA 1986a, 7, 9; van Gorkom 1997, 174). Advanced states with strong safety protections were possibly concerned that greater international regulation could actually weaken national regulations, and developing states were unwilling to further tip the balance against nuclear promotion with greater regulation (Fischer 1997, 118).[9] In the end, the Board increased the Secretariat's Nuclear Safety budget only to $8 million from $5 million (van Gorkom 1997, 174). Barkenbus (1987, 484) compares this to the US Nuclear Regulatory Commission, which at the time had a $400 million budget and staff of 3,400.

Expanding the Secretariat's supply of nuclear safety occurred but was supported through voluntary contributions from individual states. With advice from the International Nuclear Safety Advisory Group, the Secretariat again revised the Nuclear Safety Standards. It also drafted new Basic Safety Principles for Nuclear Power Plants and a Code of Practice on the International Transboundary Movement of Radioactive Waste, endorsed first by the Board and later by the General Conference (van Gorkom 1997, 176). As Munir Ahmad Khan (1997, 309), a former governor from Pakistan, argued, "Safety now constitutes one of the major activities of the Agency." However, these limited resources were diffused over so many disconnected groups, reports, and programs that they were quite ineffective.

"The Director General and the Secretariat of the Agency," argues van Gorkom (1997, 182), "have been alert and forward looking" in the aftermath of the Chernobyl accident. The Agency launched and the Secretariat managed an extensive number of internal advisory groups and an even larger number of programs and publications on nuclear safety (Fischer 1997, 119; Findlay 2012a, 124). However, these investments were largely short term and supported by a few influential members. The initiatives were also disjointed, nonbinding, lacked broad political support, and were managed by a low-profile department without a strong core program around which to organize itself. Some of the weakness of the responses can be attributed to the policy uncertainty of trying to supply global standards in a low-growth industry constructed of nearly unique facilities. Even the Agency later acknowledged it gave inadequate attention to building political support for a more systemic approach to nuclear safety (IAEA 2011b, 11). In short, the IAEA had made limited investments in international nuclear safety but lacked the power to issue rules and commands with which others expected they must comply.

Peaceful Uses

Technical assistance in the 1970s had shifted from short-term capacity building projects toward larger, longer-term, and more diverse development initiatives. The Secretariat came to offer agricultural and industrial applications to less-developed members while middle-income members benefited from medical and energy projects (including fuel-cycle development). Middle-income and advanced states both asked the Agency to act as a broker or hub for hundreds of annual meetings, conferences, and seminars (Jönsson and Bolin 1988, 307).

Demand for commercial nuclear energy had also continued to decline after energy prices renormalized and policymakers updated their beliefs about safety risks after Chernobyl. Nuclear energy production capacity had continued to increase after 1979 as in-progress constructions completed but, the IAEA would note, "there was still no general upturn in the ordering of nuclear power plants" (IAEA 1986a, 7, 9). Capacity dropped off immediately after 1987 and by 1989 was almost stagnant (see figure 4.1), although the location of new constructions would increasingly occur outside the West. Uranium oversupply also continued. Commercial nuclear energy simply was not cost competitive with cheaper fossil fuels.

The Department of Technical Cooperation had become by 1990 an example of successful international functionalism. It was an attractive source of nuclear-related assistance, willing to facilitate any project that on its own appeared legitimate as long as recipients accepted IAEA safeguards and applied IAEA safety standards on all assistance. But the Agency did not require nuclear assistance to be efficient, effective, or complementary with the recipient's broader development goals (GAO 1997). It also would not consider nonproliferation goals when approving projects. The priorities of the General Conference remained distinctly different from the Board's, which in 1991 was focused on problems with safeguards implementation in Iraq and then in South Africa and North Korea. As these challenges threatened the Agency's future, for example, the General Conference in September 1991 approved a resolution on "Strengthening of the Agency's Main Activities," which only mentions safeguards as an ancillary mission and "requests the Director General to enhance technical co-operation activities" (IAEA 1991).

Despite changing development norms in the 1980s, Technical Cooperation appeared poorly integrated with national development programs or international priorities in the 1990s. This problem was persistent but was only a conflict over development priorities and was of much smaller scale than at the UN Development Program or the World Bank. The IAEA's major donors did not expect the Agency to review assistance projects for potential contributions to weapons proliferation because, as US officials state, they did not believe any sensitive technologies were involved (GAO 1997, 3). For example, the Secretariat continued to provide North Korea with assistance in mining and processing uranium ore until 1994.

Agency support for peaceful uses, therefore, did not solve persistent distributional problems in nuclear assistance or reduce uncertainty about its technological, economic, or other developmental effects. The Secretariat's technical assistance primarily existed, believed the US GAO (1997, 5), to "ensure support for safeguards and the NPT." However, in doing so, it affirmed the norm that all states had the unconditional right to access peaceful uses of the atom. It also strengthened its monopoly over international supply of peaceful uses, requiring other international organizations to cooperate with the IAEA on any projects with nuclear components even as no such obligation existed for state-to-state supply. The IAEA in the challenge period therefore acquired a limited authority with the power to issue rules over the international supply of peaceful nuclear uses.

Disarmament

The norm of non-use had further strengthened in reaction to the Reagan administration's apparent willingness to fight a nuclear war (Tannenwald 2007). When the United States and the Soviet Union restarted down the arms control road, however, they did so to build strategic stability and possibly a foundation for larger reductions in strategic forces in the future. Although START I provided for extensive data exchanges and on-site inspections, it and other US–Soviet agreements were specifically designed to focus on easily observable measures of compliance—delivery systems and nuclear testing—to limit the need for verification. Nuclear deterrence might have been politically ignored but remained necessary. Disarmament, non-use, and even promises of "no first use" were still a long way off.

The international community was reassured by Russia's declaration that it would accept its forerunner's international legal commitments but pressed other successor states to join multilateral institutions. The coercive effect of the norms of nonproliferation and disarmament was potentially in doubt, and Western states were concerned that states with former Soviet weapons programs lacked the will or resources to secure materials, technologies, and personnel against leaking to insecure states. The reinvigoration of NSG export controls and accepting the NPT and stronger IAEA safeguards, already in the works because of Iraq, were possible solutions. Still, many emerging nuclear supplier states were less likely to demand the same level of safeguards against proliferation (Dunn 1985; Subramanian 1985). The accessions of former Soviet republics to the NPT affirmed the nonproliferation regime and international reliance on IAEA safeguards, although the IAEA played no direct role in achieving or verifying their disarmament.

The IAEA did not have a monopoly to issue rules and commands on disarmament, but it is significant that it acquired even some authority in this area because the international community demanded, and the Agency supplied, verification of the absence of weapons and weapons capabilities in Iraq and then South Africa. Its supply of disarmament verification was in some ways an extension of its supply of nonproliferation safeguards. For example, the director general could draw upon decades of experience with institutionalized processes used for administering safeguards. And its investment in impersonality, described in contexts outside of the Iraq experience by ElBaradei (2011, 17) as being "respectful" with inspection targets, aided in interacting formally and informally with targets and other members. The director general also had some flexibility, with the Board's support, to reallocate personnel and financing among all its activities. Although South Africa paid for its verification and the Iraq mission was funded under Resolution #687 (but mostly through voluntary contributions), these did not quite meet the Agency's full resource needs. It was therefore important to the Agency's success that the director general had the autonomy to choose to cut some scheduled safeguards inspections, postpone international meetings, and defer capital investments for Agency laboratories (IAEA 1992 Annual Report, 136). The two missions, therefore, required more of a difference in scale rather than kind of investment in impersonality and policy bias.

In South Africa, two years into ad hoc inspections, the government itself chose to request that the Secretariat unravel the full history of its nuclear weapons program (Stumpf 1995; von Baeckmann, Dillon, and Perricos 1995). It did so even though verifying correctness and completeness under INFCIRC/153 required only an accurate accounting of what currently existed to be sure future diversions could be detected (Rosenthal, Saum-Manning, and Houck 2010, 13). Rich Hooper, who participated in fifteen on-site inspections in Iraq and was the Secretariat's manager of the 93 + 2 Program for strengthening safeguards, would laud South Africa's cooperation with inspectors' requests to access records, locations, and personnel (Kratzer, Hooper, and Wulf 2005). Without this access, the IAEA would not have been able to reach its conclusions. Successful verification in South Africa went beyond standard nonproliferation activities and demonstrated the supply of disarmament authority in three ways.

First, the Agency could assert new political authority because it had supplied the requisite policy partiality without the external help of others who also had the technical capacity. The IAEA rejected, for example, US offers to assist with analyses of South Africa's records (Richelson 2006, doc. 34). It did hire new expertise to assist, but a number of IAEA inspectors had come from weapons programs in nuclear weapon states, some to join the

Iraq Action Team, discussed later, providing an opportunity for the Secretariat to leverage this weaponization expertise to create new policy partiality within safeguards. The Agency's principals complied so fully with its technical judgment that the General Conference invited South Africa to resume full Agency participation in 1994 and then reelected it to the Board in 1995 (Kennedy 1997, 125).

Second, South Africa welcomed IAEA verification as an alternative to having its disarmament verified by states with a more direct stake in the outcome. The United States and the United Kingdom had hoped for direct access because they wanted to know what capabilities could leak to potential proliferators. For years to come, they remained concerned about its capabilities contributing to chemical and biological weapons proliferation and drug trafficking (Purkitt and Burgess 2002). Its government was also under pressure from diverse domestic groups (the African National Congress especially) to give a full reckoning of past government activities but to resist foreign encroachment by Western governments, which created a real tension for how to do one without the other (Purkitt and Burgess 2002). Distrust and concern that foreign governments were complicit also refreshed international demand for an impartial assessment (Richelson 2006). Desperate to avoid domestic accusations of submitting to neocolonialism, South Africa's invitation was an affirmation of the Agency's greater impersonality. Its deference to Agency verification authority set a new standard for the level of abdication of sovereign authority to the IAEA required to make credible a state's transparency into its past and current nuclear activities.

Third, and finally, the South African verification mission allowed the Secretariat to assert authority superseding the nonproliferation rules it was to verify. Inspectors with classified knowledge of weaponization techniques reviewed the weapon design schematics—the type of information transmission that the NPT was supposed to prevent—to confirm South Africa's claims about the quantities of various materials used. Even though inspectors say they did not discuss their conclusions in any detail even with each other, this was the first step in the erosion of the NPT applying to the IAEA as a potential proliferator.[10] The Agency's principals were accommodating new conceptualizations of its authority that were necessary if the Agency were to identify, much less destroy, weaponization capabilities.

The Agency's disarmament of Iraq also developed its nuclear authority. First, the mission was not a voluntary undertaking by Iraq but was demanded by the Security Council. The Board, nine of which then sat on the Security Council, had to approve the relationship, but then authority went directly to the Secretariat, bypassing the Agency's political institutions (Ekéus 2012). The director general reported directly to the UN and for the first time had direct access to a body with the explicit responsibility for enforcement. This removed the political bodies that could modify its advice or judgment. The Secretariat's power to issue rules and commands increased but was checked by its own cautious desire to stay within the limits of its policy bias and impersonality.

Second, the Iraq Action Team had to identify and integrate a much more diverse array of data to understand the full history of Iraq's program. For example, the Secretariat during the 1980s had developed, with the support of Member Support Programs, nondestructive assay techniques to supplement on-site physical measurements of the properties of nuclear materials (Thorne 1992, 16). In Iraq, the Secretariat was now also using accounting forensics, trade data from supplier states, imagery, defector reports, local documents, environmental "swipe samples" for localized sites, and wide-area air and water sampling (Tucker 1996, 10). As it did in South Africa, the Agency used the opportunity to invest further in the specific assets of verification. Also as in South Africa, this meant extending its specific expertise to include weaponization activities and their dismantlement, even if they did not directly involve the misuse of fissile materials. As important as these new techniques was its development of a systems-based approach that looked at a state's nuclear infrastructure as a whole (Frank 1997, 277).

Third, to make these investments, the Agency had to leverage its relationships with supportive constituencies. The action team assembled by Deputy Dir. Gen. Maurizio Zifferero was a core group of thirty-five people, mostly from the Department of Safeguards, but Blix solicited member expertise in enrichment, weapons technology, ordinance detection, and structural safety to fill internal gaps (Thorne 1992, 16). Many sent to the action team had previous experience with the Agency through their national support programs or as employees. Blix encouraged a strong working relationship with UNSCOM's inspectors even though the relationship with UNSCOM was made uneasy by cultural differences and because UNSCOM wanted access to Secretariat inspection results in exchange for assisting with new techniques or data analysis.

As a result, Secretariat management and staff conducted informal discussions with interested member states on Iraq, as they do on other issues, and may have provided early looks at Agency reports and documents.[11] Staff members assert that it was not to receive approval from individual influential members, only to provide warning or receive feedback as part of an ongoing but informal consultation process. IAEA officials vigorously asserted in numerous interviews that the IAEA did not pass on confidential safeguards information, as ElBaradei (2011, 18) later recounted, "to maintain its integrity and legitimacy."[12] US officials who were asked about this relationship would accept ElBaradei's description, recognizing that the appearance of excessive US influence would compromise the basis for Agency authority with others.[13] A former IAEA inspector, though, argues that Blix was fairly open about sharing information with the permanent Security Council members even if China and Russia chose to not exploit it.[14] Productive relationships with supportive constituencies enabled the Agency to draw upon their verification and disarmament expertise in exercising its political authority in Iraq.

Any argument about the IAEA's incipient disarmament authority would be incomplete without discussing its relationship with UNSCOM. First, the Iraq Action Team was made subordinate to UNSCOM because the United States had insisted on this condition for the IAEA having any role. This relationship became tense because this meant that a new ad hoc body of seconded national experts, not even truly inspectors, was given ultimate responsibility for deciding when and where inspections would occur. Some UNSCOM inspectors relished being described by IAEA inspectors as "cowboys." ElBaradei (2011, 19) argued that UNSCOM had much to learn from IAEA inspectors' past experience in Iraq and about being "respectful." However, Agency inspectors also saw that UNSCOM could accomplish some tasks better by being more confrontational. Some inspectors pushed the safeguards culture to be much more aggressive in looking for proof of noncompliance (Sigal 1998, 48). Blix and some inspectors took years to be convinced that being more aggressive in verification was more effective. Some inspectors, often those from states that were less supportive of the safeguards reform measures discussed later, were politically opposed.

Second, although the IAEA was resource-deprived overall, UNSCOM was more affected by financial instability than the IAEA. Because disarmament was expected to take just a few months, UNSCOM was required to request payments on an expense-by-expense basis from a UN fund of donations and Iraqi frozen assets.[15] This fund was quickly exhausted as Iraq obstructed the disarmament process. UNSCOM had to rely on stopgap voluntary contributions for five years until Resolution #986 (1996) finally authorized oil sales to fund, among others, UNSCOM and the Iraq Action Team (Saikal 2002, 270). Even then, nearly every report by the UNSCOM executive chairman would describe its imminent insolvency.[16]

Third, the UN secretary-general technically appointed UNSCOM's inspectors, but in practice this required the UNSCOM executive chairman to petition states to provide seconded personnel and logistics for very short tours of duty (Findlay 2003).[17] UNSCOM had a small internal intelligence assessment group, but large portions of its data were provided or interpreted by the CIA, whose goal it was to cause regime change in Iraq (Saikal 2002, 271). ElBaradei (2011, 33), Findlay (2003), and others also recount allegations that the United States wiretapped UNSCOM's communications. UNSCOM inspector Scott Ritter, chief inspector on at least fourteen missions, denied that he himself met with intelligence services. However, as recounted in the review by the United Kingdom led by Lord Robin Butler and colleagues (2004, 134–35, 170), Ritter later admitted that UNSCOM was manipulated by intelligence agencies.

Zanders and colleagues (2003) argue that this flaw only manifested because the mission lasted much longer than originally expected. As disarmament stretched into months and then years, the two-way flow of information that helped UNSCOM plan missions and kept key states appraised of UNSCOM's findings also allowed institutionalized penetration by various national intelligence agencies, compromising the mission's international nature. As stated earlier, the IAEA also fostered ties to national intelligence agencies in ways that might also compromise its objectivity and lead to misuse of IAEA information. However, it appears the IAEA acquired disarmament authority in part because of its greater impersonality than the national alternatives.

Fourth, the UN secretary-general's official oversight role for UNSCOM also later enabled Kofi Annan to intervene in UNSCOM, as he did in February 1998 to negotiate an agreement gaining access to the now-infamous presidential palaces that also imposed new inspection limits (Black 2002, 300). International inspectors had previously relied on the directive that UNSCOM was to have complete access to any and all sites "based on Iraq's declarations and the designation of any additional locations by the Special Commission itself."

To summarize, South Africa and Iraq became success stories for the IAEA and its new role in nuclear disarmament because it supplied policy partiality and impersonality on nuclear disarmament in demand by the international community. An impartial but technical body was needed to verify disarmament in South Africa because the West might be too permissive, and in Iraq because the US-led coalition might be too harsh. The popular visibility of the Agency illustrated in figure 4.2 was certainly often critical, a reflection of both the usual media bias to negative reporting and the extreme difficulty of the Agency's mission. These were temporary missions with little expectation of future repetition, lacking the persistence hypothesized to be necessary for political authority to emerge. Rather than approach disarmament as a temporary mission, the Agency invested in internalizing disarmament capabilities and in relationships with constituencies that supported an Agency disarmament capacity. As ElBaradei (2011, 36) would later summarize, "The IAEA's successful dismantling of Iraq's nuclear program silenced many of its critics and detractors and was a testimony to the Agency's effectiveness."

Nonproliferation

Although the threat of global nuclear war in the mid-1980s remained more pressing than nonproliferation, 139 states had ratified the NPT by 1985—

the UN had only 159 members—and there were no known cases of noncompliance. The Agency's investment in the specific assets of monitoring allows it to implement a unique but credible system for verifying the non-diversion of nuclear materials from declared facilities. The Agency's approach to implementing safeguards, which relied on the objective equity of allocating safeguards burdens by the quantity (and quality) of its declared materials, built its reputation for both policy partiality and impersonality in delivering safeguards.

The slow diffusion of civilian nuclear technology began to shift the proliferation risk to developing states, which also magnified the challenge of applying safeguards to indigenous enrichment and reprocessing. Limits imposed by parity between regulation and promotion or by the unwillingness of developed states to expand assistance contributed to a growing backlog in Agency investments in critical infrastructure—human and physical—wanted by the major donors for an expansion of the safeguards system. The major donor states had already begun in the 1970s to supplement safeguards spending in the regular budget with voluntary contributions and national support programs.

Despite these dual challenges, the regime appeared healthy and effective. Reinhard Loosch (1997, 76), West Germany's governor from 1972 to 1992, argues that by 1990 even most developing states had "made their peace" with the NPT, IAEA safeguards, and the NSG. A limited agent, therefore, appeared quite sufficient to supply the collective action on nonproliferation demanded by the international community.

The end of the Cold War did not end concern about the large nuclear arsenals of the United States, Russia, and others. After the Gulf War, though, it became evident that small arsenals of just a few nuclear weapons could threaten international security and be within reach of many regional actors. The greater danger from regional proliferation greatly increased the individual demand for nonproliferation among developed states and the G-77, although G-77 states continued to collectively oppose increasing funding for safeguards, reallocating safeguards efforts away from "safe" states, or reforming technical cooperation programs. Although generally heterogeneous, the G-77 was unified in its pique over apparent Western indifference to economic and regional insecurity, Israel's mistreatment of Palestinians, and for protecting South Africa's Apartheid regime (Potter and Mukhatzhanova 2012).

It was serendipitous for the Agency that, as with the reaction to Iraq's invasion of Kuwait, there was little great power or G-77 interest in protecting North Korea. In the same speech to the General Conference in September 1991 in which he announced that inspections were set to begin in South Africa in October, and in which he outlined his imminent request of the Board for greater safeguards authority, Blix noted that the IAEA had just concluded negotiating with North Korea on its CSA (IAEA 1992b). Under pressure to be more aggressive in Iraq, the Secretariat's legal team had negotiated hard with North Korea on its CSA, already including stronger language on its rights of access. Blix also put Dimitri Perricos in charge of the Department of Safeguards, who abandoned decades of deference to aggressively pursue implementation of safeguards in North Korea (Sigal 1998, 48). The institutional and technical investments under way since the Iraq mission began enabled safeguards data to show for the first time that a state was engaged in undeclared activities (Rosenthal et al. 2010, 2–4). The norms of implementation in the past would have made this impossible for the Agency.

Perricos's request to the Board to endorse a special inspection was an unusual method to indirectly pressure North Korea because the Secretariat should have been able to directly demand one under INFCIRC/153. The report underlying the request was also unusual because there was no safeguards information indicating where to inspect. Blix's evidence was supplied by a third party, the same one the Agency was using in Iraq, but Iraq was a special case. The Board's support for a North Korean special inspection implicitly accepted using third-party information to target safeguards inspections (Kratzer, Hooper, and Wulf 2005). The IAEA subsequently made increasing use of national intelligence for safeguards when it was provided and could be somehow validated (Traub 2004). Because he developed a strong rapport with his powerful principals, most national intelligence came personally to Blix, though he was not a technical expert. As one former safeguards inspector explained, this sometimes led to mistakes in its use.[18]

The report was also unusual because Blix used the inspectors' description of the technical findings, but Blix himself drafted the key portion of the report explaining the access problem. While the Article XII.C of the Statute describes the director general as a passive conduit for the technical judgments of his inspectors, this created a norm in which it became appropriate for the director general's office to modify the inspectors' judgments. Blix continued to use his control over the Secretariat to control the language of reports as well as their content and timing. This was used to great effect in pressing North Korea to implement safeguards. In this way the director general could effectively keep North Korean noncompliance on the international agenda, raise the stakes for North Korea, and then slow the crisis to allow its neighbors to reach some consensus on their approach. The Board and the Security Council complied with the director general's specific commands in accommodating what were essentially his judgments about what to report about North Korea and when. Blix used his political expertise to supply nonproliferation policy bias over and above the bias and impersonality already present in the Secretariat.

Demand for nuclear nonproliferation authority further increased as three developments challenged international collective action. First, conflicting with a stronger norm of accession to the NPT was increasing contestation over who should be targeted for NPT noncompliance. More than 25 states did ratify the NPT between 1985 and 1992, and another 15 by 1998. Adherence was nearly universal with over 180 states when the 1995 Review Conference indefinitely extended the NPT, reflecting strong international socialization on the norms of noninterference with peaceful uses of the atom and of nonproliferation. Although the pro-controls and pro-safeguards West essentially fund the IAEA (table 5.1), developing states dominated the General Conference (figure 3.2) and the Board. As Voeten (2000) shows, many states of proliferation concern were already targeted by Western advocacy of economic and political liberalization. Demanding that they also accept stronger safeguards opened pro-safeguards states—nuclear weapon states and their most secure allies—to charges by G-77 states of political

Table 5.1. Scale of Assessments, Select Member States, and Select Years

Member State	1960 (IAEA 1959)	1985 (IAEA 1984)	1995 (IAEA 1995)	2013 (IAEA 2012)
Canada	2.89%	3.158%	3.270%	3.153%
China[1]	4.65%	0.764%	0.626%	2.690%
France	5.94%	6.668%	6.301%	6.020%
Germany[2]	4.95%	8.749%	9.383%	7.885%
India	2.28%	0.275%	0.260%	0.451%
Italy	2.09%	3.831%	5.514%	4.915%
Japan	2.03%	10.572%	13.082%	12.332%
Russia[3]	12.64%	10.799%	7.053%	1.575%
Spain	0.086%	1.9774%	2.079%	3.124%
United Kingdom	7.22%	4.783%	5.277%	6.494%
United States	32.51%	25.8866%	26.122%	25.509%

Data Sources: IAEA (1959). GC(III)/RES/49: Revised Scale of Members' Contributions for 1959. Vienna, The International Atomic Energy Agency.
IAEA (1984). GC(28)/RES/435: Scale of Assessment of Members' Contributions For 1985. Vienna, The International Atomic Energy Agency.
IAEA (1995). GC(38)/RES/5/435: Scale of Assessment of Members' Contributions for 1995. Vienna, The International Atomic Energy Agency.
IAEA (2012). GC(56)/12/Rev.1: Scale of Assessment of Members' Contributions for 2013. Vienna, The International Atomic Energy Agency.

1. Prior to 1984, "China" was represented at the IAEA by Taiwan; the 1985 and 2010 scale rates are for the People's Republic of China.
2. 1960 and 1985 scale rates are for Federal Republic of Germany.
3. 1960 and 1985 scale rates are for the Soviet Union (excluding Ukrainian and Byelorussian Soviet Socialist Republics).

bias in enforcing the NPT. The G-77 directed the Board to require the Secretariat to verify the completeness of South Africa's declaration in the hope that the Agency's impersonality could overcome what it saw as persistent and increasing politicization by the West. This decision perversely handed pro-safeguards interests a victory when the Secretariat would then turn in just a few months to also demand completeness from North Korea.

The 1995 Review Conference and 93 + 2 safeguards reform debates further exposed rifts not only among the Agency's most powerful principals but also between them and the G-77. States participating in these debates disagreed over the appropriateness of enforcing nonproliferation through discriminatory trade controls or allowing accusations of noncompliance when nuclear weapon states were failing to comply with apparently equal norms of nuclear disarmament. While a cohesive Security Council in the early half of the 1990s could signal the impersonality of nonproliferation enforcement, its increasing discord undermined this signal (Thompson 2006). The apparently persistent but increasing risk of distributional effects from future cases of enforcing nonproliferation or disarmament created persistent demand for an international political authority with credible impersonality.

Second, the persistent demand for impersonality coincided with new sources of technical uncertainty from advancing globalization, economic development, and the diffusion of nuclear technology. The IAEA had not in its history been invited to implement Comprehensive Safeguards as late in a program's development or with facilities of such unique design as in South Africa. North Korea's program was also sufficiently old and advanced that, while smaller than South Africa's, many small but not insignificant activities could be hidden. Iraq's ability to advance its nuclear program showed that Comprehensive Safeguards were made inadequate by the Board's constrained focus on verifying non-diversion in the 1960s and 1970s. In threatening the effectiveness of the London Club export controls and IAEA collegial verification of non-diversion from declared activities between strategic points, all three cases complicated the technical task of verifying cooperation.

Third, the effort necessary in all three cases indicated that any doubt in the target's political commitment introduced great uncertainty about the effectiveness of incomplete transparency. Nonproliferation would require the indefinite supply of deeper and broader policy bias and impersonality than in the past to provide assurances of the absence of undeclared activities. The persistence of this demand required supply by an international organization capable of designing and implementing a technically effective yet impersonal transparency regime that accommodated norms of state sovereignty.

The Board and the Secretariat contributed separately to the successful supply over time of policy bias and impersonality beyond its judgments or commands in the ad hoc challenges. The Agency's reconceptualization of the meaning of compliance with international norms and rules through the strengthening of the safeguards system and the subsequent pull felt by states to comply caused authority to accrete to the Agency's component bodies. The Board's success with managing the political and technical aspects of nonproliferation helped it develop as a collective agent. The Agency's principals benefited from continued specialization on nuclear policy by many of its individual governors and their collective defense of closed meetings, exclusion of broader political questions from the agenda, and the norm of consensus decision making that was still only very rarely violated with actual votes. These features represent one aspect of the Agency's investment in specific assets and supportive constituencies, and assisted the Board's emergence as something more than a multilateral forum. However, the evolution of these characteristics would not necessarily enable the Agency to survive in the new political and technical environment of the challenge period.

After Blix approached his principals to seek reforms of the safeguards system, the Agency's authority over nonproliferation expanded in an iterative process as the experiences of its inspectors in South Africa, Iraq, and North Korea gave ammunition for negotiations in the 93+2 program. Blix formally approached the Board in November 1991 to ask that his inspectors have access to state nuclear export data, facility design information before construction, stronger rights to inspect suspected activities, more flexible visas, and direct access to report to the Security Council (Rosenthal et al. 2010, 15). Blix also wanted the Board to agree that NPT states were obligated to share their "third-party" information about potential violations of the NPT, which the United States and others had begun to do with the Iraq mission. The Board decided to confirm the general right to special inspections months before the request for North Korea or Romania's request that one be used to make its commitments credible. The Board also authorized the Secretariat to use nonsafeguards information to target activities, to create new units to analyze incoming nonsafeguards information, and to study mechanisms to strengthen the NPT safeguards system (Rosenthal, Saum-Manning, and Houck 2010, 20; Findlay 2012b, 137–38).

Nuclear weapon states had encouraged these proposals. Other developed states, as they had been when INFCIRC/153 was originally negotiated, were concerned about its sovereignty and economic costs. Germany even voiced anxiety about a police-like Agency emerging (Rosenthal, Saum-Manning, and Houck 2010, 22). The G-77 made weak statements of support but were clearly opposed to strengthening safeguards even though many were accepting new IAEA roles in regional agreements, including the

1991 Brazilian–Argentine Agency for Accounting and Control of Nuclear Materials, the 1995 Bangkok Treaty, the 1996 Treaty of Rarotonga, and the 1996 Treaty of Pelindaba regional nuclear weapon–free zones. They feared strengthened safeguards would undermine the Agency's promotion mandate, especially without compensatory progress on nuclear disarmament (Rosenthal, Saum-Manning, and Houck 2010, 23).

Blix first took the Board consensus in September 1992 to members participating in "Committee 24," the director general's Standing Advisory Group on Safeguards Implementation, or SAGSI (see chapter 4). SAGSI returned by April 1993 with specific recommendations for reforms that Blix took to the Board. The Board's initial reaction, however, portended a dangerously drawn-out debate. SAGSI had noted, for example, the challenge of redirecting resources from traditional safeguards, using the objective quantities of materials under safeguards, to a new model using more subjective indicators of risk without sacrificing impersonality (Rosenthal, Saum-Manning, and Houck 2010).

Sensing failure, Blix proposed that he take the reins, and the Board approved the 93+2 Program. A dedicated Secretariat team drafted much of the legal text and conducted technical field trials while using Committee 24 and SAGSI to advise and consult throughout the process (Rosenthal, Saum-Manning, and Houck 2010, 35). As one specific example, an expanded state declaration proposed in GOV/2784 (March 1995) was controversial because it required states to declare a greater range of nuclear activities, information about activities near declared facilities, and use "critical proliferation pathways" to safeguard activities that did not directly involve special nuclear materials. While states like Canada, Japan, and Sweden joined the United States in supporting these measures, others were less sure. India feared references to the strengthened measures being extendable to non-CSA agreements; Brazil, Cuba, and Mexico were concerned that some reforms exceeded the IAEA's NPT authority; and Sudan and Poland believed too little attention had been given to compromises necessary to reduce the safeguards budget, even if it meant continuing to rely on less effective measures (IAEA 1995, annex 3). The Board was so divided that the Secretariat simply dropped references to these authorities when it revised its proposal (Rosenthal, Saum-Manning, and Houck 2010, 48).

When the Secretariat finally had a proposal it believed was technically sound and supported by the members, it submitted GOV/2807 (June 1995) to the Board (IAEA 1995). Part 1 of GOV/2807 requested that the Board authorize the Secretariat to access undeclared locations, require earlier reporting of facility designs, and allow inspector use of environmental sampling and satellite imagery.[19] The Board approved the Part 1 measures, agreeing with the Secretariat that these reforms were sufficiently compatible with the 1970s consensus that the Secretariat could simply renegotiate strengthened CSAs (IAEA 1999b).

There remained a number of measures the Secretariat thought were desirable but that the debate over GOV/2784 had shown many members believed were beyond the Agency's existing authority. The Secretariat outlined in Part 2 of GOV/2807 those measures that might require some additional complementary authority. The Board also wanted to be able to assure states of the absence of undeclared activities but, as Rich Hooper states, "there was simply no way, no magic that could be sprinkled over [Comprehensive Safeguards] that would stretch so far as to include the declaration basis required for those kinds of activities" (Kratzer, Hooper, and Wulf 2005, 33). The Board also authorized the Secretariat to continue to study and consult with members on the part 2 reforms.

As active as members were, safeguards strengthening had succeeded because the Secretariat developed, tested, and legalized much expanded conceptions of nuclear safeguards against nonproliferation.[20] Blix (2004) and ElBaradei (2011) separately recount, for example, their disagreement over when to return to Committee 24 over the Part 2 measures. Blix wanted the staff to complete the proposal before bringing it to the Board but followed ElBaradei, his senior advisor, who wanted him to gain their support earlier in the process.[21] Rich Hooper and Laura Rockwood have been singled out by Myron Kratzer and colleagues (2005) and others as managing the process and drafting the text, but as Hooper (1999, 11) states, it is at least clear that "a small core group of staff within the Agency and a handful of member state experts wrote the text of the Additional Protocol."[22] This was a significant deviation from the previous safeguards systems, which had been directly negotiated by the Board and then proclaimed to the Secretariat for it to implement.

When the director general presented his final report to Committee 24 in December 1996, GOV/2863 was a nearly final draft of what became the Model Additional Protocol (Rosenthal, Saum-Manning, and Houck 2010, 49). The reconceptualization of the steps minimally necessary to prove nonproliferation was possible only because of the Secretariat's extensive investment in specific assets of nonproliferation policy and the active consultation and negotiation by its safeguards experts with external governmental and nongovernmental experts. Crucial to this process was the strong participation of states supporting safeguards reform but also the Secretariat's demonstration in the negotiations and ongoing safeguards implementation of strong impersonality.

The Board consented to the assertions of authority by the Secretariat but was also an active partner in this process. The cross-cutting divisions over GOV/2863 in the Board's debate were almost identical to those during Part 1 and, unsurprisingly, as when INFCIRC/153 was originally negotiated

(IAEA 1995, annex 5; Rosenthal, Saum-Manning, and Houck 2010, 49–50). Yet, after six years of Secretariat development, consultations, and field testing, the Board finally approved the AP in INFCIRC/540 on May 15, 1997 (IAEA 1997a).[23] The revised INFCIRC/540 requires new reporting on fuel-cycle-related activities and "complementary access" outside regular inspections, which includes "short notice" but managed access (to protect sensitive information) to locations about which the Agency has questions (Schmidt 1997; Rockwood 2002).

When Blix retired in 1998, the Agency was asserting, and its principals appeared to acknowledge, authority over nuclear nonproliferation. The Secretariat emerged as an internationally recognized political authority on the conception, design, and implementation of safeguards. It had successfully wrestled control of the reform agenda away from its principals, controlled the agenda with the strategic manipulation of compliance reports in Iraq and North Korea, excluded the United States in South Africa, and avoided political compromise in Iraq. It achieved compliance with its rules and commands by the Board and General Conference because of its ability to balance a strong bias toward verifying nonproliferation (policy bias) with the nondiscriminatory application of safeguards (impersonality).

The Board then asserted its independent authority as an agent whose own expertise and decision-making culture made it more than the sum of its collected member representatives. Just as the Board chose to not micromanage the Secretariat in the safeguards implementation or reforms process, neither the members (through the General Conference), the NPT states, nor the Security Council chose to marginalize the Board by micromanaging it, bypassing it to directly manage the Agency, or empowering alternative actors.

First, states partially complied with Agency authority when they collectively accommodated its demand for resources. Safeguards spending in the regular budget doubled in real terms between 1986 and 1996, ending in 1998 at 185 percent of pre-Chernobyl levels despite "zero growth." Staffing similarly increased from 1,630 staff in 1986 to a peak of 2,295 in 1996, a net increase of over 30 percent. The Secretariat continued to speak about the need for more resources to supply strengthened safeguards with policy bias and impersonality. The winding down of the intensive efforts in South Africa and Iraq would also mean reductions between 1996 and 1998—the safeguards budget lost 14 percent, and total staff declined 7 percent. Many members would also continue to expect ever-greater efficiency gains out of safeguards and demand balance between "regulation" and "promotion."

The Agency's principals collectively accepted Agency authority also in accommodating its agenda setting, conceptualization, and regulation of nuclear nonproliferation. They deferred to its diversion of resources from other areas to support critical missions, its testing and proposing of legal texts, and participation in policy debates. They collectively complied with the Board's assertion of its authority to define and verify a wider nonproliferation mission through the AP. They also complied with the Board's reliance on the Secretariat's authority to negotiate, implement, and judge compliance with a new, much broader conception of "safeguards."

Second, states individually accommodated Agency general authority to make new nonproliferation rules and commands. Individual states consented to IAEA authority by signing strengthened CSAs. By the end of the decade, fifty-three states had also signed an AP. This legal accommodation strengthens an emerging norm that all states should accept the IAEA authority to access any location where the Secretariat believes the undeclared use of nuclear materials may be occurring.[24] Individual accommodation also occurs with some member's ongoing support in national support programs and encouraging their experts to become employees.

Third, states also complied with specific Agency commands. The South African government opened itself to whatever the IAEA believed it required to achieve first "completeness" and then endorsement of its claimed disarmament. The Secretariat's principals complied with its judgment of South African compliance by restoring South Africa's full participation in Agency policy bodies and other benefits of membership. The North Korea case led in the 1990s to North Korea and the international community also complying with IAEA authority. North Korea tried quite hard to avoid getting caught violating the NPT and its CSA, but its behavior acknowledged the verification authority of the IAEA: it was initially very open to IAEA visits and, after challenging the IAEA, was forced to accept that safeguards compliance was necessary for any deal. The refusal of the United States to exclude IAEA verification of North Korea's obligations provided the IAEA with a continuing and central role in North Korea. This later placed the IAEA in a position to insist it would not engage in "ad hoc verification" without a safeguards agreement in place. Even though the Agreed Framework undercut the norm of internationalization in tacitly endorsing the bilateral resolution of violations to an international treaty, it did so to reinforce the norms of nonproliferation and international verification. That is, the Board's growing monopoly on international nonproliferation policy was temporarily undermined but ultimately reaffirmed when "action for action" was conditional on compliance with IAEA verification. This verification was limited but is widely believed to have been the best possible deal that North Korea would accept (Heinonen 2011).

A brief word must be said about two alternative international suppliers of nuclear policy. First, the NSG that reemerged in 1991 made significant advances in suppler controls on nuclear technology. However, a more inclusive membership caused greater political division as interests on nuclear and other issues increasingly came into conflict, just as was occurring at the

Security Council. Although not obvious to the public as this period came to a close, the NSG was also less sufficient. The NSG's control over the nuclear supply market was being marginalized by the emergence of second-tier suppliers and black-market networks beyond its direct reach.

Second, the 1996 opening for signature of the CTBT is a mixed message for IAEA authority. The CTBT further institutionalized the norm of nuclear non-testing that had strengthened beyond the Limited Test Ban Treaty and Threshold Test Ban Treaty (and Peaceful Nuclear Explosive Treaty) with the continuing US–Russian moratorium. It had the misfortune, though, of being concluded as the window of optimism about internationalization was closing. The CTBT did not enter into force by 1998 because so many statutorily necessary states did not accede. Particularly relevant was the decision to create a new international organization to implement the CTBT when Blix had pursued and others had considered the IAEA. The discussions largely left who the implementing agent would be vague but the IAEA was ultimately rejected explicitly because it had acquired too much independence and states were concerned the IAEA would not yield to states the ultimate authority to judge compliance. Some Western states also worried that adding new regulatory functions would renew demands by developing states for parity with the IAEA's promotion mission.

CONCLUSIONS

By 1986 the IAEA managed to invest in the specific assets of nuclear policy bias and impersonality then in demand by its multiple principals. It remained very much a creature of its states, a community of developed states aligned on the need for nonproliferation but still divided by the Cold War. Its Secretariat had demonstrated an ability to supply niche peaceful uses, safety standards, and monitoring of non-diversion for safeguards, although with little agency in what services it offered to whom and when. It could respond only when there was a clear consensus among its principals, and the Board had emerged as a useful forum for members to engage each other. But the Board also decided that the Agency was not a forum for cooperation on international disarmament, enforcing nuclear safety, or resolving larger problems in the international system. Although the United States and the Soviet Union were beginning to negotiate controls on offensive nuclear arms in 1986, the overriding concern of the international community was still the Cold War and the overhanging threat of global nuclear war. The taboo against nuclear use was strong, but massive nuclear arsenals backed by robust conventional forces remained the means to protecting the way of life each side believed preferable.

The Chernobyl meltdown occurred within this politically divided environment and put the future of nuclear energy in doubt. Both the Board and the Secretariat advanced international cooperation on nuclear safety but in distinctly separate and nonbinding ways, following a different model from that chosen for nonproliferation. The Board served as a negotiating forum and then depository of a series of treaties that establish a foundation of international nuclear safety obligations. Its efforts were restrained when national regulators and national nuclear industries closed ranks to oppose international safety regulation. The Secretariat still found nuclear safety demand that it could meet, and over the next several years the Secretariat supported national approaches to nuclear safety by supplying international technical conferences, publishing standards applicable at the national level, and offering safety training and missions.

The end of the Cold War signaled the apparent triumph of liberal democracy, free markets, and international institutions that produced international consensus on the means and ends of peace. However, the end of the Cold War and the fall of the Soviet Union triggered regional insecurity, elevated the North–South conflict, and unleashed greater demand by regional powers for nuclear arsenals that, even if small, provided for them a deterrent utility that was disappearing for those with the largest arsenals. The revised nuclear threat became fully evident when the IAEA and UNSCOM revealed the extent of Iraq's weapons programs. After years of economizing and accommodating states to stretch safeguards resources to cover more states, the credibility of the safeguards regime, and therefore of the entire nonproliferation regime, was called into question.

The Secretariat seized upon disarmament in Iraq and verification in South Africa and North Korea as its best opportunities for redemption. It adapted but also built specific assets for verifying the absence of misuse, including weaponization. It aggressively implemented the existing safeguards system in South Africa and North Korea. Blix was not content to defend the credibility of the Agency but also initiated and then shepherded a reform of the safeguards system to ensure its central role in the nonproliferation regime. Over the next several years it pushed its inspectors to abandon their past culture of passivity and collegial verification while pulling its principals to support a major reconceptualization of the requirements for making nonproliferation commitments credible.

Using its investment in policy bias and behavioral impersonality, the Secretariat leveraged working relationships with supportive constituencies to become proactive in the redesign of the safeguards system. It offered solutions that overcame its principals' political differences to produce nonproliferation policy. Individual states actively accepted in bilateral treaties the communally negotiated model CSAs and APs. It is also observed in member compliance with Blix's specific declarations to the Board that South Africa was clean, to the Security Council that the IAEA was done in Iraq, and to the international community the conditions under which inspectors can return to North Korea.

The Board supported these moves, but the power of the Secretariat to issue rules and commands, ranging from safeguards system proposals to judgments about compliance, was also recognized by actors outside the Board at the Security Council, the NPT Review Conference, and among influential individual principals. In supporting the Secretariat's authority, and by serving as a useful body for moderating conflict over nuclear policy, the Board also began to assert political authority on nuclear nonproliferation and disarmament. The Board not only unilaterally approved a rewrite of the NPT verification system; it also inserted itself into international politics in judging compliance by sovereign states with their international nonproliferation agreements.

By the end of the challenge period, the international community must account for the Agency as an international authority on nonproliferation. As more states in the international community saw their national interests come into greater conflict with those of the West, and especially the United States, it was more important to hear what exactly the Board would (or would not) report to the Security Council. It was necessary to hear what was reported to the Board by the Secretariat about a nuclear program or what the director general said about a state's compliance. The Agency's demonstrated policy partiality and impersonality, attributes adhering to both the Secretariat and the Board, helped insulate it from international discord over Iraq and, more generally, the appropriateness of democracy, globalization, and military intervention, discord that increasingly blocked consensus policy responses, including to challenging Iraq when it expelled inspectors in 1998.

In short, by successfully deploying its investment in supplying nuclear policy, combining strong policy bias and impersonality to effectively bargain, verify, and implement nuclear safeguards and disarmament, the IAEA began to emerge as an autonomous agent of global governance: an international nuclear authority. The international community complied with Agency authority by accommodating its general outputs of rules and services, complying with its specific commands on the construction of and compliance with the nonproliferation regime, and transferring responsibility over nuclear issues from themselves and from other international organizations.

NOTES

1. "Fukushima Accident 2011," World Nuclear Association, http://www.world-nuclear.org/info/Safety-and-Security/Safety-of-Plants/Fukushima-Accident/. Many of the long-term health effects were due to people consuming contaminated food products. See Harris (2012).

2. UNSCOM's responsibilities are described in Resolution 687 (1991), but this mandate was subsequently modified by Resolutions 707 (1991), 715 (1991), 1051 (1996), and 1154 (1998).

3. For imagery of safeguarded and clandestine facilities, see, for example, Albright, Gay, and Hamza (1999).

4. Interview with a retired IAEA Safeguards official, September 20, 2011.

5. North Korea did not have diplomatic relations with many countries and therefore had limited diplomatic staff. North Korea also required all communications, at least through the mid-1990s, to be through teleprinter exchange (telex), in which each word had to be manually typed without error (these were legal documents), because it lacked even a fax machine (which had become a ubiquitous means of communication by the early 1980s). It is arguable, of course, that communicating this way also served the North Korean's interests.

6. Presentation by retired IAEA official, March 6, 2012; and Fischer 1997, 288.

7. The full name is the Joint Declaration of South and North Korea on the Denuclearization of the Korean Peninsula.

8. Interview with retired IAEA official, January 18, 2012.

9. Similar patterns have been observed for international cooperation on human rights, and the United States has made a similar argument to justify its continuing refusal to ratify the Convention on the Physical Protection of Nuclear Materials.

10. Group interview of IAEA officials, July 20, 2005, Vienna, Austria.

11. Interview with retired IAEA official, January 18, 2012.

12. Group interview of IAEA officials, July 20, 2005, Vienna, Austria; interview with government official of Arab Republic of Egypt, July 14, 2005; and interview with government official of Israel, July 15, 2005.

13. Interview with US National Security Council advisor, August 20, 2004. Other US officials interviewed asserted a very porous relationship existed.

14. Interview with retired IAEA Safeguards official, August 13, 2012.

15. Interview with Ewen Buchanan (UNMOVIC public information officer), October 14, 2005.

16. See various United Nations reports: Reports of Executive Chairman of the Special Commission and Reports by the Secretary General on the activities of the Special Commission: S/23165 (October 25, 1991), S/23268 (December 4, 1991), S/24108 (June 16, 1992), S/24984 (December 17, 1992), S/25977 (June 21, 1993), S/26910 (December 21, 1993), S/1994/750 (June 24, 1994), S/1994/1422/Add.1 (December 15, 1994), S/1995/494 (June 20, 1995), S/1995/1017 Annex I (December 7, 1995), S/1995/1038 (December 17, 1995), S/1996/258 (April 11, 1996), S/1996/848 (October 11, 1996), S/1997/301 (April 11, 1997).

17. Interview with Ewen Buchanan (UNMOVIC public information officer), October 14, 2005. Also, see UN (1991).

18. Interview with retired IAEA official, January 18, 2012.

19. Interview with US Department of Energy employee, July 2011.

20. Interview with IAEA official, July 20, 2005; interview with IAEA Safeguards operations director, July 2008; interview with IAEA official, July 2011; and interview with retired IAEA Safeguards official, September 20, 2011.

21. Interview with retired IAEA official, January 18, 2012.

22. I discussed authorship in an interview with a US Department of Energy employee, July 2011.

23. The full title of INFCIRC/540 (Corr.) is "Model Protocol Additional to the Agreement(s) between State(s) and the International Atomic Energy Agency for the Application of Safeguards."

24. These rights exist when a state has both a revised CSA and an AP in place.

6

Nuclear Authority, 1998–2013

THE IAEA SUPPLY in 1998 of international nuclear safety and security policy and of assistance with peaceful uses reflected the real but very limited power to affect state behavior that scholars of international institutions would expect. However, the Board and the Secretariat were already demonstrating a much greater power to issue rules and commands on nuclear safeguards and nuclear disarmament with which states felt obligated to comply. Authority attached to both as they defined the standards and processes for compliance, and as they judged compliance with nonproliferation and disarmament rules. The consensus among the great powers that had allowed states to cooperate to extend the Nuclear Non-Proliferation Treaty (NPT), disarm Iraq, negotiate the Comprehensive Test Ban Treaty (CTBT), and legalize a more intrusive IAEA safeguards system had weakened, making international coordination progressively less effective as the millennium came to a close. The reemergence of legitimate exceptions to the norm of nuclear nonproliferation would introduce new sources of political uncertainty, but this only increased international demand for a political authority capable of overcoming the persistent barriers to international nuclear policy cooperation.

THE CONTEMPORARY WORLD

US national security strategy during the presidency of Bill Clinton centered on democracy promotion; multilateral military operations in regional conflicts in Bosnia and Haiti; and missile strikes against Afghanistan, Iraq, and Sudan (Clinton 1996, 1998). NATO expansion was also pursued to assuage

Eastern European insecurities. Many of the interventions that were under-taken to support the new international order were opposed by Russia and China in defense of the norm of sovereign authority and because Russia and China themselves feared becoming targets.

India's decision to test a nuclear weapon in 1998 surprised many, and this action was followed by Pakistan's own test. Neither posed a strong challenge to the nonproliferation regime because both had long maintained a principled objection to an almost universal NPT (see figure 1.1). International sanctions did not try to address the insecurities that motivated their tests and so did little to roll back their nuclear programs (Cortright and Ahmed 1998). Pakistan said it tested because India had, but India claimed it was reacting to China's military modernization and increasing assertive-ness in the region, including by conducting missile tests in 1995 and 1996 over the Taiwan Straits. China appeared motivated by the US "revolution in military affairs" displayed in the 1991 Gulf War and then in NATO's air war over Bosnia. US conventional superiority, combined with the eastward expansion of NATO, also contributed to Russia's reinvigorated reliance on nuclear forces. Nuclear weapons were for the West relics of the Cold War, but all the nuclear weapon states (and NATO) continued their strategic prominence and many were still building more. The United States, for example, was investing heavily to enable "stockpile stewardship" without testing.

The pursuit of nuclear deterrent forces reinforced the existential "come-back" of nuclear weapons for deterrence (Kristensen and Handler 1996, 387; Morgan 2003, 2006–25). To the many potential targets of Western intervention, the choice was to move "up" to so-called "weapons of mass destruction" or "down" to asymmetric strategies (Freedman 2003, 456). The United States had shown that its military was incredibly capable but that it and its allies, which the United States realized could be exposed to the threat or use of violence in a regional intervention, were also sensitive to casualties. For example, the 1991 Gulf War put US power on display as well as the risks to allies like Israel and Saudi Arabia of Iraqi missiles and potential weapons of mass destruction. Insecure and aggressive regional powers learned that this cost aversion made even a few nuclear weapons militarily significant.

The new millennium saw greater resistance to the Western strategy of promoting international institutions, liberal democracy, and free markets (Voeten 2000, 2004). Echoing concerns by developing states first enunciated at the 1955 Bandung Conference, Indian nuclear strategist Brahma Chel-laney (1999, 389) argued that the Security Council, IAEA, and other in-ternational organizations did not promote truly collective interests but "supplement the great powers' unilateral strategies." Advanced economies argued more with developing states over the global economy, democracy, terrorism, human rights, economic development, and, of course, nuclear proliferation. Opposition also was linked to the rise of violent extremist religious movements and international terrorism targeting the United States (Cronin 2003).

Diverging interests among the major powers prevented a Security Council consensus over Iraq, Bosnia, Sudan, Somalia, or North Korea years before George W. Bush became US president in 2001. The new US administration intended to exploit its "unipolar moment" (Krauthammer 1990–91) to pursue a more aggressive foreign policy. The Bush administration saw a greater threat from the nuclear and missile arsenals of "rogue" states like North Korea, Iran, and Iraq but also rejected multilateralism and internationalization as costly and unnecessary compromises of American interests. After suffering NATO expansion in the 1990s, Russia assumed it was the target when the United States announced it was withdrawing from the 1972 Antiballistic Missile (ABM) Treaty to pursue missile defenses. The Bush administration tried repairing relations with Russia by concluding the Strategic Offensive Reduction Treaty (SORT),[1] which fulfilled both states' interest in reducing their nuclear arsenals but did not include the Strategic Arms Reduction Treaty's verification mechanisms. Importantly, it was also arms control, not disarmament, and Russia continued to modernize its arsenal. The Bush administration likewise, arguing that the US nuclear arsenal was aging and inappropriate for contemporary threats, requested that the US Congress fund a "robust nuclear earth penetrator" warhead to target deeply buried or hardened underground targets, and then a "reliable, replacement warhead" (Brooks 2005; Brown 2005).

The US desire for active defenses and preemptive action was clear before al-Qaeda's attacks of September 11, 2001. The United States responded forcefully by leading a NATO invasion of Afghanistan to eradicate al-Qaeda. The 9/11 attacks were symbolically important to upending the conventional wisdom that terrorists only "want a lot of people watching and a lot of people listening and not a lot of people dead" (Jenkins 1975, 15). Security analysts had considered the possibility of nonstate actors acquiring nuclear, biological, or chemical capabilities or weapons (OSD 1997), but 9/11 was terror on a mass-casualty scale. Scholars like Graham Allison (2004), Robin Frost (2005), and Michael Levi (2007) began to think seriously about demand for, and nonstate actor capacity to supply, nuclear terrorism. Potential targets expanded their cooperation on counterterrorism and renewed efforts to secure nuclear materials against theft.

For influential US neoconservatives, 9/11 also confirmed the gathering menace from rogue regimes developing missiles and weapons of mass destruction. Despite broad support for invading Afghanistan, the international community hesitated when President Bush (2002b) used his State of the Union address to threaten the "Axis of Evil" with regime change. In the colorful phrasing of US National Security Advisor Condoleezza Rice when she was interviewed by Wolf Blitzer (2003), the United States could not wait for "the smoking gun to be a mushroom cloud." The Bush administration distrust of international institutions, assumed US primacy, and perceived acute foreign threat combined to reject patient diplomacy.

Bush had first included North Korea in the "axis of evil." The IAEA had returned in a limited capacity in 1996 and was reporting that North Korea's declared facilities were still "frozen" but that it had not yet resolved the original questions that led to the 1994 crisis. Ignoring a nearly complete deal negotiated by outgoing Secretary of State Madeline Albright, the Bush administration chose instead, within months of invading Afghanistan, to accuse North Korea of a secret uranium enrichment program. When North Korea appeared to confirm the accusation, the United States had its hoped-for opportunity to force a suspension of the Agreed Framework (Pritchard 2007, 39). North Korea responded in January 2003 by destroying IAEA monitoring equipment and expelling IAEA inspectors—destroying any safeguards on the program—and then announcing the completion of its withdrawal from the NPT (IAEA 2006 Annual Report). It restarted its nuclear program and in October 2006 conducted its first nuclear weapon test.

In the absence of diplomatic progress, North Korea's nuclear program became a story about China. China did criticize North Korea, including for its withdrawal from the NPT, its nuclear tests, and other aggressive behaviors, but weakly. China blocked strong Security Council action and, as North Korea's primary economic partner, was responsible for undermining the effectiveness of even the consensus sanctions (Haggard and Noland 2007; Noland 2008). China fears that public criticism could harm its leverage over North Korea or cause its collapse (Funabashi 2007, 300, 328), likely allowing the United States to dominate the peninsula. Russia, like Iran and others, has been publicly sympathetic as it tries to again be taken seriously as a global power (Pritchard 2007, 95).

One month after accusing North Korea, in October 2002, President Bush (2002a) announced his judgment that Iraq, another named member of the "axis of evil," "possesses and produces chemical and biological weapons; it is seeking nuclear weapons; it is giving shelter and support to terrorism and practices terror against its own people." Threatened with military force, Iraq begrudgingly reopened to inspectors from the IAEA and the UN Monitoring, Verification, and Inspection Commission (UNMOVIC), but US officials dismissed their effectiveness. As Vice President Dick Cheney (2002) told the 103rd National Convention of the Veterans of Foreign Wars, "inspectors would provide no assurance whatsoever of compliance with UN resolutions." ElBaradei (2011, 53) writes that Cheney had privately threatened that the United States would "discredit the inspections in order to disarm Iraq." Treasury Secretary Paul O'Neill, who left the administration in December 2002, was quoted by Ron Suskind (2004, 86) as saying that by February 2001, "we were building the case against Hussein and looking at how we could take him out and change Iraq into a new country."

Despite intense US pressure, Director General ElBaradei (2003c) reported to the Security Council that 218 inspections at 141 sites, wide-area radiation sampling, and interviews "found no evidence or plausible indication of the revival of a nuclear weapons program in Iraq." Blix (2003), now head of UNMOVIC, reported that Iraq was only reluctantly cooperating but also found "no evidence of proscribed activities." Canada, China, France, Russia, and others wanted more time for diplomacy and international inspections (Fenton 2004). The United States demanded immediate military action,[2] however, and in March 2003 the United States launched the second Gulf War. The United States did not secure sites known to the IAEA (and under safeguards) against looting but did deploy three weapons inspection teams that were soon afterward replaced by the Iraq Survey Group (Cleminson 2003). When President Bush declared an end to major combat operations in May 2003, the Iraqi Survey Group had not yet found evidence of continuing or new programs. The Iraq Survey Group would continue searching, and its final report in September 2004 would describe only very limited attempts to retain capabilities (Duelfer 2004).

Although the United States would later add Libya, Syria, and others to the "axis of evil," Iran was the third state named to this group, included because of its support for terrorist groups; the United States also suspected Iran was attempting to acquire nuclear weapons (OSD 1997). China and Russia had each signed numerous agreements throughout the 1990s to supply Iran's nuclear energy program and were less concerned about its risks. The West, though, believed the investments were of rather large scope and scale for a country with plentiful natural energy resources from oil. Concern crested in August 2002 when an Iranian dissident group revealed the location of a previously secret centrifuge enrichment plant at Natanz. This, along with intelligence information provided to the Secretariat in 2002, suggested that Iran was violating its Comprehensive Safeguards Agreement (CSA) by not reporting uranium enrichment activities.

Iran blocked IAEA access to key locations until France, Germany, and the United Kingdom (the "EU-3") pressed it to cooperate. Iran accepted the EU-3's demand to voluntarily implement an Additional Protocol (AP), signing but not yet ratifying it, and to suspend all uranium enrichment and reprocessing. The suspension was useful for the IAEA to fully verify Iran's nuclear past but was supported by the West—and problematic for Iran and others—as a precedent for limiting the norm of unfettered access to peaceful uses. Iran allowed IAEA inspectors to inspect several suspected sites in February 2003, even as the IAEA and UNMOVIC were investigating Iraq, and Iran admitted to undeclared enrichment and heavy-water production.

Exploiting the expanded rights under the AP, inspectors left Iran with environmental samples that revealed the presence in Iran of uranium enriched to levels far higher than it had declared. The IAEA's strengthened safeguards system had caught Iran, ElBaradei (2003b) reported, engaging in a "pattern of concealment." ElBaradei also reported that Iran "has failed to meet its obligations under its Safeguards Agreement" (IAEA 2002 Annual Report). Whereas the Bush administration had dismissed the IAEA's findings in Iraq just months earlier, in 2003 it now demanded that the IAEA report Iran to be in "noncompliance." However, ElBaradei refused. Israeli officials also began accusing the Agency of withholding information about suspected weaponization work.[3]

IAEA (2004) inspectors then reported evidence that Iran had been helped by what it termed "foreign sources." Peaceful nuclear supply was not a problem, but as Albright and Hinderstein (2004) reported, IAEA verification pointed to an illicit nuclear supply network. While US and other intelligence agencies were not unaware of the role Abdul Qadeer "A. Q." Khan played in building Pakistan's nuclear program, including procuring centrifuge technology in the 1970s, they had missed his network spreading to supply states beyond Pakistan. If Pakistan was not aware of the network, argued journalist David Sanger (2004, 2), this was a major threat to the state-centric nonproliferation system.

Investigations by Western intelligence into the Khan network led in October 2003 to the seizure of the ship MV BBC *China* on its way to Libya with centrifuge parts. The seizure had been enabled under the Proliferation Security Initiative (PSI), a program launched by the United States in 2003 to facilitate cooperation on counterproliferation among traditional allies but also key transshipment ports and major "flag of convenience" countries. PSI created a web of bilateral agreements that allowed partners who signed formal Statements of Interdiction Principles to interdict international shipments of proliferation-related materials (Beck 2004; Dunn 2006). This seizure provided the United States and United Kingdom with the leverage to negotiate Libya's announcement in December 2003 that it would verifiably destroy its weapons of mass destruction capabilities, sign an AP, and ratify the Chemical Weapons Convention (Boureston and Feldman 2004).

The United States saw coercive nonproliferation successful not only with Iraq and Libya but also in the Security Council support for Resolution #1540 (April 2004), which requires that all states adopt effective domestic measures to prevent nonstate actors from acquiring weapons of mass destruction. Emboldened, the United States revealed in 2004 that it had come to possess a laptop computer that purportedly contained documents describing Iranian studies related to nuclear weapon research and development. These documents were shown to the IAEA and became another issue for its inspectors to investigate, but IAEA inspectors could neither keep the documents nor examine the laptop. ElBaradei accepted that his inspectors did have many questions about Iran's program, but he argued he was constrained because he could neither verify the validity of third-party intelligence nor share it with Iran to document his demands of them. Pressure increased when the US intelligence community concluded that Iran had an active nuclear weapon program (Linzer 2005). Western pressure eased when elections in Iran in 2005 offered the possibility of a reform-oriented government but then resumed when hard-liner Mahmoud Ahmadinejad was elected. Israel stepped up its rhetoric, drawing red lines that implied it was prepared at any time to strike at Iran's nuclear facilities, and was accused of assassinating Iran nuclear scientists. This magnified domestic pressure in the United States to also act more strongly against Iran.

The decision of the Nobel Committee to give the 2005 Prize for Peace to ElBaradei and the IAEA was a surprise. Comments by the chairman of the Nobel Committee, Ole Danbolt Mjøs, left many wondering if ElBaradei was really being rewarded for opposing the Bush administration on Iraq and Iran. Mjøs pointed to contemporary nuclear challenges being magnified by political discord: "At a time when disarmament efforts appear deadlocked, when there is a danger that nuclear arms will spread both to states and to terrorist groups, and when nuclear power again appears to be playing an increasingly significant role, this work is of incalculable importance" (Mjøs 2005). The Agency, at least as perceived by the Nobel Committee, was being rewarded not simply for "safeguards" but "for their efforts to prevent nuclear energy from being used for military purposes and to ensure that nuclear energy for peaceful purposes is used in the safest possible way."[4]

With threats of violent solutions to Iran's program percolating in the United States and Israel, Russia and China finally consented to Security Council sanctions under Resolution #1737 (December 2006). The Board followed by terminating twenty-two (of fifty-five) Technical Cooperation projects involving Iran (Boureston and Lacey 2007). Support for coercion evaporated, though, when a new US National Intelligence Estimate in 2007 indicated that Iran's nuclear weapons program had stopped years earlier. The international community appeared ready to pause on further action as it waited to see how US foreign policy would change after the presidential election.

Tensions did ease when President Barak Obama's inauguration in January 2009 promised a more collaborative approach to international system management. Obama's (2009) first speech abroad in Prague singled out nuclear and missile programs in Iran and North Korea as threats to international security but also promised to pursue "a world without nuclear weapons." Obama forced nonproliferation and disarmament onto the global agenda by promising in a major foreign policy speech to reduce US reliance on nuclear weapons, negotiate stockpile reductions with Russia, seek US ratification of the CTBT, reopen negotiations on a Fissile Material Cut-Off Treaty (FMCT), and promote international civil nuclear cooperation under stronger international safeguards.

Although locking down nuclear materials and ensuring the safety of nuclear facilities was not new, the Prague speech helped launched the issue of "nuclear security." The first Nuclear Security Summit in April 2010 drew more than forty heads of state and anchored the G-8's Global Partnership Against the Spread of Weapons and Materials of Mass Destruction. A second Nuclear Security Summit in Seoul, South Korea, occurred in March 2012 but was overshadowed by economic problems in Europe and a threat by North Korea to launch a satellite. The third, held in the Netherlands in March 2014, was also overshadowed, this time by the Russian annexation of Crimea from Ukraine.

When ElBaradei's third term ended in 2009, the Board recommended Yukiya Amano to replace him. Japan's ambassador to international organizations in Vienna, Amano had not been the first choice of many governors, but the United States asserted his capacity to manage the Secretariat and represent the interests of the Board.[5] Amano won by a two-thirds majority of the General Conference after strong lobbying on his behalf by US Secretary of State Hillary Clinton.[6] Amano's first term is remembered most for his poor reaction when a natural disaster returned nuclear safety to international salience for the first time since the Chernobyl accident in 1986. When the Great East Japan Earthquake struck Japan on March 11, 2011, several tsunami waves hit the coast, killing more than fourteen thousand people and hitting Fukushima's Daiichi power plant.[7] The designed safety systems of four of the reactors were overwhelmed, causing them to melt down and putting the spent fuel ponds at risk of exploding. The danger of radiation exposure led to the evacuation of nearly one hundred thousand people, but millions more were in potential danger. Findlay (2012a) reports that IAEA staff mobilized within hours; hundreds volunteered both to prepare information that the Agency and members would need and to assist in the emergency response. However, without direction from Amano to do so, the Agency did little to provide information or analysis useful to the international public. The worst nuclear accident in history was brought under control, but the complete remediation of Fukushima Daiichi is expected to take forty years, and a report by Congressional Research Service analysts Mark Holt, Richard Campbell, and Mary Beth Nikitin (2012, 1) predicted the total cost would exceed $75 billion.

Amano was more willing than his predecessor to press Iran to fully cooperate with IAEA verification. Whereas the IAEA had previously referred to Iran's "alleged studies" on weaponization, Amano moved to give a much more detailed reporting on the "possible military dimensions." In

2011 Amano reported to the Board that the Secretariat had also acquired since 2004 new evidence of weaponization (IAEA 2011c), providing new impetus for international sanctions. The ratcheting up of sanctions by the United States and the European Union from 2011 to 2013 was quite damaging to Iran's economy. Pressure also came from Israel's threat to repeat the disarmament strategy used in 1981 against Iraq to set back Iran's nuclear program. The Ahmadinejad government still refused to constrain its program, even temporarily, or allow IAEA inspectors to access the sites where weaponization was suspected.

Iranian elections in June 2013 replaced Ahmadinejad's government with one expected to ease the pressure of sanctions by engaging the international community. President Hassan Rouhani replaced Iran's nuclear negotiators, which paved the way for more productive talks with the "P5+1"—the EU+3 and the United States, Russia, and China—and the first direct talks with the United States since the 1979 hostage crisis. These finally yielded the Joint Plan of Action in November 2013 to freeze large parts of Iran's nuclear program in exchange for a reduction of sanctions (IAEA 2013a). Reductions, however, were conditional upon "enhanced monitoring" by the IAEA, which would be "responsible for verification of nuclear-related measures . . . to facilitate resolution of past and present issues of concern" (2013a, 1). With Iran appearing to implement its commitments and the IAEA reporting it had verified that Iran had not diverted materials from safeguarded facilities (the "correctness" standard), the policy problem could shift away from reducing Iran's stockpile of enriched uranium to whether Iran would allow IAEA verification to resolve the alleged "possible military dimensions."

As the international community approaches the 2015 NPT Review Conference, concern extends beyond Iran and North Korea to a number of aspiring or threshold states. Allegations in the recent past of undeclared nuclear activities had also arisen against Syria, where construction of an alleged North Korean–style reactor was bombed (allegedly by Israel), and against Myanmar.[8] Prospects also appear slim for the CTBT entering into force, for progress on an FMCT, or for new US–Russian arms reductions.

AGENCY AUTHORITY

Political discord between the West and Russia, China, and developing states persisted after 1998 over the structure of the international system. This increased the distributional effects of cooperation on nuclear issues, cooperation complicated by changing technical demands for achieving collective nuclear goals with new standards for judging nonproliferation, safety, and security cooperation. The changing political and technological environment has ultimately created persistent demand for international political authority on some issues, and the Agency clearly gained greater power on nonproliferation and disarmament to issue rules and commands with which states feel pulled to comply. The Agency also has some power over nuclear safety, nuclear security, and peaceful nuclear uses but remains a limited agent because the demand for its policy partiality and impersonality is much weaker and less persistent. The IAEA has also been less successful in these areas at exploiting opportunities to seize authority.

Unipolarity

In the years following the 1995 NPT Review Conference, many non–nuclear weapon states felt cheated by the failure of the United States to follow through on the many promises it made to secure the indefinite extension of their commitments to nonproliferation under the NPT. However, the anticipated beginning of a multipolar international system had also failed to materialize, locking the United States into its role as an international system manager. The US testing moratorium continued, but so did its reliance on nuclear deterrence.[9] Relations with Russia had deteriorated with the Clinton administration's push to expand NATO and to somehow amend the ABM treaty to allow missile defense research. The United States was also heavily investing in the scientific infrastructure necessary to assure its military that the nuclear stockpile was safe and reliable despite the end of testing.

President Bush believed that the real threat to US interests was rogue states. Invested in US primacy, there was little reason to attend to the needs of Russia, just emerging from years of economic contraction, or China, which was growing but still lacked the military capability to threaten even its smaller neighbors. This did not change with the 9/11 attacks, and President Bush (2001) publicly declared that all governments "will be held accountable for inactivity" in the US war on terror and rogue regimes. Even allies were told, "You're either with us or against us."

The Bush administration was successful with Libya, PSI, and Resolution #1540. It also pushed through the IAEA the first deviation from the "zero real growth" budget since the 1980s (and increased its voluntary contributions for IAEA safeguards and nuclear security). However, the long-term health of the nonproliferation regime was undermined by its unwillingness to address the interests of others (Dunn 2006, 5). Erik Voeten (2004) shows that the hegemon became progressively more isolated at the United Nations. US system management also worsened divisions among the Board. The United States saw ElBaradei's actions—and the unwillingness of others to support his ouster—as disobedience. Even former US diplomats would blame discord equally on US unilateralism (Hibbs and Persbo 2009, 22).

The United States' hegemonic approach achieved policies but denied a new, sustainable consensus on the Agency's missions. The United States—distracted by two wars and, beginning in 2008, by a mounting economic crisis—lacked the capacity or legitimacy to lead the international community on North Korea or Iran. It began to step back, opening space for the EU-3 to negotiate with Iran, although the EU-3 also remained divided among themselves and with the United States over how to press forward.[10] The G-77, China, and Russia opposed Western efforts to roll back Iran's nuclear program, defending Iran's right to peaceful uses and its decision to protect its nuclear energy program against Israeli strikes by hiding its existence from the world, including the IAEA. They accused the West of hypocrisy in ignoring Israel's, India's, and Pakistan's nuclear programs. They entertained the possibility that the evidence of Iran's weaponization could be fabrications by the US and Israeli governments, as the United States had done against Iraq in 2002–3.[11]

President Obama promised a return to international institutions as a means to accomplish US interests. His administration appeared more receptive to ratifying the CTBT, advancing the FMCT, and political compromise generally, including acceding to demands for reforms at other international institutions like the IMF and World Bank. Obama had little success at advancing his nuclear policy initiatives because of the hardening political divisions at home and because of resistance from non-Western states, each with their own individual reasons for rejecting elements of the American order. Middle Eastern states already divided over Israel, the wars in Iraq and Afghanistan, and Iran were further divided over the "Arab Spring" wave of internal revolutions. They criticized the US failure to close the Guantanamo detention center and the increased US reliance on drone strikes and Special Forces for assassinations. The killing of Osama bin Laden, for example, was a US victory important to talking about an end to the war on terror, but reactions to how it was accomplished also widened the political chasm between the United States and others. Meanwhile, Russia's approach to Iran, Syria, Georgia, and Ukraine, and China's greater aggressiveness in asserting its territorial claims have presented alternatives to accepting the US-led international order.

The international cooperation we observe on nuclear issues as elsewhere does not reflect obedience to US hegemony. Whereas one could be uncertain whether the divergence in interests had been as great as that proclaimed by the Bush administration, even under Obama the most successful US nuclear policy initiative has probably been in the area of nuclear security, where leadership encouraged a normative shift in the importance of national attention rather than international institutionalization. US leadership is still important, and without it major international initiatives will fail, but the United States has continued to experience diminishing influence over others.

Norms of Behavior

India's and Pakistan's nuclear tests were obvious markers of antinuclear norm fracturing that continued when others also defended the continuing utility of nuclear weapons for deterrence. The United States appeared to undermine the norm of disarmament and non-use when the Bush administration sought new nuclear weapons to supply missions that its military believed defied conventional solutions and proposed a warhead intended to be interchangeable among multiple delivery systems. Russia did as well when it decided to rely on nuclear weapons for a wider range of contingencies that its conventional forces could no longer supply. China, fearing it could not ignore conventional US compellence in the event of a regional crisis, also began nuclear force modernization. The greater utility of proliferation for serving higher order norms of sovereignty and freedom from (Western) intervention undermined the international nonproliferation norms that had strengthened since the NPT entered into force. The coercive effect of nonproliferation norms was also undermined by the United States' misuse of international nonproliferation to achieve other goals. In short, even though many states were more adamant about nonproliferation, the norms of nonproliferation, disarmament, and non-use only weakened.

The Bush administration was also responsible for promoting nuclear energy as an environmentally acceptable strategy for meeting the predicted increase in global energy demand while also supplying energy independence.[12] It heavily supported the Generation IV International Forum, launched by the Clinton administration in 2000, and successfully reframed the debate away from the environmental fear of radioactive waste and accidents. The program fostered new international demand for nuclear energy as an environmentally friendly alternative to fossil fuel energy, supporting research to develop reactors designed to operate more safely, efficiently, and offer enhanced "proliferation resistance."[13] The range of energy proposals it included indicates a demand for technically effective strategies (policy partiality), but the United States, while promoting nuclear power, still held the parallel goal of limiting access to "sensitive" fuel-cycle capabilities for potential proliferators.

The Bush administration reversed Clinton's (1998, 3) pursuit of "continued US engagement and leadership abroad" and rejected internationalization as a valued signal that goals and procedures were collectively deemed legitimate or appropriate. Its approach to Iraq at the Security Council well exemplified how the United States now avoided international institutions except when it could use them as a truncheon against its enemies. As with PSI and the Moscow Treaty, the United States preferred more flexible arrangements. The weakening of internationalization norms had help from states upset by misbehavior by UN peacekeeping troops (Ledgerwood 1994; Lynch 2005), the World Health Organization's response during the SARS and avian influenza epidemics (Choi 2008), or the greater chaos of democratic governance and globalization (Wade 1998; Kahler and Lake 2003; Milanovic 2003). The economic crisis after 2008 saw even European states resisting IMF authority. International institutions came under attack from so many directions for their ineffectiveness at achieving collective aims and for imposing policies that primarily benefited their most powerful principals that the norms of internationalization also weakened.

President Obama (2009) promised the international community that the United States would adopt a more collaborative approach to its foreign policy. His promise to work toward a world without nuclear weapons, as a "moral responsibility" for the United States, inspired an international return to nuclear disarmament, nuclear nonproliferation, and nuclear security. Although nuclear security was described as useful to improving the material security of all states, Obama's attention to nuclear issues promoted antinuclear norm internalization. Obama's shift also began to return US leadership to international institutions, which together contributed to support a more authoritative IAEA. However, beyond its nuclear security initiative, the Obama administration has done a poor job of articulating a broader US foreign policy agenda that the Prague vision could support. It also continued a big surge in funding to the US nuclear weapons infrastructure and in 2013 proposed reducing the number of US warheads further by developing a new "interoperable" warhead that, much like the Reliable Replacement Warhead, could be used on multiple delivery platforms. As a result, neither the weakening norm of internationalization nor the fracturing of antinuclear norms could be the cause when IAEA authority increased after 1998.

Agency Autonomy

Hans Blix had cleared major issues before retiring in 1998, completing the 93+2 safeguards strengthening process and Iraq's disarmament. The Secretariat had been integral to international nonproliferation efforts, and Board negotiations had become so important that in 1999 the US permanent representative to the IAEA began to reside in Vienna. Munir Ahmad Khan (1997, 310), Pakistan's governor to the IAEA for twelve years, argued that Blix deserved special credit for establishing the IAEA as "a technically strong, professionally capable, financially viable and administratively well managed organization" with the respect of the international community. Blix was also respected and was soon recruited to head UNMOVIC. Blix's long-time advisor, Mohamed ElBaradei, promised to follow in Blix's footsteps and was selected as his replacement, delivering a turn at "control" to G-77 states. However, this was a gift given over the objections of his own government. Egypt had preferred its own candidate but, supported by the United States and others, ElBaradei's appointment marked an end to the traditional veto members had over their own nationals working at the Agency.

The IAEA budget had been in decline since 1995 (see figure 1.2), but attempts to incrementally economize had been ongoing since the 1980s. IAEA inspectors commented in interviews that the Agency's laboratories used for many of its safeguards analyses were outdated, with needed investments having been postponed for years, and inspectors were spending fewer days in the field conducting fewer inspections. ElBaradei even rejected a proposed reform of the "significant quantities" standard because, he said, "we're barely surviving right now with the resources we have" (quoted in Redden 2003, 39). ElBaradei (2011, 165) later described the inability of the members to fully fund the responsibilities they expected the Agency to fulfill as "another distressing indicator of the North-versus-South divide."

Major budget increases began in 2003 when, despite ElBaradei earning US enmity for opposing the invasion of Iraq, the US government pushed the Board to approve the first "real" increase since zero real growth began in 1985: $15 million in 2004 to $260 million, and another $25 million by 2007. Although supported by pro-safeguards members, the United States succeeded because ElBaradei had created the appearance of an economic crisis at the Agency.

When he and the Agency were awarded the Nobel Prize, ElBaradei (2011, 189–90) would later write, "I felt far more immune against accusations of being biased or soft and against those who would question my integrity. . . . I began speaking out more publicly and with greater vigor about the need to bolster the IAEA's independence with enhanced legal authority, technological capabilities, and financial support." His acceptance speech challenged the West by supporting the G-77 narrative that nuclear proliferation was a problem but was also symptomatic of a larger problem of global inequality and insecurity. This view resonated with the many who feared that the IAEA was all that stood between the United States and more wars for regime change. And when the US government failed to prevent his reappointment because he retained the support of China and Russia as well as Germany and France, ElBaradei could rightly claim that he served the entire Agency, not one or a few of its powerful Board members.

ElBaradei continued to publicly criticize the Board, in 2007 arguing that the Board's budget would not "by any stretch of the imagination meet our basic, essential requirements" (Kerr 2007). Four days later ElBaradei told the Board that the "dichotomy between increased high priority activities and inadequate funding, if continued, will lead to the failure of critical IAEA functions" (Kerr 2007). In 2009 Europeans on the Board still appeared ready to continue zero growth and again reject an increase sought by the United States, though weakly supported also by China and Russia. ElBaradei aggressively interrupted their debate, as a US internal document paraphrased: "Member States had resisted a budget increase, and that they would eventually 'reap what they sowed.' He warned Member States not to 'come to me in a couple of years, after there is another Chernobyl, a terrorist attack, or a country develops a clandestine nuclear program.' . . . Asking the Agency to 'pass the hat' was a 'bastardization' of an important international organization" (Schulte 2009).

His intervention succeeded, and the Board finally approved real budget increases. Although only half what ElBaradei was seeking, the IAEA budget more than doubled from 2000 to 2010 to $402 million, not including another $167 million in voluntary and extrabudgetary contributions (IAEA 2011a). In 2011, the United States GAO (2013) would report, the regular budget reached $433 million, supplemented by another $317.3 million in extrabudgetary cash contributions. In short, by 2011 the Agency was consuming over $750 million each year in direct spending, not counting other "off voluntary" contributions of equipment, training, seconded staff, and other assistance from Member State Support Programs. Compared to other international organizations like the IMF and World Bank, only a small portion of this support was as a pass-through for assistance.

The Agency's resource constraints under zero growth, even with the recent exceptions, have eroded the Agency's capacity. The influx of staff that joined in the 1970s expansion are beginning to retire, and the remaining professional staff are being stretched over more responsibilities, problems that are repeated in reports by the US GAO (2013) and elsewhere.[14] IAEA hiring procedures also limit the overlap between outgoing and incoming staff. For example, replacement inspectors cannot be recruited until a position is vacated, and it may take six months to hire and then a year of training for a new inspector to be ready for the field.[15] Meanwhile, anti-tenure policies implemented under ElBaradei were limiting most new employees to three-year contracts, which is most painful for divisions reliant on technical expertise and institutional memory.[16] The proliferation of safety and security programs, described in more detail in the following, has largely been supported by voluntary contributions, preventing the Secretariat from developing more comprehensive approaches to nuclear policy problems. This requires direct ongoing efforts by members or the director general to sustain and bridge disparate programs and initiatives.

The Agency launched several management reforms that promised to further economize and would also justify its need for greater resources. The

GAO (2013) reports that, beginning with the Safeguards Department, many departments initiated medium- and long-term planning in an attempt to anticipate changes likely needed in the Agency's roles and resources. The Agency began using "results-based management" to evaluate its programs, beginning with the Department of Technical Cooperation as it tried to accommodate the UN's Millennium Development Goals.[17] Since the G-77 acquired a majority in the Agency, developing states have resisted long-term planning that could justify greater spending on "regulation" or greater scrutiny of "promotion." Agency inefficiencies remain because member constituencies protect some areas, such as the continued separation of the Department of Nuclear Applications from Technical Cooperation described in internal US documents as one of the "stubborn redundancies."[18]

Resource-management issues highlight the difficult position of the director general as the agent of multiple principals. The minimum share of members able to impose—or, in this case, block—major institutional changes as expressed in the budget through the Board continued to decrease to just 11 percent of the 158 members by 2011 (see figure 3.1). Although he is practically speaking accountable only to the thirty-five governors, he is ultimately the agent of the General Conference and less directly of the Security Council and NPT Review Conferences, where worsening politicization has left the membership divided over the solution. A proposal to amend Article VI of the Statute to expand the Board to forty-three governors, for example, remains far short of the needed two-thirds approval. Among those who have not ratified the amendment are the United States, Russia, China, India, and Israel. A similar debate has been ongoing at the Security Council where it is widely accepted that reforms, including changes to the veto or an expansion of the number of veto-wielding seats, would benefit institutional action and legitimacy (Hurd 2008b). Persistent disagreement remains, however, over how institutional power should be distributed.

ElBaradei (2011, 125) would later write, "The distrust between nuclear haves and have-nots, already palpable, was exacerbated and continued to dominate the back corridors of international nuclear diplomacy." After Iraq, analysts were beginning to wonder whether the IAEA could resist the intense political pressure put on its judgments (Redden 2003, 34–35). Still, even as late as 2005, US government and Agency officials were commending the level of Board consensus on Iran.[19] It was "a rare event" and "not a good sign" when the Board finally referred Iran to the Security Council in February 2006. Whereas almost every decision was by consensus, in line with the "Vienna Spirit," ElBaradei (2011, 193) reports that this was decided by a vote with five of the thirty-five governors abstaining and three voting "no."

Despite his increased international stature, ElBaradei faced increasing internal opposition. Safeguards experts who were interviewed noted that he became increasingly aloof, isolating key decisions at the Agency from the staff.[20] John Carlson, the former head of the Australian Safeguards and Nonproliferation Office, said staff morale was "appalling" and that even very senior staff, including deputy directors general Pierre Goldschmidt and Olli Heinonen, were complaining about ElBaradei's mismanagement. El-Baradei (2011) himself hinted later at disagreements between himself and Heinonen over safeguards issues.

US government internal memos show that the members expected a major opportunity to affect the development of the Agency when ElBaradei announced he would retire in 2010.[21] Amano was elected with wide international support, but the strength of US support caused concern by Russia, China, and many developing states (Crail 2009). Leaked US government cables describe Amano as "solidly in the US court on every key strategic decision, from high-level personnel appointments to the handling of Iran's alleged nuclear weapons program."[22] Still, internal US discussions urged a lobbying effort because the United States could not dictate Amano's selections for his senior management.[23] Amano and his first deputy director general for Safeguards (until late 2013), Herman Nackaerts, were also seen as being more aggressive with Iran, reflecting Western priorities. Secretariat reports on Iran have been more uncompromising, and Amano pressed the Board and the Security Council to support Agency verification efforts.[24]

Amano is seen inside the Agency as less aloof, making a point of building staff loyalty by having open discussions in meetings and often eating in the communal cafeteria, something ElBaradei never did.[25] IAEA staff note that Amano was quite deliberately maintaining diverse geographic representation in his management team but had also removed some of ElBaradei's closest advisors.[26] Trevor Findlay (2012b) argues that Amano's reorganization of management sought to reduce the outsized influence over policy of the "foreign office" and reduce inefficiencies of ElBaradei's "flat" management structure. Others are concerned that these reforms increase the political role of his office and ultimately compromise IAEA analysis and credibility (Borger 2012).

In short, the last fifteen years have seen more states join and demand expanded IAEA services but without a corresponding increase in the Agency's funding or staff levels. ElBaradei successfully challenged the membership to increase the Secretariat's funding but he, and Amano after him, also successfully engaged the international community on some nuclear issues. Taking the issues one by one examines how the IAEA confronted new political and issue complexity and in the process acquired international political authority.

Peaceful Uses

IAEA support for expanding peaceful uses of the atom is not large by development bank standards. It disbursed $64.5 million in 1998, which it believed to be an outlier year on the low end (IAEA 1999b). While in 2012 it completed nearly nine hundred active projects and delivered thousands of hours of offered safety, security, and applied uses training, it still disbursed only $80 million (IAEA 2013a). In comparison, the World Bank Group in 2011 executed over $43 billion in loans and is increasingly consulting to states on their economies. The IAEA supply of international nuclear assistance is also relatively small compared to state-to-state supply that includes reactor fuel or turn-key facilities, such as reactors or fuel-cycle facilities (Fuhrmann 2009a; Kroenig 2009a, 2009b). However, nuclear energy production had declined in the 1980s and grew only slightly with Bush administration encouragement (see figure 4.1). The IAEA reports there were 434 operational reactors in 1997 and just one more by 2011, but in a major shift from the Cold War era, now the vast majority of new reactor construction is occurring in developing states; China alone plans more than 100 new reactors.[27] Electrical capacity grew only slightly from 348 to 369 gigawatts (electric) but has declined since peaking in 2006.[28]

A decade previously, as the GAO (1997) notes, developed states were voicing concern that IAEA projects were not integrated into recipients' larger nuclear and economic development. The Board did pursue some reforms, including Country Program Frameworks to better align Agency efforts with larger national development needs (IAEA 1999b, 2006 Annual Report, 73), but the basic guidelines have not been revised since 1979 (IAEA 1979). Technical Cooperation now also appears poorly integrated with new international development priorities under the UN Millennium Development Goals adopted in 2000: good governance, democracy, transparency, poverty reduction, education, rule of law, civil society, and human rights.

The United States in particular was concerned about the proliferation potential of Agency assistance (GAO 1997; Aloise 2011). Neither the Department of Technical Cooperation nor the Standing Advisory Group on Technical Assistance and Cooperation were considering proliferation potential or compliance with other nonproliferation agreements as a criterion for assistance (Boureston and Lacey 2007; GAO 2009). Although Barretto and Cetto (2005) would state that the review process since the 1990s officially coordinated with Safeguards, GAO reports and interviews suggest these reviews had only occurred ex post for evaluating safeguards compliance. The director general finally insisted in 2005 that Safeguards review all assistance projects in advance, but such reviews were still spotty.

To the majority of the members, the Secretariat is still the authority for providing international nuclear assistance. Other UN development bodies now require projects with nuclear components to include the IAEA.[29] Despite the problems noted earlier, the World Bank, the UN Development Program, and the UN Food and Agriculture Organization trust that the IAEA is reviewing joint projects not only for efficiency and effectiveness. Of course the Agency requires projects be under safeguards and comply with

IAEA safety standards, but this is not the same as ensuring that projects—such as uranium exploration in North Korea—are not, as Brown and Kaplow (2014) worry, contributing to the proliferation of nuclear weapons.

For these reasons it is easy to see that the IAEA has acquired a small amount of authority over the international supply of peaceful uses. Donors want the IAEA to continue assistance to support safety and security. Developed states also see a useful coordinating role with technical conferences and standards setting on peaceful uses, which also imposes safety standards and safeguards on its assistance. The Technical Cooperation program itself has little authority as a development agent except to developing states that try to protect this mission fiercely. They argue that Technical Cooperation is not only useful but also their right under the nonproliferation bargain. Attempts by the Board to impose discipline in the review of individual projects have proven politically dangerous, as the GAO (2009) found when the United States challenged programs for Iran in 2007.

Safety

It was plausible after the 1986 Chernobyl accident to describe the Agency, as did UK senior nuclear safety official Mike Weightman (2011a), as becoming "the appropriate international focal point for strengthening the global nuclear safety framework." The list of IAEA nuclear safety activities is extensive: depository for eleven international nuclear safety conventions, publisher of greater than 120 safety standards (only 8 are older than 2000 and more than 50 were written or updated after 2007), thirty-one types of safety-related review missions to review everything from a member's nuclear regulatory structure to its locating and operation of nuclear facilities, eighteen "special projects" on safety (which range from the safety of different aging facilities to environmental modeling and facility decommissioning), and innumerable training programs through the departments of Technical Cooperation and Nuclear Safety and Security.[30] To implement its responsibilities under the various conventions, the Agency created its Incident and Emergency Center, which establishes the Agency's internal Response Plan for Incidents and Emergencies, clarifies states' expectations of the Agency's role in these events under the Emergency Notification and Assistance Technical Operations Manual, and coordinates assistance in a nuclear accident, when such assistance is requested, through the Response and Assistance Network. The center also includes a small office staffed twenty-four hours a day, seven days a week, as a contact point for notification of emergencies and requests for response and assistance.[31]

However, the poverty of the international response to the Fukushima nuclear accident, argues Monica Washington (1999, 194), reveals the collective choice after Chernobyl to not internationalize. Many might have inferred that the Agency would assist in a nuclear emergency by collecting, analyzing, and communicating useful information or deploying trained personnel. The IAEA did offer assistance to Japan within two hours of the earthquake and put its Incident and Emergency Center into full emergency response mode to receive and transmit information. Amano, however, explicitly directed the staff not to talk to the public about the crisis except with his specific approval.[32] The IAEA (2012a) would only transmit information to the public that it deemed "validated" by Japan. Amano did not make his first public statement, or travel to Tokyo, until four days after the crisis began and reportedly only then because the US ambassador told Amano to go. Many members were upset, trying to decide whether to evacuate their citizens from Japan.[33]

The Fukushima crisis showed that any expectation of IAEA authority on nuclear safety hinged on several false premises. First, the Secretariat offers many safety codes, programs, and units, but they are poorly supported. IAEA Safety Standards are universally recognized as good assurances of safety when followed but are not legally required except on assistance that the IAEA supplies (Bunn and Heinonen 2011; Lochbaum 2012). The Agency's safety missions occur only at the request of the member, and the results are confidential and also nonbinding. Further, few advanced states request them, and the safety missions may be too expensive for developing states to host even when developed states pay for the mission staff's time and international transportation. For example, missions can still require the translation of complex documents into English and the local costs for international mission personnel (Washington 1999, 207).

Second, the various conventions are legally binding but impose few obligations. The Convention on Nuclear Safety, for example, uses closed "peer review" meetings with no legal or moral obligations. Although few states make their reports public, Findlay (2012a) argues that the process may still be productive for those seeking to improve their safety practices. The conventions also require designating contacts for emergency notifications, but an IAEA test in 2010 reportedly found that only 21 percent of states' nuclear emergency points of contact responded within thirty minutes; half did not respond at all (Findlay 2012a). Japan (2011b, 37) could not fully exploit foreign assistance because, despite the Convention's obligations, "there was not a specific structure in the government to accommodate such assistance." No one in Japan knew who was ultimately responsible for public safety in a nuclear emergency (Weightman 2011b, 128; Japan 2011a, 4–11; 2011b, 36). The crisis was worse, residents in Japan reported, because the government and major national and international news outlets provided little useful information.[34] This weakness of international regulation allowed, as Japan (2011b, 31) acknowledged, emergency response preparations to be "regarded as voluntary efforts by operators, not legal requirements."

Third, Amano chose not to act because he apparently believed the conventions require a state to specifically request assistance. The IAEA's Incident and Emergency Center, for example, was explicitly created to help IAEA members "enhance their own preparedness" (Washington 1999, 217). Findlay (2012a), though, argues that Amano underused his authority and failed to seize numerous opportunities to leverage the Secretariat's expertise and information in ways that would have been useful and welcome to his principals. Even when the immediate crisis was over and an IAEA Ministerial Conference requested the Secretariat to prepare a plan for advancing international nuclear safety, the resulting action plan relied on member consultations (IAEA 2011b, 1; 2012a). It offered only limited, hortatory references to "strengthening" and continued to emphasize that safety is a national responsibility. Again, if Amano had wanted to seize leadership, according to a former IAEA official, the Agency should have drafted the action plan internally and then used it to set the agenda with members.

States remain uninterested in internationalizing nuclear safety. Findlay (2012a) reported that the Obama administration, for example, blocked a larger IAEA role in nuclear safety. Reviews by the US Nuclear Regulatory Commission addressed the specific causes of the Fukushima crisis but expressed a continued reliance in the United States on a cooperative review system that includes private operators and their industry organizations (NRC 2011). The Institute of Nuclear Power Operators, established after Three Mile Island, and the World Association of Nuclear Operators, established after Chernobyl, both publish standards and conduct safety reviews, with the World Association of Nuclear Operators claiming to have inspected every commercial power reactor in the world. This hybrid review system is also nonbinding and confidential, presenting the same transparency issues as IAEA reviews, but Lochbaum (2012) argues that it is supposedly effective at detecting safety problems.

In summary, the Secretariat has some authority to promote nuclear safety because it has invested in specific assets useful to supplying safety expertise independent of industry and their organizations, and independent of governments. However, Amano sacrificed authority by not exploiting opportunities during and after the Fukushima accident to fill an obvious vacuum in the international supply of nuclear safety. In light of the ineffectiveness of the domestic and international response, the IAEA could have supplied assistance and public information with greater behavioral impersonality. Instead, the IAEA (2011b, 1) abdicates: responsibility "lies with each Member State and operating organization."

Security

The international community began raising nuclear security as an issue in the mid-1970s, but the Convention on the Physical Protection of Nuclear Materials did not enter into force until 1987 and was still, in 1998, the only legally binding nuclear security treaty. The Agency supported the Convention and later launched negotiations to amend it to cover domestic nuclear security. Although the parties officially began considering this amendment in February 2001, negotiations did not conclude until 2005 and had not entered into force by 2014. The Secretariat also promotes nuclear security within the safeguards mission, offers training, and shares information about interdictions, which is why the 2001 General Conference meeting, just days after the 9/11 attacks, directed the Board to examine how the Secretariat could help prevent terrorism involving nuclear materials or attacking nuclear energy facilities (IAEA 2006, 1).

With this encouragement, a new Office of Nuclear Security within the Department of Nuclear Safety and Security was created in 2002 to be responsible for coordinating IAEA efforts on nuclear security. This includes updating its publications on security standards and offering nuclear security and physical protection training workshops and courses (four hundred were conducted in 2002–11 for more than ten thousand individuals). The Agency renewed its promotion of its security evaluation missions and, from 2002 to 2011, the International State System of Accountancy and Control Advisory Service conducted thirteen missions; the International Nuclear Security Advisory Service, thirty-nine missions; and the International Physical Protection Advisory Service, forty-one missions (IAEA 2012b). The missions can help states to develop Integrated Nuclear Security Support Plans, and thirty-one states had approved plans by 2011. The IAEA began promoting how its contributions align with all three elements of the "3S Initiative"—safeguards, safety, and security—coming out of the 2008 G-8 Summit, issued a nonbinding Code of Conduct for the Safety and Security of Sources, launched the International Nuclear Security Education Network to help members collaborate on training programs, and created an Interdepartmental Special Training Centre in Obninsk, Russia.

While members increased funding in 2002 from $1 million a year to $30 million to support these efforts, these were largely voluntary contributions. The Office of Nuclear Security received only about $15 million a year during 2006–9, more than 90 percent through voluntary contributions. The tens of millions of dollars that briefly flowed into Agency programs therefore paled in comparison with other efforts. The US Cooperative Threat Reduction program alone received closer to $1 billion each year (Bunn and Wier 2006). Although the actual contribution levels have fallen quite short, the G8's Global Partnership Against the Spread of Weapons and Materials of Mass Destruction pledged in 2002 to raise $20 billion over ten years to fund nonproliferation efforts and help states destroy their weapons of mass destruction.

Whenever Agency meetings try to bring attention to new threats to the physical protection of nuclear materials, delegates argue that security is a state responsibility and that the IAEA should stick to safeguards.[35] Fewer states have exploited these missions than could because governments and the nuclear energy industry fear revealing to others or to their own publics any weaknesses in facility or materials protection. The IAEA does benefit from a multiplier effect with Nuclear Suppliers Group (NSG) members now including in their bilateral supply agreements requirements to apply INFC-IRC/225, the IAEA's "guidance and recommendations for the physical protection of nuclear material against theft in use, storage and transport." For example, the 2007 US–India "123 Agreement" (2007) requires that India apply these standards to materials transferred to India under this agreement.

However, members rejected substantial new programs. For example, one proposal was to create an IAEA database of nuclear materials to assist states with identifying the source of the material after a radiological interdiction or terror event.[36] States feared, however, that participation would compromise confidential commercial information or make them responsible if their nuclear materials were used in an attack. States also resisted building the international capacity to respond after a terrorist event involving radiological materials, despite widespread acknowledgment that such capabilities were limited (May 2008).[37] The strongest internationalization of nuclear forensics was an International Technical Working Group on building technical and legal frameworks.[38]

While the IAEA has not added substantial authority for nuclear security, it is still clear that other international efforts also remain limited and ad hoc. All states are to report to the Security Council on their implementation of Resolution #1540 (2004) but progress and reporting has been slow and uneven. As the IAEA has found with safeguards, many developing states lack the capacity to implement #1540 (Findlay 2012c, 134–35). Some feared becoming targets despite the resolution's focus on nonstate actors.[39] Despite holding similar interests as the permanent members of the Security Council, Rosand (2004) argues that others simply reject the Security Council's authority to legislate new rules and commands, whether on nuclear security or any other issue. The International Convention for the Suppression of Acts of Nuclear Terrorism (ICSANT) finally entered into force in 2007, despite being first proposed by Russia in 1996, after Chechen rebels planted a container of radioactive cesium in a Moscow park.[40] ICSANT requires states to adopt domestic legislation on nuclear terrorism and place any seized materials or weapons under IAEA safeguards.

The United States has been at the forefront of nuclear security initiatives, supporting nuclear security multilaterally (G-8 initiatives and the International Technical Working Group), bilaterally (information sharing, training, and conversion programs), and through unilateral action (PSI and counterterrorism programs). While the Bush administration's nuclear security initiatives were confrontational, President Obama's Nuclear Security Summits were not intended to commit states to legally binding international standards but to strengthen domestic advocates (Guarino 2012). As one foreign diplomat said, Obama's invitation to attend the first summit forced many state leaders to tell Obama what their country was doing to improve nuclear security.[41] The most tangible outcomes are the "gift baskets" or promises made by the participants as nuclear security gifts to the host. For example, Japan at the 2014 Nuclear Security Summit promised to send five hundred tons of plutonium and highly enriched uranium to the United States.

Statements at the summits suggest that some do want greater legalization. For example, the announced goal in 2012 was to bring the amendment to the Convention on the Physical Protection of Nuclear Materials into force by 2014. Then, in 2014, thirty-five of the participating states recognized the IAEA's contributions to nuclear security when they signed a pledge to incorporate into domestic law the Nuclear Security Fundamentals outlined in the IAEA Nuclear Security Series publication NSS20, to "meet the intent of the recommendations" in INFCIRC/225 and other Nuclear Security Series recommendations, and to periodically host IAEA International Physical Protection Advisory Service missions. Another sixteen states, including Russia, China, India, and Pakistan, refused.

The summits succeeded in part because they offered new options for cooperation outside the ossified divisions over nonproliferation and rights to peaceful uses but may have now run their course. Even before the 2014 summit (and before it was announced that the next summit in 2016 would occur in Chicago), the Secretariat began suggesting the Agency take over as a host of future ministerial nuclear security meetings.[42] In 2013, for example, the IAEA did hold a ministerial-level conference with 125 participating states. The final declaration acknowledged the contributions of the many IAEA initiatives to nuclear security but also noted the many ways states can use the IAEA (2012 Annual Report): responsibility for nuclear security "within a State rests entirely with that State," nuclear security measures should not "hamper" cooperation on peaceful nuclear uses, and IAEA nuclear security efforts should not duplicate other effects.

In summary, 9/11 inspired significant fear of nuclear or radiological terrorism, but there has been little substantive internationalization. Despite #1540, ICSANT, the G8 Global Partnership, Security Summits, and donor state demand and support for IAEA nuclear security programs, including the 2014 summit commitment to implement INFCIRC/225 and security missions, Bunn and Wier (2006, 57) note that "the world is still a long way from having effective global nuclear security standards." Industry resists new legal standards, and many states see too great a cost to implementing nuclear security measures when others are the likely targets. Just as international nuclear security norms are still weak, neither the Secretariat nor the Board has a strong nuclear security mandate. The Agency is investing in and supplying nuclear security expertise in narrow programs that largely serve less advanced states, and serve as a bureaucratic and international forum for negotiating collective responses such as INFCIRC/225 and the ministerial conference. The Secretariat's contributions primarily extend its promotion of safeguards, helping to secure materials against misuse, and of safety, helping to protect against and respond to accidents. It therefore lacks the authority over nuclear security to issue rules and make commands, but authority on nuclear security also does not reside elsewhere at the international level.

Disarmament

The Clinton administration made grand promises to extend the NPT indefinitely, but global disarmament efforts were undermined by its failure to fulfill them and by the weak international response to India's and Pakistan's tests. The Bush administration could have greatly affirmed nuclear nonproliferation and disarmament norms when it negotiated the Moscow Treaty, but it also withdrew from the 1972 ABM Treaty and sought new warhead designs. Although the US Congress rejected the "new" nuclear weapons, and senior former government officials repeatedly called for disarmament (Shultz et al. 2007), these policies reinforced demand for nuclear weapons elsewhere, fulfilling the basic predictions of the security dilemma.

Excluding the Iraq case, discussed later, demand for international disarmament was sporadic. Neither bilateral nor international verification was desired by the United States or Russia for the Moscow Treaty. In a major change from the 1990s, when the Agency hoped states would share information, ElBaradei became aggressive when US and UK diplomats announced that Libya would dismantle its weapons programs. ElBaradei (2011, 150) reports telling US and UK officials the next day that their governments had violated the NPT by not informing the IAEA when they first became aware of Libya's noncompliance. ElBaradei was asserting the authority of the IAEA that required states to share information about noncompliance. Although the US government had supported a similar position during the 93+2 safeguards strengthening process, the Bush administration demurred. Libya's disarmament was a major victory for the nonproliferation regime even if the "why" is contested. Libya may have wished to avoid an Iraq-like experience, which Bruce Jentleson and Christopher Whytock (2005–6) and others saw as a success for US aggressiveness. Others argue it was a success for sanctions and careful diplomacy (Mark 2005).

This spilled over into the practical debate over "how": who would disarm Libya? Within days of the deal being announced on December 19, 2003, ElBaradei visited Libya and announced that the IAEA had the legal mandate and that it planned to verify Libya's disarmament. He was invited by Libya because it, like South Africa a decade previously, wanted to avoid the appearance of US suzerainty. Bush administration officials dismissed this as a publicity stunt, and the diplomatic battle escalated when both US–UK and IAEA teams arrived to begin their separate investigations (Boureston and Feldman 2004). Journalist Judith Miller (2006) reported a "standoff" when Agency inspectors asked US experts to hand over warhead design blueprints that the United States planned to remove from the country. ElBaradei (2011, 156) relates that he called in the UK ambassador to the IAEA and told him that if equipment was removed before the IAEA completed its work, "I will report to the Board that I am no longer in a position to perform my responsibilities under the NPT because of interference by the British and Americans." They quickly struck a deal: the IAEA would verify dismantlement of Libya's nuclear program and then the United States and the United Kingdom could remove the surrendered equipment and materials.

This is not behavior appropriate to an agent without the power to issue rules and make commands to states. ElBaradei was asserting an IAEA monopoly over the authority to verify disarmament in pursuance of verifying NPT and safeguards compliance in Libya. Even the United States, which then held international organizations to be anathema, had to acknowledge this authority. Libyan interest in international verification helped but received additional support with the discrediting of US nuclear authority when it had not found anything in Iraq to support its claims.

Meanwhile, North Korea became a disarmament challenge with its 2006 attempt to test a nuclear weapon. When the Board condemned North Korea's decision in 2003 to end its cooperation with the IAEA and withdraw from the NPT, the Board declared North Korea "to be in further noncompliance" and referred it to the Security Council. Especially after this first nuclear weapon test, the interested states still have had few attractive options that would not undermine the NPT or otherwise legitimate North Korea's nuclear program (Funabashi 2007, 328). North Korea still professes to desire talks on its nuclear program and on occasion has invited the IAEA to visit for talks. Though North Korea wished it could keep the IAEA out, it recognizes that IAEA involvement in any North Korean verification is "very important" and "indispensable."[43] The IAEA's continuing involvement has been facilitated by the refusal of the NPT depository states, the NPT Review Conferences, and the IAEA to acknowledge its renunciation (IAEA 2006 Annual Report). ElBaradei and inspectors visited in 2007, performing some safeguards activities, but then left in 2009 when North Korea again announced an end to its cooperation. The IAEA has itself demurred from serving as an ad hoc inspector, with ElBaradei (2011, 107) stating, "Either we would perform verification under the auspices of the international community . . . or they could find someone else to do the job."

Disarmament received a big push when President Obama promised to pursue a "world without nuclear weapons" and negotiated New START. The reductions, as Hans Kristensen (2014) complains, are too few and US strategy is too reliant on nuclear weapons to convince others to follow. Even if the United States were willing to give up its deterrent, Russia's annexation of Crimea from Ukraine in April 2014 has tempered any interest in engaging Russia in further reductions, especially since the next step would involve the tactical nuclear forces Russia now sees as integral to deterrence.

The Obama administration also appears unlikely to make progress on disarming North Korea. The Security Council expanded sanctions four times, most recently after its January 2013 nuclear test. Amano, like ElBaradei before him, continues to raise the "application of safeguards in North Korea" in reports to the Board on a regular basis. Although Amano rejected talks with North Korea in 2012, the invitation signaled North Korea's continuing recognition that the IAEA must be a part of any eventual deal. In this regard, the IAEA retains the support of its principals. For example, Assistant Secretary of State Thomas Countryman (2014) even remarked, eleven years after its announced withdrawal from the NPT, that North Korea was still required to comply with its NPT commitments.[44]

In short, there is no request yet for IAEA authority on superpower disarmament but there may be demand for an IAEA role in verifying the FMCT or whatever follows the follow-on to New START, if the US and Russia arsenals become small enough to make others' arsenals numerically significant. There was recurring demand for IAEA authority to supply behavioral impersonality and policy bias in disarming regional powers, especially relative to alternative verification agents. The IAEA's willingness to challenge the United States to supply disarmament in Libya and Iraq openly clarified its authority in this area for the international community.

Nonproliferation

Demand for an international nonproliferation authority increased after 1998. Smaller countries whose interests were ignored or under attack by the

West had begun seeking nuclear weapons before the 9/11 attacks proved that powerful states could be easily hurt. Allegations of proliferation became contentious because the accused states were simultaneously resisting other aspects of the US international order. Russia and China shared with the West some common aversion to proliferation but, as seen in the debate in 2002–3 over Iraq and subsequently over Iran, they also saw their interests served by defending G-77 states against Western coercion. Greater risk of and danger from nuclear proliferation and exogenous and endogenous sources of policy uncertainty persist, increasing demand for an impersonal arbiter as enforcing international nonproliferation rules becomes more divisive. Still, as much as resistance was motivated by the divisiveness of the Bush approach, the substance of the conflict of interests between the United States and others remained real with Obama's election, and demand for nuclear policy impersonality persists.

The strengthening of the safeguards system in the 1990s meant that new standards being issued by the IAEA would demand greater policy bias in two regards. One was the employment of new techniques for verifying safeguards compliance. The approaches incorporated into the AP and revised CSA had been field-tested and were accepted by the members, but there were still questions about the IAEA's ability to deploy these measures in a consistent and equitable manner. The other endogenous source of greater demand for policy bias occurred after Iraq, South Africa, and North Korea, with the shift from a standard of "innocent until proven guilty" to a presumption of noncompliance when states failed to disprove IAEA suspicions.

Exogenous to these sources of policy uncertainty were changes to the nonproliferation monitoring problem. There were fewer operational reactors in the United States and European Union but more elsewhere, and reactor construction starts were planned in countries of recent proliferation concern, including Egypt, Iran, India, and North and South Korea. The spread by Khan's network of centrifuge enrichment and weaponization showed there was also a supplier network beyond the reach of the NSG that made it easier to keep these capabilities hidden from international verification.

These developments show persistent demand for proliferation but also a persistent problem for the international community with impersonal and expert verification and enforcement of nonproliferation rules. The international community did perform some nonproliferation cooperation experiments, but states increasingly were pulled to comply with the authority of the IAEA to achieve nonproliferation outcomes. Since 1998, as the remainder of this section shows, (1) states accommodated the IAEA with greater transfers of resources and autonomy; (2) states accommodated the IAEA conceptualization and implementation of nonproliferation rules; and (3)

IAEA commands elicited compliance by target states and its collective principals.

First, states are observed accommodating the authority of the IAEA through their transfers of autonomy and resources for nonproliferation. Transfers of autonomy occur at a general level when states choose to become members and accept some level of IAEA safeguards on their programs. Thirty states joined the IAEA (but North Korea left) and now 162 states are members (see figure 3.2). As there is no obligation for IAEA membership under the NPT, and therefore states are choosing to join, this number compares favorably to other nonproliferation institutions to show strong demand for the IAEA: Ten more states acceded to the NPT for a total of 190 states (see figure 1.1), making it nearly universal, as the UN reaches 193 members. The NSG also invited ten more states to participate, reaching forty-six. For example, China was admitted to the Nuclear Suppliers Group in 2005, despite numerous incidents of US sanctions against Chinese companies for exporting weapons of mass destruction–related materials (Prosser 2004), while Russia was excluded from the NSG because of its poor record implementing other export controls.[45]

However, while these numbers have brought greater legitimacy, continued zero growth forced the Secretariat to rely increasingly on voluntary contributions. Until, that is, the three significant exceptions to the zero-real-growth limit in 2002, 2009, and 2012 occurred to specifically offset concern about the IAEA's nonproliferation mission. Safeguards spending in the regular budget had declined over 30 percent in real terms between 1995 and 2002, making it all that much more remarkable; by 2012 the safeguards spending in the regular budget had doubled in real terms.[46] These increases occurred despite developed pro-safeguards states experiencing domestic demand for fiscal austerity and developing anti-safeguards states pressing the Secretariat to somehow make strengthened safeguards cost neutral. The Board also decided in 2000 to begin erasing a deal made decades previously with many smaller (and poorer) members over the cost of safeguards. The process of "deshielding" to ensure that all members pay their full share began in 2006 but will not be complete until 2032 (Rosenthal et al. 2013, 219–24). In short, states increased their accommodation of IAEA authority over nonproliferation by accepting safeguards in greater numbers and granting it greater resources to supply its nonproliferation mission.

Second, states accommodated the Agency's nonproliferation authority to define and implement the verification rules when they accepted its recasting of safeguards. States with a CSA already in force accepted the renegotiated CSA and quickly acceded to an AP, accommodating IAEA authority when the Board had unilaterally stretched the original verification mandate. Specifically, the number of states (and Taiwan, China) under any safeguards grew from 138 in 1998 to 179 in 2012 (more states than are members). Of these, 119 had an AP in force, and the number of states with both a CSA and an AP in force grew from 28 states in 2002 to 75 by 2006 (IAEA 2006 Annual Report, 11).[47] In 2005 the IAEA began to convince many Small Quantities Protocol states to accept CSAs and even the AP. The quantities of plutonium and uranium (excluding unenriched source material) also increased from 50,157 tons in 1998 to 132,000 in 2010 (IAEA 1999a, 2011a). The autonomy to use member intelligence after 1992 to target safeguards in North Korea already led to G-77 fears of being targeted by Western intelligence agencies through the IAEA, but equally as intrusive was the reframing of safeguards after approval of the AP to verify the absence of undeclared dual-use nuclear activities or weaponization activities that do not (yet) involve nuclear materials.

The IAEA (2002 Annual Report, 65) asserted that only when both a CSA and an AP are in force "are Agency safeguards able to provide credible assurance of the absence of undeclared nuclear material and activities." Dual accessions were also creating an unsustainable resource burden because, as legalized, the Secretariat had to implement each separately. With the behavioral impersonality of the system threatened, the Secretariat argued that it could balance policy bias, behavioral impersonality, and budgetary limits with "integrated safeguards." The Secretariat proposed that an intensive initial implementation of the AP could enable the Agency to draw "broader conclusions" that certain diversion scenarios were excludable so that some CSA efforts could be reduced (Bragin, Carlson and Leslie 2001, 105). A key component was dropping the requirement for facility-by-facility verification activities dictated by a formula measuring timely warning for a given quantity and quality of materials under safeguards. Instead, traditional safeguards activities could be integrated with information from the Safeguards Information Management group, with several units collecting and analyzing nonsafeguards information about states' activities acquired from proliferation pathway analysis, state reporting of supply requests and denials, satellite imagery purchased from commercial companies, open-source media and literature reviews, and third-party intelligence from states.

G-77 states rallied behind suspected proliferators to oppose shifting inspection efforts from the states with the most nuclear material—Canada, Japan, and Germany—without evidence of noncompliance. Without a Board consensus, the Secretariat could apply integrated safeguards and draw a "broader conclusion" about safeguards compliance only with states open to a more intense initial verification effort (Bragin, Carlson and Leslie 2001). Only three states accepted integrated safeguards in 2003, but by 2011 another forty-eight would also do so (IAEA 2003; IAEA 2011 Annual Report). This conflict could also be resolved if states agreed to make the AP a mandatory component of the CSA system, although the 2010 NPT Review Conference rejected doing so.

To institutionalize behavioral impersonality under "differentiation not discrimination,"[48] Safeguards created a team of Agency experts for each country over the traditional safeguards inspection teams to produce state-level evaluation reports, reviewing all data available to Safeguards. As Pierre Goldschmidt (2008a, 294) describes, the single report would provide all-source analysis using data from inspections, unattended monitoring systems, state declarations, environmental sampling, and the new Safeguards Information Management unit.[49] Approximately one in ten State Evaluation Reports is then subjected to a "red team" analysis. If there is a dispute, the reports go to an Information Review Subcommittee, chaired by the deputy director general, with participation by the operational directors of the various safeguards divisions and section heads from the Office of Legal Affairs and Department of External Relations and Policy Coordination, or *EXPO* (although the latter was folded into the director general's office under Amano).[50] Drafts are then sent to the director general's office where his senior advisors may amend it before reports go to the director general, along with the several previous drafts, for final review. State Evaluation Reports are continually updated and are closely held by the Department of Safeguards, though their conclusions are collected for the public Safeguards Implementation Report delivered annually to the Board.

Safeguards experts outside the Agency, including Jim Casterton (2007, 7), note that the increased subjectivity and decreased transparency of criteria is weakening the ability of external observers to directly observe the policy bias and behavioral impersonality of the inspectors. However, this process improves accountability by documenting inspectors' conclusions and their review by management better than in the past, argues Hooper (2003). The director general's political judgments have the power to affect staff technical judgments, but this power is limited, noted inspectors in interviews, by the willingness of staff to leak their disagreements.[51]

A continuing question is whether, as the Secretariat and some Board members sought, the Secretariat had the authority to use non-inspection data when judging compliance. "Information-Driven Safeguards" were first proposed in the late 1990s to describe how inspectors could employ all-source analysis to report compliance judgments or questions about compliance to the Board (Carlson 2006). This would shift the burden of proof by requiring states to resolve inspectors' uncertainties rather than requiring inspectors to find proof of diversion or misuse.[52] The cultural code of safeguards now encouraged asking questions, Scheinman (2004) argues, but by 2010 the Secretariat was backing away from Information Driven Safeguards to avoid any implication it was relying too heavily on third-party information (GAO 2013).[53]

Third, IAEA authority is observed in how states comply with specific IAEA commands on nonproliferation, such as in the cases of Iraq (2002–3), of South Korea and Egypt (2004), and of Iran (2002–). In Iraq, the need for IAEA authority is evident when the policy bias and impersonality that supported its judgments was compared in retrospect to that of the United States, the major alternative authority on proliferation. While the United States had in several cases ignored proliferation for strategic reasons, including Iraq in the 1980s, its significant investment in intelligence and bias against proliferation led foreign audiences to generally trust the United States when it made accusations of nuclear proliferation. The IAEA and UNMOVIC had also demonstrably put great effort into the verification of Iraq when they returned in 2002, but at least its judgments relied on a safeguards system being transparently applied in so many states around the world with success. It was also important to audiences estimating the impersonality of the Agency that ElBaradei was from a developing state and appeared sensitive to the perceptions of the nonaligned states, especially in the Middle East. ElBaradei (2011, 55) writes that he had to balance charges by both sides of bias by encouraging "a focus on technical objectivity" and the airing of dissenting views. An Egyptian official stationed in Vienna said, "The IAEA has been the domain of developed countries, at least this is how developing states perceived the IAEA up until this point. . . . If there had been a developed state person at the head of the organization these last years I think it would have hurt the process. There would have been more problems."[54] ElBaradei's position on Iraq successfully countered concerns that the IAEA could be turned against states whose interests diverged from those of the United States, but there was still uncertainty about who was correct when ElBaradei and Blix contradicted Colin Powell's (2003) allegations that Iraq had active weapons programs.

It was not public until later that, as UK Foreign Secretary Jack Straw admitted, "the case was thin."[55] When ElBaradei and Blix complained about not receiving Western intelligence before the invasion, ElBaradei (2011, 66) says French president Jacques Chirac reportedly replied, "You know why you don't get the information. . . . It is because they don't have any." Even US intelligence analysts, writes Craig Unger (2007, 278–81), were worried that US claims were "unsubstantiated" or "weak" and that there was no "direct evidence that Iraq had used the period . . . to reconstitute its weapons of mass destruction programs."[56] A study by Charles Lewis and Mark Reading-Smith (2008) found that President Bush and three top administration officials falsely stated Iraq had or was trying to produce weapons of mass destruction, or had ties to al-Qaeda, on 532 separate occasions between September 2001 and September 2003.[57] Also, while UNMOVIC and the IAEA combined had a few dozen people and an annual budget of about $100 million, for example, the Iraq Survey Group had a staff of nearly 1,400 and a monthly budget of $100 million (Rosenberg 2004). Although several years would first pass, Iraq demonstrated IAEA authority to provide verification that was relatively more objective, effective, and cost efficient. As along as the war that began over US allegations of Iraqi weapons programs continued, it served as a continuous reminder of the cost to the superpower and to international community of ignoring IAEA authority.

The Board also accepted the Secretariat's authority when Egypt and South Korea agreed to ratify an AP, and initial implementation in 2004 revealed they had both engaged in unreported enrichment activities.[58] These were safeguards violations that did not substantially differ from the accusations being leveled against Iran and Libya. They were serious enough that South Korea threatened to oppose ElBaradei's reappointment to another term if he made the report public (Kang et al. 2005; Pinkston 2004). Findlay (2012b) reports that, with Egypt, ElBaradei directed the Secretariat to handle the case, essentially recusing himself to avoid accusations of bias for his home country. Despite their desire for secrecy, both states complied with IAEA commands and cooperated with the Agency's investigations. Although some governors wished to also charge Egypt and South Korea with noncompliance to treat them equally with Iran, the Board also complied when ElBaradei (2004b) argued that the violations could be dismissed from the agenda as substantively insignificant.

Finally, Iran and the international community acknowledged IAEA authority when they complied on three primary dimensions with the Secretariat's judgments on Iran. The first dimension of compliance concerned the initial right to investigate Iran in 2002 when the quantities involved were below the "significant quantities" threshold used traditionally to evaluate safeguards compliance. ElBaradei (2003a, 7) claimed, however, that the Agency could investigate if activities were "not insignificant in terms of a State's ability to conduct nuclear research and development activities." This has been described by Australian safeguards expert Carlson (2006) as a "revolutionary" change in part because it is also one in which "expert judgment is coming to the fore in drawing safeguards conclusions." IAEA "judgment," aided by national intelligence, introduced inherently less objective factors and could allow the intrusion of political bias. The Secretariat was asserting a mandate, one unilaterally offered by the Board under INFCIRC/153 (Rev.), that none of its collective principals have rallied to oppose.

Some members (and individual inspectors) would contest this shift in authority. They defend Iran's legal right to pursue dual-use activities and, as ElBaradei (2011, 119) found, some even sympathize with its keeping peaceful activities secret to prevent their destruction (Findlay 2012b). Developing states, writes Chellaney (1999, 380–81), were loath to join the condemnation of Iran because they as a group felt forced to disprove unfounded Western suspicions. As the presumption of innocence was disappearing, Chellaney continues, they feared that "IAEA inspectors would have the right to roam around in [non-nuclear weapon states] like supercops, and demand immediate access to places, persons, and data." They therefore contest inspectors' increased reliance under the state-level approach on qualitative evaluations of state responses to safeguards efforts—the transparency and cooperation of the state—and of how disparate activities integrate into the state's nuclear program (Casterton 2007, 31).

Iran was applauded by ElBaradei (2004a) for accommodating IAEA safeguards authority with acceptance of a strengthened CSA and voluntary implementation of an AP. Even when it later renounced this level of cooperation, after the Board referred it to the Security Council, Iran did not challenge the Agency's safeguards authority. Instead, it challenged only minor legal points over what verification was within its rights. For example, Iran attempted to unilaterally revoke its acceptance of revisions to its CSA, specifically Subsidiary Arrangements General Part, Code 3.1, which obligates early reporting of preliminary facility design information. Most legal scholars, however, reject Iran's authority to unilaterally revise this international treaty.[59] In short, the Iran case first shows compliance by collective and individual principals—including Iran—with safeguards expanded by unilateral mandate of the Board, and then further actions by the Secretariat are more intrusive and subjective.

With Iran having, since 2006, increasingly cooperated with IAEA verification of its declared activities but still blocking efforts to resolve the "possible military dimensions" (de Jong 2011), the second dimension concerns the IAEA's authority to investigate these allegations. The question is whether the IAEA has the authority to investigate them as a violation of safeguards activities when there is no clear evidence of the misuse or diversion from peaceful uses of nuclear materials. On the one hand, the IAEA may lack the requisite staff expertise for on-site verification of weaponization. The IAEA lost through attrition some of the expertise it had during the South Africa and Iraq missions and by 2014, claims nuclear physicist and policy analyst Yousaf Butt, had only two inspectors with a significant nuclear weapons background (Hibbs 2014). Iran has also used its right to delist inspectors from conducting safeguards in Iran to effectively exclude many of those qualified to conduct verification there.[60]

On the other hand, the debate over IAEA authority to investigate weaponization is a legal dispute. In a 2005 interview ElBaradei said inspectors "don't have an all-encompassing mandate to look for every computer study on weaponization" (Kerr and Pomper 2005). ElBaradei focused instead on the IAEA mandate to verify the completeness and correctness of state declarations as sufficient authority. Daniel Joyner is among those who argue that the IAEA exceeded its authority, pointing to Iran's retraction of its strengthened CSA, to Iran's renunciation of its voluntary implementation of an AP, and to objections during the 1990s negotiations by some governors of some provisions of INFCIRC/153 (Rev.). One feature of the Board, despite its preferences for consensus, is its power to impose such changes despite opposition by individual principals. While it is clear the Agency should investigate if activities involve nuclear materials, and can under the CSA even without an AP, the debate over its independent authority to investigate weaponization in Iran shows an incredible leap in IAEA authority. Only a few years previously the Agency would have been precluded from considering this a safeguards issue without first having clear evidence that significant quantities of nuclear materials had been diverted.

The third dimension of compliance with the IAEA authority is the Secretariat's power to judge, or choose to not judge, Iran's noncompliance with nonproliferation rules. IAEA inspectors, reports Gregory Schulte (2010, 3), found Iran's cooperation from the start in 2002, "minimal at best—forced and partial, rather than fully forthcoming." Still upset over being challenged on Iraq, the Bush administration challenged ElBaradei over his decision in 2003 to not use the term "noncompliance." They complained that ElBaradei was not acting as the executor of safeguards and was instead playing "shuttle diplomacy" (Traub 2004). ElBaradei (2011, 122) countered before the Board that his diplomatic approach kept the IAEA involved and, as a result, made "more progress in ten months than the world's best intelligence agencies had come up with in the previous ten years . . . because of our objectivity." After this clear reference to the greater relative credibility of the IAEA after Iraq, ElBaradei (2011, 123) said, "The boardroom was hushed. People were stunned at this public exchange between the Americans and the IAEA Director General in a diplomatic setting. . . . A number of delegations told me after the meeting that this had been a 'historic day' to see an international civil servant stand up to bullying by the United States." ElBaradei may have overstated the reaction, and perhaps his approach pushed against the boundaries of behavioral impersonality. However, the purpose of the exercise of Agency authority was not to punish noncompliance but to convince the "State or States to take requested corrective steps within a reasonable time."[61] ElBaradei (2011, 85) also feared the consequences for the Secretariat if his reports led to war but were later found to have been based on faulty third-party intelligence.[62] Portraying himself, Blix, and UN Secretary-General Annan as jointly responsible for allowing the 2003 invasion of Iraq by not opposing the US claims strongly enough, ElBaradei (2011, 316) feared that, as the "custodian of the Nuclear Non-Proliferation Regime," his actions could directly lead to another Middle East war.

The US pressure on ElBaradei would continue after its attempt to remove him, but ElBaradei was unwilling to report that his efforts were unsuccessful (Albright and Shire 2009; Spector 2007). The US Permanent Representative to the IAEA in May 2007 delivered a message from Secretary of State Condoleezza Rice, "saying that, to her deep disappointment, my media statements were undercutting the unity of the international community and their diplomatic efforts" (ElBaradei 2011, 252). The IAEA-brokered "work plan" was also criticized as compromising IAEA safeguards implementation in the hopes of achieving progress when the US and others were trying to push the Security Council for sanctions. The *Washington Post* would well summarize the US problems with ElBaradei when it editorialized, three months before the public summary of the 2007 National Intelligence Estimate eased pressure, "Rather than carry out the policy of the Security Council or the IAEA board, for which he nominally works, Mr. ElBaradei behaves as if he were independent of them, free to ignore their decisions and to use his agency to thwart their leading members—above all the United States."[63]

By resisting the demands of the solitary superpower, ElBaradei clearly elicited compliance with the IAEA power to judge for itself whether states were in compliance with their safeguards. With the Board and the Security Council politicized by growing conflicts of interests, the international community was forced to rely on the Secretariat to set the agenda on Iran (de Jong 2011, 4). A former IAEA official who has otherwise been critical of ElBaradei's record at the Agency argues that "it wasn't because of ElBaradei or the Secretariat" that the world missed a chance to shut down a possible Iranian weapons program (Hibbs and Persbo 2009, 16). Instead, the IAEA was caught, argues Pierre Goldschmidt (2008b, 301), because turning Iran over to the Security Council could cause Iran to stop all its cooperation with the IAEA and would only encounter deadlock there. In many ways, ElBaradei was simply reusing Blix's playbook from the first North Korea crisis when it was left to the head of this "technical agency" to balance in Iran, in ways its collective principals could not, the short-term desire for verification with the long-term health of the nonproliferation regime. Therefore, despite the expectation since the 1990s that the Board should judge compliance with the nonproliferation regime, ElBaradei's position reflected another shift in this authority: It was not the Board but the director general that ultimately decided whether to refer Iran to the Security Council.

To conclude, the Agency's nonproliferation authority results from its success in meeting the persistent demand by its principals to supply policy bias and impersonality on nonproliferation. The Secretariat not only defines and implements an evolving nuclear safeguards regime but also achieves accommodation and compliance with IAEA nonproliferation authority:

states transfer greater autonomy and resources for nonproliferation, accommodate its implementation of expanded verification rules, and comply with its specific commands when it judged compliance with the nonproliferation regime by key states. The IAEA capacity to elicit compliance resulted from its continued investment in the implementation of safeguards—a verification function—but also its investment in adapting the legal application of safeguards. The Agency also continued to invest in supportive constituencies, welcoming contributions from Member State Support Programs but also pursuing informal engagement as it brokered agreements on adapting safeguards and on noncompliance by Iran, South Korea, Egypt, and others. The nonproliferation authority of the IAEA is not limited to its Secretariat but intimately involves the Board, which acted unilaterally over the past two decades to legislate a significantly expanded safeguards system and then compelled states to accept it. The Board is receptive to regular reporting by the director general on North Korea, Iraq, and Iran, as Schulte (2010) describes, exploiting the Secretariat's reports as opportunities to keep cases on the international agenda and to maintain pressure to comply with Security Council resolutions.

CONCLUSIONS

Under Dir. Gen. Mohamed ElBaradei and then Yukiya Amano, the Agency leveraged the autonomy acquired during Hans Blix's tenure to assert greater power to issue rules and commands across a range of nuclear issue areas after 1998. Leadership by the United States remained necessary for the IAEA's success, and the United States is often actively leading others, if not coercing them, to accept IAEA authority by transferring more resources and autonomy, accommodating its conceptualization and implementation of regulations, and complying with its judgments on compliance with international norms and rules. At the same time, the United States is occasionally also the greatest continuing source of competition for international authority on nuclear issues because it has the capacity and often the interest to supply nuclear policy public goods. It supports IAEA rules and commands most consistently on nonproliferation, sometimes on disarmament, but only as voluntary obligations for safety and security. US challenges to IAEA authority are episodic and inconsistent. And the IAEA's other competition at the international level is initiatives intended to be limited in scope or accountability, including the Nuclear Security Summits, the Nuclear Suppliers Group, Resolution #1540, and the many conventions on nuclear security and nuclear safety.

The widening gap between US interests and those of others made exercising US hegemony through the IAEA and other international institutions less effective, which prompted the Bush administration to reject the utility but also the legitimacy of internationalization relative to unilateral action. The allure of internationalization weakened progressively because of dissatisfaction by non-Western states, some of whom saw the utility of nuclear weapons as alternative solutions to their insecurity before President Obama inspired a return to international approaches to nuclear nonproliferation and disarmament. This initially delegitimized Bush policies that had reinforced the appropriateness of nuclear deterrence, but this social pressure has not proved sufficient to overcome widening political gulfs in the international community. Therefore, in addition to encouraging national approaches to nuclear safety and nuclear security, the United States has done little to deter the national solutions to insecurity and has itself sought to renew investments in its nuclear weapons infrastructure.

The accumulated power of the IAEA to issue rules and commands over nuclear issues observed in 2014 is the result of IAEA success in exploiting new opportunities to meet persistent demand by the international community for nuclear policy expertise and impersonality. The IAEA still has the authority to frame, implement, and judge compliance with nuclear safeguards, but its members also acknowledge its authority to verify the absence of undeclared nuclear activities. It also acquired the authority to verify disarmament in non–nuclear weapon states asserting their compliance with the NPT, several times in direct conflict with powerful individual principals. The Agency is now also claiming the authority to verify the absence of activities that do not involve nuclear materials but suggest the intent to pursue nuclear weapons. This authority far exceeds the limited role it played in the 1980s in verifying the non-diversion of nuclear materials and providing assistance with peaceful uses. The IAEA is also the only significant international supplier of policy bias and impersonality over nuclear peaceful uses, nuclear safety, and nuclear security, even if its authority in these areas is much more limited.

The authority of the IAEA encompasses the partiality and impersonality of the Secretariat but also that of the Board. Despite some internal opposition, and with little if any clear direction from its collective principals, the Board has used the Vienna Spirit to legislate a significantly expanded verification system, allow the Secretariat to supply disarmament, and exploit Secretariat reports to keep cases on the international agenda. The changes in IAEA nuclear authority that we have observed since 1998 are not epiphenomenal to US hegemony. They are also neither the reflection of a consensus on international action created by effective multilateral coordination at the IAEA nor coerced by powerful international norms of nuclear behavior. The authority of the IAEA in 2014 is the accumulated result of its repeated success in meeting the persistent demand for nuclear policy bias and impersonality, success that is evident in its power to elicit accommodation with its rules and commands by the international community.

NOTES

1. Also known as the Moscow Treaty, the full name is Treaty between the United States of America and the Russian Federation on Strategic Offensive Reductions (The Moscow Treaty), signed May 24, 2002, by George W. Bush and Vladimir V. Putin (http://www.state.gov/t/isn/10527.htm).

2. For example, see Russert (2003).

3. Interview with government official of Israel, July 15, 2005.

4. "The Nobel Peace Prize 2005," http://www.nobelprize.org/nobel_prizes/peace/laureates/2005/.

5. Glyn T. Davies, "IAEA: Replacement Needed for Deputy Director General Taniguchi," 09UNVIEVIENNA536. USMISSION UNVIE VIENNA; and Mark Tokola, "HMG Has Not Decided Whom to Support for IAEA Director General," US Embassy London, 09LONDON1104, 5/11/2009 13:24.

6. Hillary R. Clinton, "Demarche: IAEA Director General Election," 09 State 046302, May1.

7. On the timeline, see also NRC (2011), Weightman (2011b), and "Fukushima Accident 2011," World Nuclear Association, http://www.world-nuclear.org/info/Safety-and-Security/Safety-of-Plants/Fukushima-Accident/.

8. Neither Israel nor Syria would even admit a strike occurred. The IAEA was admitted to the site but only after Syria bulldozed the area. For example, see Erlanger (2007).

9. "The 1994 Nuclear Posture Review." *Nuclear Strategy Project*. Nautilus Institute. http://oldsite.nautilus.org/archives/nukestrat/USA/Npr/npr94.html.

10. Craig Roberts Stapleton, "P3 Consultations on Nonproliferation and Disarmament in Paris," US Embassy Paris, 08PARIS2134.

11. For example, see Hibbs and Persbo (2014).

12. "Outline History of Nuclear Energy," World Nuclear Association, http://www.world-nuclear.org/info/Current-and-Future-Generation/Outline-History-of-Nuclear-Energy/.

13. See, for example, "Generation IV Nuclear Reactors," World Nuclear Association, http://www.world-nuclear.org/info/inf77.html; and Generation IV International Forum, http://www.gen-4.org/.

14. Interview with retired IAEA official, December 9, 2011.

15. Interview with IAEA official June 15, 2012.

16. BLN, "International Atomic Energy Agency: Recruitment Brochure." *International Safeguards Project Office*, (2008), http://www.bnl.gov/ispo/recruitment/recruitment_brochure.asp.

17. On the UN Millennium Development Goals, see the United Nations website, http://www.un.org/millenniumgoals/bkgd.shtml.

18. Geoffrey R. Pyatt, "IAEA/DG: Amano Sketches Ambitious Transition Agenda," UNVIE VIENNA 000331, July 10, 2009, 15:41.

19. Interview with IAEA official, July 20, 2005; and interview with IAEA employee, July 20, 2005.

20. Interview with retired IAEA official, September 27, 2011.

21. John Thomas Schieffer, "NPT Envoy Ambassador Sanders Hears Australian Ideas to Prevent a Third Term for IAEA DG ElBaradei," 05CANBERRA322. Embassy Canberra.

22. Glyn T. Davies, "IAEA: Amano Ready for Prime Time," UNVIE VIENNA 000478, 16 October 2009, 16:12; and Geoffrey R. Pyatt, "IAEA Leadership Team Transition and US Influence in the Agency," UNVIE 000322, July 7.

23. Geoffrey R. Pyatt, "IAEA/DG: Amano Sketches Ambitious Transition Agenda," UNVIE VIENNA 000331, July 10, 2009, 15:41.

24. Interview with retired IAEA official, July 2011.

25. Interview with retired IAEA official, September 27, 2011.

26. Interview with IAEA official, July 2011.

27. "Power Reactor Information System (PRIS)," http://pris.iaea.org/public/; and "Outline History of Nuclear Energy," World Nuclear Association, http://www.world-nuclear.org/info/Current-and-Future-Generation/Outline-History-of-Nuclear-Energy/.

28. "Outline History of Nuclear Energy," World Nuclear Association, http://www.world-nuclear.org/info/Current-and-Future-Generation/Outline-History-of-Nuclear-Energy/.

29. Interview with IAEA official, June 15, 2012.

30. See the IAEA Nuclear Safety & Security website, http://www-ns.iaea.org/.

31. The Incident and Emergency Center also has two web-based reporting systems and access to the Agency's (non-safety-related) Illicit Trafficking Data Base and Incident Reporting System.

32. Interview with retired IAEA official, January 18, 2012.

33. Interview with retired IAEA official, September 27, 2011.

34. Interview with resident of Japan, April 2012.

35. Lawrence Scheinman, interview, Washington, DC, 2005.

36. Each batch of fissile material exhibits unique impurities, isotopic concentrations, and decay signatures that make them distinguishable from not only other sources but even the same source across time.

37. Experts interviewed would state several years after the 9/11 attacks that even the US government only had a few people working full time on the problem.

38. The Nuclear Forensics ITWG website, which appeared to be last updated in mid-2013, is http://www.nf-itwg.org/home.

39. Lawrence Scheinman, interview, Washington, DC, 2005.

40. See Lexi Krock and Rebecca Deusser, "Dirty Bomb: Chronology of Events," PBS.org, http://www.pbs.org/wgbh/nova/dirtybomb/chrono.html.

41. Interview with IAEA official, June 15, 2012.

42. Ibid.

43. John Thomas Schieffer, Tenth US–Japan Commission Meeting (07TOKYO5492). Embassy Tokyo.

44. There were multiple reasons for this requirement in the US view, as Countryman explained: "The DPRK was not in compliance with its IAEA safeguards obligations when it announced its withdrawal from the NPT in 2013. The DPRK committed in 2005 to return to the NPT and IAEA safeguards. . . . It is also required by the UN Security Council to act strictly in accordance with the obligations that apply to parties under the NPT."

45. Louis B. Susman, "U/S Tauscher's Bilateral Meetings Russian, Chinese, and French Officials," 09LONDON2214, September22. US Embassy London.

46. In nominal dollars, safeguards spending increased from $70 million in 2001 to $156 million in 2012.

47. China ratified the AP in 2005 under a voluntary offer, like the United States, the United Kingdom, and France.

48. See, for example: INMM and ESARDA (2005) *Changing the Safeguards Culture: Broader Perspectives and Challenges*. Institute of Nuclear Materials Management-European Safeguards R&D Association Workshop, Santa Fe, New Mexico, 11.

49. Confidential presentation by US Department of Defense official, July 16, 2008; and interview with retired IAEA official, September 27, 2011b.

50. The IAEA has one director general but many directors, which direct groups below the level of deputy director general, such as Safeguards Operations A and Safeguards Operations B.

51. Interview with retired IAEA official, January 18, 2012; interview with retired IAEA official, July 2011; and confidential presentation by Safeguards inspector, July 16, 2008.

52. Interview with retired IAEA official, September 27, 2011.

53. Lawrence Scheinman, interview, Washington, DC, 2004.

54. Interview with government official of Arab Republic of Egypt, July 14, 2005a.

55. UK government officials, as leaked in the 2005 "Downing Street memo," reported the US felt "military action was now seen as inevitable . . . but the intelligence and facts were being fixed around the policy." See: Rycroft (2002).

56. While the case was stronger for biological and chemical weapons, there was "no clear intelligence" on nuclear weapons and "no intelligence on any BW agent production facilities." See Butler et al. (2004, 59, 63, 107).

57. See also Center for American Progress, "Neglecting Intelligence, Ignoring Warnings" (Washington, DC: Center for American Progress, 2004).

58. The two cases are unrelated.

59. See the discussion in Joyner, Ford, and Persbo (2012).

60. Interview with retired IAEA official, July 2011.

61. Art. XII Para. A.7 and C, IAEA (1957). On the distinction between punishment and rehabilitation goals, see, for example, Wright (1973).

62. Interview with IAEA Safeguards operation director, July 2008.

63. Editorial, "Rogue Regulator: Mohamed ElBaradei Pursues a Separate Peace with Iran," *Washington Post*, September 5, 2007.

7

Conclusion

THIS BOOK began with an empirical puzzle about the power of the IAEA to affect state behavior in some areas of nuclear policy: States accommodate and comply with IAEA rules and commands on non-proliferation but less on disarmament, and even less on nuclear safety, security, and peaceful uses. In the absence of the capacity to coerce, this power to change behavior is political authority. To explain international political authority, this book unpacked the puzzle of international nuclear policy cooperation, derived a theory to explain nuclear authority, and compared the authority of the IAEA across four historical periods and across four nuclear issue areas. This concluding chapter offers first a retrospective look at the arguments and findings of the book. If "what's past is prologue," then the retrospective analysis can guide expectations on nuclear policy for coming years and prescriptions for policy. Finally, if the IAEA possesses international authority, then authority is probably also held in other issue areas by other international organizations or other actors. This book concludes by considering the implications of the theory of political authority for the study of international organizations and for global politics more generally.

IAEA AUTHORITY

This book argues that we are observing the rise of international political authority at international organizations that is the product of persistent demand and successful agent supply rather than an artifact of hegemonic coercion, multilateral coordination, or coercive norms of behavior. When changing technologies, new conceptions of a policy problem, or increased problem complexity prevent collective action, then states should seek the assistance of an agent capable of providing the policy partiality necessary to enable cooperation. Policy partiality requires an investment in policy-relevant expertise, but the agent is also motivated to be biased toward a particular outcome. When conflicts of interest on other issue dimensions create concerns about politically motivated biases among the states seeking to cooperate, states should seek the assistance of an agent capable of acting with impersonality. Only when this demand is persistent do states move beyond the demand for temporary or limited solutions to demand political authority.

Demand for Nuclear Policy Partiality

Beliefs about the causal structure of the various areas of nuclear policy have evolved substantially since the nuclear age began, presenting states with persistent policy uncertainty and creating demand for an international authority with policy partiality. The inability to limit access to the basic knowledge of how nuclear weapons worked created demand to prevent proliferation by coordinating to prevent peaceful nuclear supply from being misused. Most controls on dual-use materials, experience, and equipment that could contribute to a nuclear weapon program for most of the Cold War assumed that a plutonium-based weapon was the easiest route. Early nonproliferation efforts therefore safeguarded peaceful programs against diversion but focused on controlling access to reprocessing technologies. The diffusion of gaseous centrifuge enrichment in the 1980s, however, made covert acquisition of enriched uranium cheaper, easier, and easier to hide.

Safeguards against proliferation were also premised throughout most of the atomic age on the belief that an effective nuclear arsenal required hundreds of warheads whose design was proven by rigorous testing. Even as the Comprehensive Test Ban Treaty (CTBT) was concluded, the received wisdom began to question whether testing was necessary for a credible nuclear deterrent, though this belief was also challenged by North Korea's failed test in 2006. Smaller states with less expansive security problems also challenged the premises of the superpower strategy of overwhelming nuclear arsenals, believing they could rely on a "minimum" deterrent force with dozens rather than hundreds of warheads. Today, however, a greater sensitivity to the costs of war means that North Korea has a credible deterrent with a handful of possible devices that nowhere near meet the advanced state definition of a deployable warhead. In short, nonproliferation has encountered persistent policy uncertainty as nuclear technology diffused and nuclear strategy developed.

Demand to internationalize peaceful nuclear uses and nuclear safety and security has historically been weaker. Nuclear power was commercially competitive with other energy sources for only a few short periods of time while other peaceful uses occupy niche contributions to quality of life issues for which wealthy states, like nuclear safety and security, could provide indigenously or through direct state-to-state supply. Although developed states benefited from internationalizing the process of delivering nuclear-related development assistance and in building some consensus on how to invest in nuclear technology, demand for international supply has largely come from poor and middle-income states seeking development assistance. It was assumed that states and operators would take measures to protect their investments that were sufficient to ameliorate the localized effects of safety or security failures. The diffusion of nuclear technology contributed to increased international demand only as the effects of failures became more clearly transnational: after Chernobyl in 1986 for nuclear safety, and after the 9/11 terrorist attacks for nuclear security.

Uncertainty over the effects of international nuclear policy choices was magnified as the population of relevant actors grew and diversified with independence and economic development. For example, the UN in 1945 included only 51 states and was dominated by economically developed and industrial states in Europe. By 2010, a majority of the 193 members of the UN were developing states that became independent after World War II and after colonial occupation by a European power, and that were at greater risk of experiencing political violence. Irrespective of how their specific interests vary (and conflict), more states are relevant to international nuclear policy issues but also have different developmental needs and are more varied in their economic, cultural, and political institutions. This contributes to policy uncertainty when, for example, seven developed states may have been sufficient in 1975 to initiate the London Club, but today there are forty-eight "participating governments" attempting to coordinate within the Nuclear Suppliers Group and still analysts look at excluded (and some included) states and even nonstate networks that undercut their export controls.

In short, the history of the atomic age has been relatively short but suffers from a continuously changing population of relevant actors, diffusing and evolving peaceful nuclear technologies, and inconsistent assumptions about the value of nuclear weapons and other nuclear uses. States attempting to produce national security by limiting access by others to nuclear weapons and by making their own self-restraint credible have faced continuing, if not increasing, uncertainty about the effectiveness of their policies. In this highly uncertain policy environment, states experienced persistent demand for a political authority with the policy partiality to choose, implement, and enforce some nuclear policy strategies. Demand was weak, however, for international policy solutions to national problems of nuclear safety, security, and the supply of peaceful uses.

Demand for Policy Impersonality

The high stakes of political competition outside nuclear policy issues threatened persistent distributional effects from collective action on nuclear policy, creating demand for a political authority with policy impersonality. Most of the atomic age was concurrent with an intense ideological divide in which a zero-sum game infected attempts to solve communal problems. The Cold War became less a barrier to collective action on nuclear issues when both the United States and Soviet Union acknowledged their need for an impartial agent that could verify compliance by the other's allies. It quickly became apparent that superpower interests differed from those of their developed allies who supported nonproliferation but feared the costs and intrusiveness of a verifiable regime. A third cleavage emerged by the 1970s as developing states rejected both the US and Soviet international order. Although the Global South rarely achieved sufficient unity to take a combined stand, this alignment resurfaced after the end of the Cold War as the G-77 saw itself increasingly under economic, political, and cultural attack by a global system constructed by the United States and its allies.

Nonproliferation, disarmament, and assistance with peaceful uses enjoyed broad international appeal and acquired increasing social power, but the distributional effects of these policies fell persistently and with great cost upon developed non–nuclear weapon states in the 1960s and then upon the G-77 after the 1970s. Demand for behavioral impersonality in the delivery of nuclear cooperation was briefly supplied by effective multilateral coordination in the early post–Cold War period but increased again in the later post–Cold War years with greater willingness of major and minor powers to challenge US primacy. In short, the incredible and increasing variation of the international distribution of interests on non-nuclear issue dimensions has created persistent demand for an international authority capable of supplying collective nuclear policy with impersonality.

The Supply of Nuclear Authority

States may experience persistent demand for policy bias and impersonality, but international authority requires an agent to supply collective action successfully and repeatedly over time. Political authority is the power, without the threat or use of violence, to issue rules and commands that elicit compliance by others. States accept authority when they accommodate how an agent conceptualizes, regulates, or structures an issue with resources and changes in behavior. They accept authority also when they comply with its orders or rules in specific events or cases. Political authority is always contested, and actors continuously compete over the best or appropriate location of issue authority, if any, but the claim to authority is greater the more an agent monopolizes the supply of policy in an issue area to the exclusion of other actors. Any agent that fails to assert authority can become highly circumscribed (limited), dismissed (temporary), or replaced (experimentation).

During the past more than fifty years, the Agency has grown in the number of its staff, the regular budget, the voluntary and extrabudgetary resources it receives, the breadth of its responsibilities, and its political salience. These changes are summarized in previous illustrative graphs and need not be repeated here except to note the simple comparison:

* In 1958, after its first full year in operation, the IAEA's budget was $4.1 million ($26 million in 2003 inflation-adjusted US dollars), received about $1.85 million in voluntary and extrabudgetary contributions, and had 393 staff (IAEA Annual Report 1959). However, it also had no safeguards responsibilities, provided no technical assistance to its members, and was at best a gamble by its members that cooperation to promote the peaceful use of incredibly scarce nuclear materials could keep them from being used for nuclear weapons.
* In 2012, the IAEA had 2,474 staff and its 158 members provided a regular budget of $420.5 million (IAEA 2012 Annual Report). They also contributed more than $185 million in additional voluntary and extrabudgetary cash contributions, not to mention hundreds of millions spent in more than twenty official member programs to support IAEA operations with research, equipment, training, and seconded staff. In exchange, the Secretariat implemented safeguards against proliferation in 179 states and each year provided members with nearly 900 Technical Cooperation programs, issued hundreds of publications on all aspects of nuclear technology and policy, and had responsibilities to implement aspects of dozens of active international or multilateral nonproliferation, safety, and security conventions.

In the regular supply of services to the international community, but also in a number of crises, the IAEA has exhibited surprising power to issue rules and commands on aspects of international nuclear policy. There are many current examples of its authority being contested—states that challenge its expertise, its legal authority in specific cases, or its legitimacy to engage in certain behaviors—but the trend toward the IAEA's increasing international nuclear authority is clear across time when one compares across the four distinct areas of nuclear policy.

Peaceful Uses

The Statute of the IAEA identifies the promotion of peaceful uses of the atom as the Agency's primary purpose, but the Board was quickly forced to solicit voluntary contributions from its members to finance limited nuclear assistance projects. The Technical Cooperation program thereby grew from a few fellowships to offering over $115 million a year in training, equipment purchases, capital investments, and implementation of programs to support members' agricultural, medical, and industrial development. To developing states—the majority of its members—this is the most legitimate purpose of the IAEA. They directly benefit from its development assistance but also defend this assistance against restrictions or reductions to protect what they argue is their right to peaceful uses under the Nuclear Non-Proliferation Treaty (NPT). Advanced states benefit from its many technical conferences and middle-income states from its training and consulting, both of which help inform their domestic nuclear policies, but the major donors of Technical Cooperation predominantly view it as an inefficient but symbolic incentive for some to accept the Agency's regulative functions. The IAEA also has a monopoly on international nuclear cooperation as a supplier of niche nuclear applications. Even if the Secretariat moves to offer fuel-cycle services, such as fuel guarantees, its role is likely more regulative than as an authority on nuclear supply.

Nuclear Safety

The Statute of the IAEA also identifies the adoption of nuclear safety standards as a key function of the Agency. The Board, though, removed monitoring safety conditions from inspections in the early 1960s to gain greater willingness to accept safeguards. Nuclear safety became a national concern, and state regulators relied heavily on commercial nuclear suppliers for facility-specific advice. The Secretariat did not abandon its safety mission, turning to developing nonbinding standards and facilitating information sharing. The Secretariat assisted with information sharing during the 1986 Chernobyl accident and afterward acquired roles from helping develop the first international nuclear safety conventions. Its investment in extensive safety-related training programs, expert missions, and publications gave it some authority over drafting and monitoring performance with safety standards. The Agency may be the locus of international nuclear safety standards, especially for developing and middle-income states, which lack an independent capacity to develop effective safety practices, cultures, or regulations. IAEA authority over nuclear safety remains limited by a norm of national responsibility and exists in competition with industry-sponsored organizations such as the World Association of Nuclear Operators and the

Institute of Nuclear Power Operations. These limits on Agency power to issue rules and commands on nuclear safety were highlighted when its own director general refused to take an active role in the 2011 Fukushima accident. The international safety authority vacuum, however, is exactly why Agency advocates viewed Fukushima as a major missed opportunity.

Nuclear Security

International pressure to attend to the security of nuclear facilities and materials is not evident prior to 1975. The Convention on the Physical Protection of Nuclear Materials, intended to commit states to securing international shipments of nuclear fuel and waste against accident or theft, was concluded in 1979 but did not enter into force until 1987. The Agency quickly sought an amendment to add domestic security of materials transport and storage, which did not conclude until 2005 and has still not entered into force. Prior to 2001, the Secretariat supplied nuclear security largely by aiding states in securing materials against state diversion or misuse: safeguards.

After 2001 the Secretariat invested more in supplying training, consulting missions, international meetings, and information sharing relevant to nuclear security. These efforts have occurred largely by moving activities from Safeguards to Nuclear Safety and Security, although these departments have been less enthusiastic about prioritizing nuclear security. The Agency's efforts suggest a proliferation of disconnected initiatives funded largely through ephemeral voluntary contributions. The members have actively resisted major IAEA initiatives on monitoring or enforcing nuclear security standards or responding to nuclear security failures.

The Agency faces little competition for nuclear security authority, however. The Physical Protection Convention remains the only legally binding international nuclear security convention, outside UN Security Council resolutions whose legislative authority is debated, and its amendment has yet to enter into force. The Nuclear Security Summits, G-8 efforts, and bilateral assistance programs also compete. Reliance by developed states on these initiatives supporting national capacity building suggests they believe that, like nuclear safety, states require more encouragement and mentoring than regulation.

Nonproliferation

President Eisenhower's vision was an international body that could dissuade proliferation, but the early safeguards system was rudimentary and "amateurish," held back by Soviet opposition and US unwillingness to transfer its bilateral safeguards to the Agency. Director General Eklund, though, directed the Secretariat's investments in policy bias and impersonality in safety and peaceful uses with sufficient success that the IAEA was a credible if risky bet when the NPT negotiators had to select an agent to implement the compulsory safeguards they envisioned. The members designed, and the Board approved, the Comprehensive Safeguards Agreement (CSA) safeguards system described in INFCIRC/153. The CSA focused on the physical verification by Secretariat inspectors of the non-diversion of nuclear materials between strategic points in declared facilities. Each element of this compromise was believed to be the minimum necessary to protect the sovereignty of those developed states whose accessions were necessary for success while still verifying non-diversion. States began complying with this IAEA conception, regulation, and implementation of safeguards by accepting safeguards—under the NPT, nuclear weapons–free zones (NWFZ), and voluntarily—in increasing numbers.

When the CSA system was challenged in the 1990s, the Board relied heavily upon the Secretariat when negotiating reforms that would better enable the Secretariat to identify undeclared activities. States explicitly accepted the broader legal requirement to provide the IAEA with information and access under the revised CSA and the Additional Protocol (AP). IAEA authority expanded over subsequent years, and inspectors now may report to the Board that a state is in noncompliance because of its failure to resolve IAEA questions about compliance, even if raised using noninspection data or without proving diversion. Further, with the revised implementation of integrated safeguards and the state-level approach, the IAEA is better able to focus its inspection efforts on where it believes is the greatest risk of proliferation.

The Secretariat has played an active leadership role in developing, proposing for adoption, and implementing the expansions of this system for verifying nonproliferation. The Secretariat's nonproliferation authority was reinforced by successes throughout the past two decades, including affirmation that it was right and the United States wrong in Iraq in 2002–3, and by its receipt of the Nobel Prize in 2005. The United States rejected the IAEA's judgments in isolated cases even as it accommodated IAEA authority by supporting safeguards strengthening and pushing for a much larger IAEA budget, but its subsequent difficulty in attracting international support also reinforced the power of IAEA authority on nonproliferation.

The Board was established as a representative body to manage the day-to-day activities of the Secretariat but has acquired a corporate identity that is more than a forum for its governors to bargain. The early norms of consensus and closed meetings built behavioral impersonality, enabled investment by individual governors in policy expertise, and ultimately pulled the

Board back from day-to-day management to play a more important strategic role. The Board in the 1990s not only demonstrated it could act as a competent technical judge of compliance with the NPT but by the early 2000s was increasingly seen as the only actor with the authority to do so.

IAEA nonproliferation authority now supersedes the prevailing international norm that individual states ultimately hold the power to judge compliance with their international commitments. Even inside the IAEA, where authority to judge compliance in the 1990s was reserved for the Board, even the Board refused to consider noncompliance without the recommendation of the Secretariat when it came to allegations against Egypt, Iran, and South Korea. While the international community determined that the Agency should not be the implementing organization for the CTBT in the mid-1990s, largely over concern about expanding IAEA authority and the mismatch between Board and the parties, there appears to be growing consensus that the IAEA should implement a future Fissile Material Cut-Off Treaty (FMCT) despite similar concerns.

Disarmament

Whereas the political authority of the Agency—both the Board and Secretariat—over nonproliferation is clear, growing, and growing in exclusivity, IAEA authority on disarmament is less well defined. The Secretariat demonstrated it could supply dismantlement and verify disarmament in the 1990s in South Africa, an entirely voluntary mission, and in Iraq, imposed by the Security Council. By a decade later, when ElBaradei claimed that the IAEA had the right and responsibility to verify Libya's disarmament, he was drawing on the international expectation that an Agency role was appropriate and expected in order for the international community to have confidence in the outcome. These experiences implementing and verifying nuclear disarmament have facilitated the Secretariat extending its safeguards authority beyond non-diversion to include undeclared activities. This authority was unilaterally asserted by the Board on behalf of its various collective principals but without their express approval. Its experiences with disarmament could become the basis for also extending the Secretariat's safeguards authority to include activities that demonstrate the intent to proliferate but that do not yet include the misuse of nuclear materials: weaponization.

Alternative Explanations

The IAEA's power to issue rules and commands may not be a result of its authority but could have alternative explanations. Authority could be an artifact of strengthening nuclear norms. The earliest nuclear norms were of non-use and disarmament, given the horrors of their use in the Second World War, and then of non-testing because of the environmental dangers. The norm of disarmament, one component of "complete and general disarmament," faded with its complete apparent impracticality and was replaced with a norm of nonproliferation only during the adoption of the NPT. The norm of disarmament may be resurgent in recent years but remains contested. Many states see persistent utility for deterring major powers, and even in the United States many accept significant reductions but not "disarmament."

None of these norms acquire an ineffable, coercive effect; they are at all times attenuated by caveats, exceptions, and conditions. The norms of non-use and nonproliferation are conditional throughout the entire period on the absence of an overriding threat to national survival that could legitimate pursuing a nuclear weapons option. The norm of non-testing is also limited, until very recently, to preventing environmental danger. This collection of antinuclear norms has become less conditional and more a constitutive part of state identities, making nuclear behavior less a strategic choice: the taboo against nuclear use is increasingly universal across actors and situations, contributing to the broader delegitimation of nuclear weapons testing or possession. Importantly, however, the strength of these antinuclear norms has not privileged any particular strategies for their realization.

Authority could result from norms of internationalization strengthening across international politics. Early pressure for atomic internationalization coincided with the idealist and legalist belief that internationalization within a world government could promote peace. These beliefs were unpopular among those who saw the League of Nations fail to prevent the atrocities of the early twentieth century and were further delegitimized during the Cold War by the repeated failures of the United Nations. Eisenhower's Atoms for Peace proposal reflected faith not in international institutions but in the power of technocratic bureaucracies and scientific rationality. Multilateralism is again "necessary" in the post–Cold War period, although it is unclear whether it was necessitated by multipolarity, as a useful signal of international legitimacy, or because even successful hegemonic coercion requires some commonality of interests among all whose positive contribution is necessary. The basic belief that mechanisms of international coordination are useful to supplying some collective goods has persisted since the late nineteenth century, but each stage of the evolution of the appropriateness of internationalization has prescribed a different strategy: from treaties to congresses, to technocratic civil servants, and, finally, to autonomous international agencies.

Comparing within issue areas across time, and across issue areas within time periods, shows that a procedural norm of internationalization is sometimes at play but is too weak to be determinate. Variation in the coercive effect of internationalization is observed in the 1950s when it was appropriate for peaceful uses and some nonproliferation efforts but not for disarmament or safety. In the 1960s there was less pressure to internationalize peaceful uses but internationalization was necessary for verifying nonproliferation safeguards. Since the 1990s there has been increasing pressure to internationalize safeguards and disarmament but largely as a hedge against great power abuses. Even after 9/11 and Fukushima, and despite many proposals for internationalizing aspects of safety and security, few states believe internationalization is the solution.

IAEA authority may be an artifact of effective multilateral coordination on nuclear policy issues by its multiple collective principals despite the increasing delegation to it of autonomy and resources. At least through the 1980s, the IAEA's principals had a limited, revocable, and hierarchic relationship with their Board and Secretariat in the international supply of technical assistance, nuclear safety and security, and even of nonproliferation in the early safeguards systems. The CSA system produced in 1972 under INFCIRC/153 (Rev.), for example, resulted from multilateral negotiations among interested members and assumed that the collective principals trusted the political commitments of non–nuclear weapon states: a restrictive legal standard, which required proving the non-diversion of significant quantities of nuclear materials from declared facilities, was further constrained by norms that inspectors would accommodate states and not challenge their declarations without objective evidence to the contrary. While there was a brief respite in the early post–Cold War years, the trend toward increasing politicization has affected international institutions that rely on effective multilateral control for their effectiveness or legitimacy. Navigating the several salient lines of political conflict among its members, even with superpower leadership, has compromised at the IAEA the ability of its multiple collective principals—the General Conference, the NPT Review Conferences, and even the UN Security Council—to achieve sufficiently strong consensus to lead a redirection of the Agency. The power of the IAEA to issue rules and commands since the 1990s, although it varies across nuclear issues, is not the result of effective delegation by collective principal.

The strongest alternative explanation is that the effects of IAEA rules and commands are actually a reflection of the order imposed upon the international community by a powerful hegemon. After multiple failures to achieve any internationalization of the atom, it is clear that support by the United States was necessary but insufficient to create and maintain the Agency. The safeguards system required Soviet support in the 1960s, and widespread adoption occurred only because states voluntarily chose to commit to nonproliferation through the NPT. As the IAEA acquired authority, it took almost Sisyphean effort by the United States to get developed and developing states to agree to significant budget increases as it fought against giving the CTBT to the IAEA in the mid-1990s and railed unsuccessfully against IAEA judgments on Iraq and Iran in the early 2000s. The Agency's power to issue rules and make commands has been supported by but is not an extension of US hegemony.

Summary

This book therefore suggests five conclusions about IAEA authority in 2014. First, its authority has been central to resolving the recurring tension over who international audiences should believe when noncompliance with international norms and rules is in dispute. The United States repeatedly contested the Secretariat's authority to judge and, in the one case in which IAEA authority was ignored, the United States and the United Kingdom were shown to have colluded to misrepresent or even manufacture evidence. In the other cases of noncompliance discussed, and in the other 170 or so states with safeguards in place, the judgment of the Agency was respected. As furious as some members were that ElBaradei refused to declare Iran was in noncompliance, without this judgment the Board also refused to find Iran in noncompliance or to refer Iran to the Security Council.

Second, the Secretariat has asserted its authority over nuclear policy by openly criticizing its principals when their choices threatened its mandate with insufficient economic, political, or materiel support. One director general felt his stature was sufficiently high after being awarded the Nobel Peace Prize that he openly berated the Board for failing to support the Agency's nonproliferation, safety, and security mandates. This same "agent" openly accused his single most powerful principal of violating its international legal obligations by withholding information about violations of IAEA safeguards and the NPT. However, a director general also chose passivity during and after a major nuclear accident despite its transnational effects, refusing an opportunity to fill an international safety vacuum. With the diffuse support of the international community, the Secretariat has chosen to exploit several opportunities to assert an activist role on nuclear policy that succeeded despite being at odds with its most powerful supporters.

Third, the Board recommended Amano to succeed ElBaradei because they believed he would be less political. In no small part due to the success of the former office holders, the director general has become sufficiently autonomous that powerful principals had to heavily lobby him as he selected which of the senior management he would keep and which he would replace. A counterfactual is illustrative: if the collective principal or individual principals had strong control over the actions of its agent, the particular interests of the director general and his Secretariat would have been less important. Rather, the independent authority of the director general has grown such that relying on the Board or the collective principals provides too weak a mechanism for agent control. And, despite Amano's hesitancy to act in the Fukushima nuclear disaster, he has been more aggressive with Iran and was selected to serve another term.

Fourth, the Board itself is acquiring an independent identity and functions as more than a forum for bargaining among national governors. The norm of consensus but the autonomy to impose its judgments by majority provides a mechanism to cope with overtly political questions. These questions are not simply important to its members, as might be the case for the IMF or World Bank, as the Board increasingly made decisions central to national decisions for or against war. The Board unilaterally granted greater verification autonomy to the Secretariat for safeguards, accepting its mandate to disarm Libya; its judgments on Iran, Egypt, and South Korea; and its exploring strengthening of international nuclear security after 9/11 and nuclear safety after Fukushima. The international response to nonproliferation and disarmament cases since 1998 showed that the Board is the authority to judge state compliance with a range of international nuclear policy commitments. The Board has asserted its authority on behalf of, but without direction from, its collective principals at the IAEA's General Conference, the NPT Review Conferences, or the various NWFZs.

Finally, authority is evident in the decline of national or international alternatives. The Agency dominates international nonproliferation and disarmament efforts, with nearly 180 states under safeguards and 120 states with an AP in force, with a central role in every critical case since 1998 including judging Iran and verifying Libya, and necessary for any North Korean deal. This authority follows acceptance by members and other states that inspectors are qualified to ask hard questions of their behavior and will feel free to do so but will also pursue their responsibilities more free from political bias than any national or ad hoc alternative. States considering future major international arms control agreements—an FMCT, multilateral nuclear fuel cycles, and even implementation of Obama's vision of a world free of nuclear weapons—are presented with the IAEA as the default implementing authority. Because the Agency possesses the technical and political authority for nuclear policy, the onus is on those contesting an Agency role or judgment to explain why. There is also no alternative source of international authority on nuclear safety or nuclear security as cooperation is decentralized. Although states generally regulate nuclear industry more heavily than many other areas, even national governments may not possess authority sufficient to prevent or remediate nuclear incidents with transnational effects. The IAEA may have little autonomy to act on safety and security, but this does not belie the fact that, in an authority vacuum, it occupies an important position in developing greater international cooperation.

The absence of alternatives is evident as the IAEA continued to grow, absorbing ever more resources and serving more often as a hub for international nuclear policy cooperation. Beyond the direct resources it receives, now over three-quarters of a billion dollars a year, it continues to be supported by large national efforts in research and development, preparation of trained personnel, and training programs for Agency staff for everything from safeguards to promotion of peaceful uses. The US government alone, for example, spends hundreds of millions of dollars each year to support IAEA programs, including recruiting qualified US citizens for Agency positions, preparing basic research on the safeguards system, developing new technologies, inviting Agency staff to the United States for training (including nationals of states with which the United States may not have cooperative relations), and regularly sending US experts on short-term consulting contracts.

A stark view of the Agency as a constrained agent that is efficiently managed by its state masters, or the international hegemon, may have been accurate in the past but cannot be justified today. Its collective principals and even powerful individual members defer judgment about matters central to international peace and security to the IAEA Board, which in turn requires action by the IAEA Secretariat. States—most ordinarily assumed to be sovereign and some outright powerful to the point of exerting hegemony in the system—have been forced in a series of strategic interactions to accommodate and comply with the power of the Agency to issue rules and commands over some areas of nuclear policy. The acknowledgment of Secretariat authority by its Board, and by the international community more broadly, siphons from its collective principals their authority and, ultimately, the independent authority of the sovereign states that populate them. The Secretariat began its life as an experiment with nuclear policy delegation, but today, despite continued contestation, the IAEA's power to make rules and take actions over much of the nuclear policy landscape reflects its emergence as the international political authority on nuclear issues.

PROSPECTIVE ON IAEA AUTHORITY

The contemporary world is threatened by nonproliferation compliance problems. To the contemporary observer these appear to be terrible challenges—as difficult to resolve as any in the past. At least the Iran case, like that of alleged covert nuclear activities in Syria and Myanmar, is occurring within the NPT framework, and this provides a legal opportunity for the IAEA to exercise its authority toward a peaceful—and proliferation-free—resolution. North Korea presents a more difficult challenge because its missile, uranium enrichment, and nuclear testing programs continue to expand, making any future verification more technically difficult, but the Agency's responsibilities remain unclear because its collective principals have yet to clarify North Korea's NPT status.

To these challenges are added a confluence of a prospective "renaissance" of nuclear power and new awareness of nuclear safety problems. The World Nuclear Association reported in 2012 that sixty reactors were under construction and dozens more planned, but the renewed commercial optimism for a climate change–friendly energy source has torn the environmental movements in many advanced states.[1] The Fukushima nuclear disaster reignited concerns about nuclear safety, slowing anticipated growth to something less than a "renaissance." The spread of nuclear energy has raised concern about supplies of nuclear fuel, which in turn feeds concern about the proliferation of sensitive nuclear fuel-cycle facilities to more states and fear that existing nuclear and radiological materials are not sufficiently secure against misuse.

As daunting as these challenges to international nuclear cooperation may be, they began to occur when there was great hope for progress on nuclear disarmament: the United States and Russia had brought into force New START, the Obama administration was considering resubmitting the CTBT for US Senate ratification, and a single country (Pakistan) was being blamed for holding up advancing the FMCT to completion. The groundswell of support after President Obama's 2009 Prague speech suggested a larger, global movement toward disarmament and the delegitimization of nuclear weapons. Unfortunately, progress on disarmament is on hold in 2014 as US relations with China, and Western relations with Russia, threaten diplomatic resolution of the problems that motivate the reliance on nuclear weapons.

Two particular developments will directly affect the international political authority of the Agency over nuclear issues in the next ten years. First, the CTBT has not entered into force because several states whose accession is required have now not ratified the treaty. Indonesia acceded in February 2012, and the eight remaining Annex II states required for entry into force are China, Egypt, India, Iran, Israel, North Korea, Pakistan, and the United States. Few expect North Korea or Iran to accede, and China is apparently waiting for the United States.[2] The US Congress has generally supported ratification but rejected the treaty under persistent opposition from the Departments of Defense and of Energy over the ability of science to ensure the safety and reliability of the warhead stockpile without testing (Medalia 1998, 2004). This opposition is mostly now dead, especially with a 2012 American Association for the Advancement of Science report defending the ability of the national labs to validate the reliability of the US deterrent force. Congressional Republicans, however, are unlikely to hand a Democratic president a foreign policy victory, especially if doing so appears to move the United States toward disarmament, a goal for which there is no US consensus.

It is difficult to imagine all the current Annex II countries ratifying the CTBT, but US and Chinese ratification would under international law increase the obligation of both to adhere to its purpose even without entry into force. This advancement might also be close enough to universal accession to trigger a renegotiation of the requirements for entry into force. Advancement of the CTBT would be a major advancement of the nuclear nonproliferation and disarmament regime, affirming the regime's norms (of nonproliferation, non-testing, and disarmament). Advancement would also legitimate an international actor that, while created to deliberately bypass the IAEA, could be a future partner.

Second, despite the success of New START, future reductions appear contingent on reducing Russian opposition to US missile defense plans and to putting on the table Russia's thousands of nonstrategic (tactical) nuclear weapons. If these issues were not deal breakers by themselves, it is hard to see how the deal after whatever follows New START will multilateralize the negotiations: if Russian and US stockpile reductions continue much further, they reach the point where the arsenals of other nuclear weapon states numerically come into play. When reaching these thresholds, the IAEA's authority may be useful in internationalizing the verification of reductions, disarmament, or dismantlement of a multilateral warhead reduction treaty. Its authority on weaponization and disarmament improves the chance of its being asked to supply verification for such a treaty.

Five specific prescriptions would offer new opportunities for the Agency to assert greater authority on nuclear issues. First, the Technical Cooperation program as it is currently structured provides private goods to a large number of its members, but it is inefficient, poorly integrated into larger development plans, and may be inadvertently supporting nuclear proliferation. To reverse its negative effect on the Agency's nuclear authority, the project review process should be reformed to enable the Board to set and enforce specific goals in the promotion of nuclear technology. These reforms might include increased integration with international financial institutions to ensure projects support broader development needs, which would increase the Technical Cooperation program's legitimacy even if in doing so it subordinates the goal of nuclear promotion.

Second, many nuclear suppliers are adding IAEA security standards to their supply agreements, but the Board could do much more to provide a safe and secure environment for the pursuit of peaceful nuclear uses. The Board should reverse its past consensus to exclude safety monitoring from safeguards, but safeguards should also verify that states have implemented sufficient controls to prevent the misuse of nuclear materials and not simply ensure it is detectable afterward. Even if their recommendations were not legally binding, the Board could incentivize participation in safety and security missions with greater subsidies by offering consultations whenever facility-level subsidiary agreements are renegotiated or whenever a state intends new constructions, and offering annual public reporting on who participates (and does not). States could be encouraged to take safety convention obligations implemented by the IAEA more seriously through more periodic system tests (and again reporting on participation). Folding the safety and security process into the implementation of safeguards would reduce the political costs of participation by making them automatic while also excluding from exposure to its costs those states for which safeguards are not required. In short, the Agency could unilaterally implement small internal changes that would increase its authority over international nuclear safety and security.

Third, the Board must recognize the increased authority of the Secretariat by adjusting its oversight process. The Board uses extensive informal consultations to supplement reporting though the director general. However, the Board could ensure that the interests of the Secretariat more closely track with the interests of its median members by extending its screening and selection power below that of the director general to include senior management. By requiring Board approval of the deputy director generals, the Board may politicize the process but would ensure that the individual appointees are acceptable to a majority of the Board. This should lead to fewer doubts, such as about whether Technical Cooperation is not contributing to proliferation or whether Nuclear Safety and Security is sufficiently proactive, and could reduce the hold some states have over senior positions. The members could also require that the director general maintain the confidence of the Board at all times. Though this could further elevate the position of the director general, much as a prime minister has more status than other members of a parliament, this reform might offer greater continuity in leadership transitions.

Fourth, the accountability of the Board to its collective principal at the General Conference and the Board has weakened because Board autonomy has increased since only 18 of the 162 members (just 11.1 percent in 2014) are required to make decisions and take actions on nuclear policy. The democratic deficit problem experienced in other international organizations is potentially magnified at the IAEA as the Board also contracts with other collective principals, from the NPT states and NWFZs to the Security Council, with prospects for adding in the future an FMCT and multilateral disarmament treaties. Democratic accountability could be increased by having the General Conference meet more often or by expanding the size of the Board to be more representative but with strong drawbacks. The Board does effectively balance interests along the several lines of political cleavage, and expansion would put this balance at risk. Expansion is also likely to increase the population of governors that follow the lead of others because they lack the independent expertise or direction from their national governments to do more. Principal–agent theory would suggest that there are multiple mechanisms for increasing oversight of the Board by the General Conference, including expanding the use of Standing Advisory Groups, but empirically the problem is not inadequate representation of interests, only the desire of individual states for a seat at the table.

Fifth, if the Secretariat wishes to become involved in the future in verifying weaponization and disarmament, this will require investing to maintain and even expand its current expertise in this area. This will present two problems for the Agency, however. First, the international community must have confidence in the results, but nuclear weapon states will be hesitant to share information with each other or with other states that may have weaponization experience. This suggests that the IAEA will need to maintain an over-large coalition of weaponization experts to guarantee both partiality and impersonality. Second, if there is a more permanent mission verifying a multilateral follow-up to US–Russian reductions, this disarmament will occur only once the parties trust initial declarations about the size and composition of their stockpiles, and then it will be black-boxed to avoid any transfer of sensitive design information. As a result, verification will more closely parallel the verification of chemical weapons disarmament by the Organization for the Prohibition of Chemical Weapons than it will the disarmament of Iraq or Libya with international (and national) inspectors roaming the countryside. In short, extending IAEA authority over weaponization and disarmament is an expensive proposition given the episodic demand for these skill sets.

Finally, the most important policy prescription concerns the necessary expansion of the budget. The zero-growth policy has over decades of imposition eroded the capacity of the Secretariat to supply international nuclear policy cooperation. The several exceptions have increased the budget and alleviated the immediate pressure, but the infrastructure of the Agency—from its laboratories to the training of its professional staff—has deteriorated in recent decades. Its ability to implement safeguards, safety, security, and technical cooperation to the standards expected by the international community is impossible without significant increases.

The authority of the Agency would be increased in two ways by the deployment of more resources to support its mandate. Expansion of the budget would allow the Secretariat to consolidate and rationalize its offerings of safety and security services, hire more safeguards inspectors and analysts for implementation of integrated safeguards, and advance internationalization of fuel-cycle services. In short, the Secretariat could accomplish more and deliver higher quality services to its members and collective principals. However, expanding its budget also requires each member to individually send a larger signal of political support by transferring those resources from other potential uses. Folding voluntary and extrabudgetary contributions into the regular budget, however, may not be in the best interests of the Agency. Principal–agent theory suggests that the flexibility of these contributions offers individual principals an opportunity to more accurately reveal their nuclear policy interests and to more closely align Agency outputs with these interests when they otherwise lack the formal or informal influence to control the Agency.

INTERNATIONAL POLITICAL AUTHORITY AND INTERNATIONAL RELATIONS THEORY

This book demonstrates that the IAEA has emerged as an international political authority over nuclear issues. The possibility that the Agency, once an agent, now has power over its principals is really only a small departure for political scientists and policy analysts who recognize that states and their citizens have relied upon international organizations—governmental and nongovernmental—to service their interests. Many international agencies may be little more than glorified institutions that allow cooperating states to manage each other's expectations by creating rules, processes, and forums for negotiation. Delegation to these institutions is limited and easily revoked, despite the value of their policy partiality or impersonality in producing outcomes of benefit to the collective principal.

International political authority is also only a small departure for political scientists such as David Lake (2009), Kathleen McNamara (2010), and Chad Rector (2009), who have recognized that, as anarchic as our global political system may be overall, hierarchic relationships are in fact endemic and widespread. Polities regularly recognize that others have the power—even if backed by the threat of coercion—to issue to them rules and commands. Finally, this view is also a small departure for those, like Alexander Wendt (1999), who have long observed the coercive power of social structure upon citizens and their leaders. This structure encompasses conceptions of appropriate outcomes and the legitimate agents and processes for producing them.

However, these individual arguments miss the totality of the IAEA as an international organization composed of egoistic individuals, endowed with resources, and tasked with discrete and exclusive nuclear missions that emerges with the power to compel state action. This book has been a test of the authority of a single international agent but one carried out using careful analysis comparing the power of the Agency to issue rules and commands in several nuclear issues. This test has required such a detailed analysis to trace the effects across time of variation in state power, expertise, norms, interests, political skill, identities, economics, and atomic power.

These findings imply that political authority should be endemic to the international system. The first and easiest step in a future research agenda would be to determine which other international organizations also possess political authority. Analyzing other international actors can allow political scientists to directly compare across time to the IAEA the structure of the principal–agent relationship, the power structure of interstate politics, and the normative social structure. The most obvious candidates for international political authority include the IMF and the World Bank, already the focus of study for many scholars in other ways. But which others have the power to issue rules and commands? And how and why did their power emerge, how contested is their authority, and what is the prognosis for its persistence?

A second step to analyzing the emergence of international political authority is to extend the universe of cases to other forms of collective action, particularly international nongovernmental organizations, that may also possess the power to issues rules and commands with which others expect they must comply. Scholars are already studying groups like Amnesty International, Greenpeace, the Red Cross, and al-Qaeda to see how these groups aggregate resources and deploy them to producing transnational outcomes in pursuit of goals whose legitimacy bears in no small part on the generalized support of individuals. But is this effect of nongovernmental organizations also political authority?

One final point to consider is the implication of the emergence of international political authority for state sovereignty. The political authority of international organizations implies that states are either actively transferring or abdicating their own authority to international actors to produce gains that the states are unable to produce in some other, less costly fashion. The political authority of international nongovernmental organizations, if it exists, implies that substate actors are recognizing and empowering the authority of nonstate actors. If so, individuals, but also other nonstate collectivities, are in practice bypassing states, recognizing as a limited sovereign some actor other than the states that claims total authority over the territory in which they happen to reside.

State sovereignty and its partner, international anarchy, are constructed concepts that reify a set of political authority relationships that have emerged over several centuries, but this description has for some decades appeared less and less accurate. The emergence of international political authority in its many possible forms does not yet challenge the state as "primus inter pares" or "first among equals," but someday they may. Certainly the IAEA, created to help states control the threat from nuclear weapons, does challenge the authority of the states that created it to independently pursue nuclear policy. Only through continued observation, exploration, and analysis will we know whether this world makes us better off, a task we as political actors must continue.

NOTES

1. "Plans for New Nuclear Reactors Worldwide," World Nuclear Association, February 2012, accessed 18 July 2012, http://www.world-nuclear.org/info/inf17.html.

2. India, North Korea, and Pakistan have not even signed the treaty. For the latest list, see the CTBTO website, http://www.ctbto.org/specials/who-we-are/.

References

Abbott, Kenneth W., and Duncan Snidal. 1998. "Why States Act through Formal International Organizations." *Journal of Conflict Resolution* 42, no. 1: 3–32.

Abbott, Kenneth W., Robert O. Keohane, Andrew Moravcsik, Anne-Marie Slaughter, and Duncan Snidal. 2000. "The Concept of Legalization." *International Organization* 54, no. 3: 401–19.

Adler, Emanuel. 1992. "The Emergence of Cooperation: National Epistemic Communities and the International Evolution of the Idea of Nuclear Arms Control." *International Organization* 46, no. 1: 101–45.

Adler, Emanuel, and Michael Barnett. 1998. *Security Communities*. Cambridge: Cambridge University Press.

Albright, David. 1994. "South Africa's Secret Nuclear Weapons." *ISIS Report*. Washington, DC: Institute for Science and International Security.

Albright, David, Corey Gay, and Khidhir Hamza. 1999. Development of the Al-Tuwaitha Site: What If the Public or the IAEA Had Overhead Imagery? *ISIS Report*. Washington, DC: Institute for Science and International Security.

Albright, David, and Corey Hinderstein. 2004. "Uncovering the Nuclear Black Market: Working toward Closing Gaps in the International Nonproliferation Regime." Institute for Nuclear Materials Management 45th Annual Meeting, July 2, Orlando, FL. http://isis-online.org/publications/southasia/nuclear_black_market.html.

Albright, David, and Jacqueline Shire. 2009. "Nuclear Iran: Not Inevitable." Paper for the Institute for Science and International Security, Washington, DC, January 21. http://www.isisnucleariran.org/assets/pdf/Iran_paper_final_2.pdf.

Aler, Bo. 1997. "Non-Proliferation and the IAEA." In *International Atomic Energy Agency: Personal Reflections*, ed. Hans Blix, 141–56. Vienna: International Atomic Energy Agency. http://www-pub.iaea.org/MTCD/publications/PDF/Pub1033_web.pdf.

Alesina, Alberto, and Guido Tabellini. 2007. "Bureaucrats or Politicians? Part I: A Single Policy Task." *American Economic Review* 97, no. 1: 169–79.

Allison, Graham. 2004. *Nuclear Terrorism: The Ultimate Preventable Catastrophe*. New York: Times Books.

Aloise, Gene. 2011. *Nuclear Nonproliferation: More Progress Needed in Implementing Recommendations for IAEA's Technical Cooperation Program* (GAO-11-482T). Washington, DC: US Government Accountability Office.

Alter, Karen J. 2008. "Agents or Trustees? International Courts in their Political Context." *European Journal of International Relations* 14, no. 1: 33–63.

Avant, Deborah, Martha Finnemore, and Susan K. Sell, eds. 2010. *Who Governs the Globe?* Cambridge Studies in International Affairs. Cambridge: Cambridge University Press.

Barkenbus, Jack. 1987. "Nuclear Power Safety and the Role of International Organization." *International Organization* 41, no. 3: 475–90.

Barnaby, C. Frank, ed. 1969a. *Preventing the Spread of Nuclear Weapons.* Pugwash monograph 1. London: Souvenir Press.

———. 1969b. "Existing Systems for the Control of Peaceful Uses of Atomic Energy." In *Preventing the Spread of Nuclear Weapons*, ed. C. Frank Barnaby, 36–49. London: Souvenir Press.

———. 1969c. "Nonproliferation Negotiations, 1961–1968." *Preventing the Spread of Nuclear Weapons*, ed. C. Frank Barnaby, 50–61. London: Souvenir Press.

Barnett, Michael, and Martha Finnemore. 1999. "The Politics, Power, and Pathologies of International Organizations." *International Organization* 53, no. 4: 699–732.

———. 2004. *Rules for the World: International Organizations in Global Politics.* Ithaca, NY: Cornell University Press.

Barretto, Paulo M. C., and Ana Maria Cetto. 2005. "IAEA Technical Cooperation and the NPT." *IAEA Bulletin* 46, no. 2: 28–30.

Barton, William H. 1997. "The IAEA as I Remember It." In *International Atomic Energy Agency: Personal Reflections*, ed. Hans Blix, 37–44. Vienna: International Atomic Energy Agency. http://www-pub.iaea.org/MTCD/publications/PDF/Pub1033_web.pdf.

Baruch, Bernard. 1946. "The Baruch Plan." Presented to the United Nations Atomic Energy Commission, June 14, 1946, http://www.atomicarchive.com/Docs/Deterrence/BaruchPlan.shtml.

Bechhoefer, Bernhard G. 1959. "Negotiating the Statute of the International Atomic Energy Agency." *International Organization* 13, no. 1: 38–59.

———. 1973. "Historical Evolution of International Safeguards." In *International Safeguards and Nuclear Industry*, ed. Mason Willrich, 21–44. Baltimore: Johns Hopkins University Press.

Beck, Michael E. 2004. "The Promise and Limits of the PSI." *Monitor* 10, no. 1: 16–17.

Bello, Judith Hippler, and Peter H. F. Bekker. 1997. "Legality of the Threat or Use of Nuclear Weapons." *American Journal of International Law* 91, no. 1: 126–33.

Bendor, Jonathan, A. Glazer, and T. Hammond. 2001. "Theories of Delegation." *Annual Review of Political Science* 4:235–69.

Bernstein, Barton J. 1974. "The Quest for Security: American Foreign Policy and International Control of Atomic Energy, 1942–1946." *Journal of American History* 60, no. 4: 1003–44.

Black, Stephen. 2002. "UNSCOM and the Iraqi Biological Weapons Program." In *Biological Warfare and Disarmament: New Problems/New Perspectives*, ed. Susan Wright, 285–309. Lanham, MD: Rowman and Littlefield.

Blitzer, Wolf. 2003. "Search for the 'Smoking Gun'." *CNN*, January 10. http://www.cnn.com/2003/US/01/10/wbr.smoking.gun/index.html?_s=PM:US.

Blix, Hans. 1985. *Safeguards and Non-Proliferation*. Vienna: International Atomic Energy Agency.

———. 1997. *International Atomic Energy Agency: Personal Reflections*. Vienna: International Atomic Energy Agency. http://www-pub.iaea.org/MTCD/publications/PDF/Pub1033_web.pdf.

———. 2003. "Transcript of Blix's U.N. Presentation." *CNN*, March 7. http://articles.cnn.com/2003-03-07/us/sprj.irq.un.transcript.blix_1_inspection-effort-unmovic-unscom?_s=PM:US.

———. 2004. *Disarming Iraq*. London: Bloomsbury.

Bodansky, Daniel. 1999. "The Legitimacy of International Governance: A Coming Challenge for International Environmental Law?" *American Journal of International Law* 93, no. 3: 596–624.

———. 2008. "The Concept of Legitimacy in International Law." *Legitimacy in International Law*. Max Planck Institute for Comparative Public Law and International Law. UGA Legal Studies Research Paper No. 07–013. *Social Sciences Research Network*, http://papers.ssrn.com/sol3/papers.cfm?abstract_id=1033542.

Boffey, Philip M. 1981. "Nuclear Cheating: Why the Experts Are Worried over Safeguards." *New York Times*, December 22. http://www.nytimes.com/1981/12/22/science/nuclear-cheating-why-the-experts-are-worried-over-safeguards.html.

Borger, Julian. 2012. "Nuclear Watchdog Chief Accused of Pro-Western Bias over Iran." *Guardian*, March 22. http://www.theguardian.com/world/2012/mar/22/nuclear-watchdog-iran-iaea.

Boughton, James M. 2001. *Silent Revolution: The International Monetary Fund, 1979–1989*. Washington, DC: International Monetary Fund.

Boureston, Jack, and Yana Feldman. 2004. "Verifying Libya's Nuclear Disarmament." In *Verification Yearbook*, 87–106. London: VERTIC. http://www.vertic.org/media/Archived_Publications/Yearbooks/2004/VY04_Boureston-Feldman.pdf.

Boureston, Jack, and Jennifer Lacey. 2007. "Nuclear Technical Cooperation: A Right or a Privilege?" *Arms Control Today*, September. http://www.armscontrol.org/act/2007_09/NuclearCoopFeature.

Boyer, Paul. 1984. "From Activism to Apathy: The American People and Nuclear Weapons, 1963–1980." *Journal of American History* 70, no. 4: 821–44.

Bradley, Curtis A., and Judith G. Kelley, eds. 2008a. *Law and Contemporary Problems*, Special Issue: *The Law and Politics of International Delegation* 71, no. 1 (Winter). http://scholarship.law.duke.edu/lcp/vol71/iss1/.

———. 2008b. "The Concept of International Delegation." *Law and Contemporary Problems* 71, no. 1: 1–36. http://scholarship.law.duke.edu/cgi/viewcontent.cgi?article=1451&context=lcp.

Bragin, Victor, John Carlson, and Russell Leslie. 2001. "Integrated Safeguards: Status and Trends." *Nonproliferation Review*, Summer, 102–111. http://cns.miis.edu/npr/pdfs/82bragin.pdf.

Brennan, Donald P., ed. 1961a. *Arms Control, Disarmament, and National Security.* New York: George Braziller.

———. 1961b. "Setting and Goals of Arms Control." *Arms Control, Disarmament, and National Security*, ed. Donald P. Brennan, 19–42. New York: George Braziller.

Brennan, Donald P., and Morton H. Halperin. 1961. "Policy Considerations of a Nuclear-Test Ban." In *Arms Control, Disarmament, and National Security*, ed. Donald P. Brennan, 234–66. New York: George Braziller.

Brewer, Thomas L. 1978. "The International Atomic Energy Agency." *Armed Forces & Society* 4, no. 2: 207–26.

Brodie, Bernard, ed. 1946. *The Absolute Weapon: Atomic Power and World Order.* New York: Harcourt, Brace.

Brooks, Linton F. 2005. "Trinity and Beyond." Presentation to the National Academy of Sciences Symposium, "60th Anniversary of Trinity: First Manmade Nuclear Explosion, July 16, 1945," July 14, 2005, Washington, DC, http://sites.nationalacademies.org/PGA/cs/groups/pgasite/documents/webpage/pga_049741.pdf.

Brown, Harold. 2007. "US Nonproliferation Policy." *Public Policy & Nuclear Threats Summer Program 2007*, La Jolla, CA, June 9–27, Institute for Global Conflict and Cooperation.

———. 2007–8. "New Nuclear Realities." *Washington Quarterly* 31, no. (1): 7–22. http://csis.org/files/publication/twq08winterbrown.pdf.

Brown, Robert L. 2005. "21st Century Deterrence: Punishment, Denial, and the Future Demand for Nuclear Weapons." *The Future Security Environment and the Role of US Nuclear Weapons in the 21st Century.* Washington, DC: Center for Strategic and International Studies.

———. 2009. *The Enforcement Powers of International Agents.* Annual Meeting of the American Political Science Association, September, Toronto, Canada. *Social Science Research Network.* doi:10.2139/ssrn.1466048.

———. 2010. "Measuring Delegation." *Review of International Organizations* 5, no. 2: 141–75.

———. 2011. *Preferences, Power, and International Cooperation.* Presentation to the International Studies Association Annual Meeting, March 19, Montreal, Canada.

Brown, Robert L., and Jeffrey M. Kaplow. 2014. "Talking Peace, Making Weapons: IAEA Technical Cooperation and Nuclear Proliferation." *Journal of Conflict Resolution* 58 (April 1). doi:10.1177/0022002713509052.

Brown, Walton Lyonnaise. 1982. "Assessing the Impact of American Nuclear Proliferation Policy, 1970–1980: An Analysis of Six Cases." PhD diss., University
of Michigan.

Büchler, Carlos L. 1997. "Safeguards: The Beginnings." In *International Atomic
Energy Agency: Personal Reflections*, ed. Hans Blix, 45–52. Vienna, Interna-
tional Atomic Energy Agency. http://www-pub.iaea.org/MTCD/publications/
PDF/Pub1033_web.pdf.

Bull, Hedley. 1977. *The Anarchical Society: A Study of Order in World Politics*.
New York: Columbia University Press.

Bunn, George. 1967. Telegram from Department of State to Certain Posts (November 11, 1967). Doc. 16. http://history.state.gov/historicaldocuments/frus1964
-68v11/d216. In *Foreign Relations of the United States 1964–1968*, vol. 11,
Arms Control and Disarmament, eds. Evans Gerakas, David S. Patterson, and
Carolyn B. Yee. Washington, DC: US Department of State. http://history.state
.gov/historicaldocuments/frus1964–68v11.

———. 1992. *Arms Control by Committee: Managing Negotiations with the Russians*. Stanford, CA: Stanford University Press.

Bunn, Matthew, and Olli Heinonen. 2011. "Preventing the Next Fukushima." Op-
Ed, Belfer Center for Science and International Affairs, May 26. http://belfer
center.ksg.harvard.edu/publication/21071/preventing_the_next_fukushima
.html.

Bunn, Matthew, and Anthony Wier. 2006. "Securing the Bomb 2006." Report for
Project on Managing the Atom, Harvard University, and Nuclear Threat Initiative, July 13. Cambridge, MA: Harvard Belfer Center.

Burr, William. 2005. "National Intelligence Estimates of the Nuclear Proliferation
Problem: The First Ten Years, 1957–1967." Washington, DC: National Security
Archive.

Burr, William, and Jeffrey T. Richelson. 2000. "Whether to 'Strangle the Baby in
the Cradle': The United States and the Chinese Nuclear Program, 1960–64."
International Security 25, no. 3: 54–99.

Bush, George W. 2001. "President Welcomes President Chirac to White House,"
November 6. http://georgewbush-whitehouse.archives.gov/news/releases/2001/
11/20011106-4.html.

———. 2002a. "President Bush Outlines Iraqi Threat," Cincinnati Museum
Center—Cincinnati Union Terminal, Cincinnati, Ohio, October 7. http://
georgewbush-whitehouse.archives.gov/news/releases/2002/10/20021007–8
.html.

———. 2002b. State of the Union, January 29. http://georgewbush-whitehouse
.archives.gov/news/releases/2002/01/20020129–11.html.

Butler, Robin, Peter Inge, John Chilcot, Michael Mates, and Ann Taylor. 2004.
Review of Intelligence on Weapons of Mass Destruction. London: House of
Commons.

Buzan, Barry, and Richard Little. 2000. *International Systems in World History: Remaking the Study of International Relations*. Oxford: Oxford University Press.

Caldwell, Dan. 1991. "The SALT II Treaty." In *The Politics of Arms Control Treaty Ratification*, ed. Michael Krepon and Dan Caldwell, 279–354. New York: St. Martin's Press.

Calvert, Randall. 1985. "The Value of Biased Information: A Rational Choice Model of Political Advice." *Journal of Politics* 42, no. 2: 530–55.

Caporaso, James A. 1996. "The European Union and Forms of State: Westphalian, Regulatory or Post-Modern?" *Journal of Common Market Studies* 34, no. 1: 29–52.

Carlson, John. 2006. "SAGSI: Its Role and Contribution to Safeguards Development." Barton: Australian Safeguards and Non-Proliferation Office.

———. 2011. "Expanding Safeguards in Nuclear-Weapon States." Presentation to the Annual Meeting of the Institute of Nuclear Materials Management, July 17–21, Palm Desert, CA.

Carpenter, Daniel. 2001. *The Forging of Bureaucratic Autonomy: Reputations, Networks, and Policy Innovation in Executive Agencies, 1862–1928*. Princeton, NJ: Princeton University Press.

———. 2010. *Reputation and Power: Organizational Image and Pharmaceutical Regulation at the FDA*. Princeton, NJ: Princeton University Press.

Carr, Edward Hallett. 1961. *The Twenty Years' Crisis, 1919–1939*. New York: St. Martin's Press.

Casterton, Jim. 2007. "International Perspectives on Safeguards" (A panel discussion with current and former SAGSI representatives, PNNL-SA-56894). *Foundations of International Safeguards: Safeguards in the Nuclear Age*. Interviewed by Rich Hooper and Tom Shea, Tuscon, AZ. http://cgs.pnnl.gov/fois/doclib/5.0Tucsontranscript.pdf.

Chayes, Abram, and Antonia Handler Chayes. 1993. "On Compliance." *International Organization* 47, no. 2: 175–205.

Checkel, Jeffrey T. 2005. "International Institutions and Socialization in Europe: Introduction and Framework." *International Organization* 59, no. 4: 801–26.

Chellaney, Brahma. 1999. "Arms Control: The Role of the IAEA and UNSCOM." In *International Security Management and the United Nations*, eds. Muthiah Alagappa and Takashi Inoguchi. New York: United Nations University Press.

Cheney, Richard. 2002. "Remarks by the Vice President to the Veterans of Foreign Wars 103rd National Convention," August 26, Nashville, Tennessee. http://georgewbush-whitehouse.archives.gov/news/releases/2002/08/20020826.html.

Choi, Kathleen J. 2008. "A Journey of a Thousand Leagues: From Quarantine to International Health Regulations and Beyond." *University of Pennsylvania Journal of International Law* 29, no. 4: 989–1022.

Churchill, Winston S. 1946. "The Sinews of Peace." Speech given at Westminster College, Fulton, Missouri, March 5. http://www.winstonchurchill.org/learn/speeches/speeches-of-winston-churchill/120-the-sinews-of-peace.

CIA. 2005. "Managing Nuclear Proliferation: The Politics of Limited Choice" (25X1A9a, December 1975). In *National Intelligence Estimates of the Nuclear Proliferation Problem: The First Ten Years, 1957–1967.* Washington, DC, National Security Archive. http://www2.gwu.edu/~nsarchiv/NSAEBB/NSAE BB155/prolif-15.pdf.

Claude, Inis L. 1964. *Swords into Plowshares: The Problems and Progress of International Organization.* New York: Random House.

Cleminson, Frank Ronald. 2003. "What Happened to Saddam's Weapons of Mass Destruction?" *Arms Control Today* 33, no. 7: 3–6.

Clinton, William J. 1996. "The National Security Strategy of Engagement and Enlargement," February. Washington, DC: The White House. http://nssarchive .us/NSSR/1996.pdf.

———. 1998. A National Security Strategy for a New Century. Washington, D.C.

Cohen, Bernard L. 1990. *The Nuclear Energy Option.* New York: Plenum Press.

Cortright, David, and Samina Ahmed. 1998. "Sanctions: Modify 'Em (India and Pakistan)." *Bulletin of the Atomic Scientists* 54, no. 5: 22–25.

Countryman, Thomas M. 2014. "US Priorities for the Nuclear Non-Proliferation Treaty (NPT) Preparatory Committee Meeting." US Department of State, April 29. http://fpc.state.gov/225407.htm.

Crail, Peter. 2009. "Five Candidates Vie for Top IAEA Post." *Arms Control Today.* http://www.armscontrol.org/act/2009_5/IAEA_candidates.

Cronin, Audrey Kurth. 2003. "Behind the Curve: Globalization and International Terrorism." *International Security* 27, no. 3: 30–58.

Cronin, Bruce, and Ian Hurd. 2008. Introduction to *The UN Security Council and the Politics of International Authority,* ed. Bruce Cronin and Ian Hurd, 3–22. New York: Routledge.

de Jong, Derek. 2011. "A Chronicle of Non-Compliance: The Iran Case." In *Compliance Briefing Note.* Waterloo, Canada: Canadian Centre for Treaty Compliance.

de Nevers, Renee. 2007. "Imposing International Norms: Great Powers and Norm Enforcement." *International Studies Review* 9, no. 1: 53–80.

Decker, Torsten, Andreas Stiehler, and Martin Strobel. 2003. "A Comparison of Punishment Rules in Repeated Public Goods Games." *Journal of Conflict Resolution* 47, no. 6: 751–72.

Dixit, Avinash, Gene M. Grossman, and Elhanan Helpman. 1997. "Common Agency and Coordination: General Theory and Application to Government Policy Making." *Journal of Political Economy* 105, no. 4: 752–69.

Dos Santos, Theotonio. 1991. "The Structure of Dependence." In *The Theoretical Evolution of International Political Economy,* ed. George T. Crane and Abla Amawi, 144–52. Oxford: Oxford University Press.

Downs, George W., David M. Rocke, and Peter N. Barsoom. 1996. "Is the Good News about Compliance Good News about Cooperation?" *International Organization* 50, no. 3: 379–406.

Dreher, Axel, and Nathan M. Jensen. 2007. "Independent Actor or Agent? An Empirical Analysis of the Impact of US Interests on International Monetary Fund Conditions." *Journal of Law and Economics* 50, no. 1: 105–25.

Duelfer, Charles A. 2004. "Comprehensive Revised Report with Addendums on Iraq's Weapons of Mass Destruction (Duelfer Report)." Washington, DC: Iraq Survey Group and Special Advisor to the Director of Central Intelligence on Iraq's Weapons of Mass Destruction.

Dunn, J. F. 1993. *The Ukrainian Nuclear Weapons Debate*, April 6. Surrey, UK: UK Royal Military Academy Sandhurst Soviet Studies Research Centre. http://fas.org/news/ukraine/occbrf18jfd.htm.

Dunn, Lewis A. 1985. "The Emerging Nuclear Suppliers: Some Dimensions of the Problem." In *The Nuclear Suppliers and Nonproliferation*, ed. Rodney W. Jones, Cesare Merlini, Joseph F. Pilat, and William C. Potter, 119–27. Lexington, MA: Lexington Books.

———. 2006. "Countering Proliferation: Insights from Past 'Wins, Losses, and Draws.'" *Nonproliferation Review* 13, no. 3: 479–89.

Eisenhower, Dwight D. 1953. "Address by Mr. Dwight D. Eisenhower, President of the United States of America." 470th Plenary Meeting of the United Nations General Assembly, December 8. New York. http://www.iaea.org/Publications/Magazines/Bulletin/Bull452/article20.pdf.

Ekéus, Rolf. 2012. "The Iraq Action Team: A Model for Monitoring and Verification of WMD Non-Proliferation." Stockholm International Peace Research Institute, September 12. http://www.sipri.org/media/newsletter/essay/Ekeus _Sep12.

Eklund, Sigvard. 1981. "The IAEA on Safeguards." *Bulletin of the Atomic Scientists* 37, no. 8: 32–33.

ElBaradei, Mohamed. 2003a. "Implementation of the NPT Safeguards Agreement in the Islamic Republic of Iran," June 6. GOV/2003/40: Report by the Director General for the Board of Governors (Derestricted June 19, 2003). Vienna: International Atomic Energy Agency.

———. 2003b. "Implementation of the NPT Safeguards Agreement in the Islamic Republic of Iran," November 10. GOV/2003/75: Report by the Director General for the Board of Governors (Derestricted November 26, 2003). Vienna: International Atomic Energy Agency.

———. 2003c. "Statement to the United Nations Security Council: The Status of Nuclear Inspections in Iraq: An Update," March 7. Vienna: International Atomic Energy Agency.

———. 2004a. "Introductory Statement to the Board of Governors," November 25. Vienna: International Atomic Energy Agency.

———. 2004b. "Implementation of the NPT Safeguards Agreement in the Islamic Republic of Iran," June 1. GOV/2004/34. Report by the Director General. Vienna: International Atomic Energy Agency.

———. 2011. *The Age of Deception: Nuclear Diplomacy in Treacherous Times.* New York, Metropolitan Books.

Epstein, David, and Sharyn O'Halloran. 1999. *Delegating Powers.* Cambridge: Cambridge University Press.

Erlanger, Steven. 2007. "Israel Silent on Reports of Bombing within Syria." *New York Times,* October 15. http://www.nytimes.com/2007/10/15/world/middle east/15mideast.html?_r = 0.

Essis, Essoh J. M. C. 2005. "From Individual State Preferences to Collective Decisions: An Analytic Account of the 1995 NPT Review and Extension Conference." *International Negotiation* 10:513–39.

Eyre, Dana P., and Mark C. Suchman. 1996. "Status, Norms, and the Proliferation of Conventional Weapons: An Institutional Theory Approach." In *The Culture of National Security: Norms and Identity in World Politics,* ed. Peter J. Katzenstein, 79–113. New York: Columbia University Press.

Fearon, James D. 1994. "Domestic Political Audiences and the Escalation of International Disputes." *American Political Science Review* 88, no. 3: 577–92.

———. 1997. "Signaling Foreign Policy Interests: Tying Hands versus Sinking Costs." *Journal of Conflict Resolution* 41, no. 1: 68–90.

Fearon, James D., and Alexander Wendt. 2002. "Rationalism vs. Constructivism: A Skeptical View." In *The Handbook of International Relations,* ed. Walter Carlsnaes, Thomas Risse, and Beth A. Simmons. London: Sage.

Feldman, Shai. 1982. "The Bombing of Osiraq-Revisited." *International Security* 7, no. 2: 114–42.

Fenton, Anne Marie. 2004. "France, Italy and the 2002/2003 Iraq Crisis." Master's diss., Naval Postgraduate School.

Findlay, Trevor. 2003. "The Lessons of UNSCOM and UNMOVIC." In *Verification Yearbook 2004.* London: Trevor Findlay.

———. 2010. *Nuclear Energy and Global Governance: Ensuring Safety, Security and Non-Proliferation.* New York: Routledge.

———. 2012a. "Unleashing the Nuclear Watchdog: Strengthening and Reform of the IAEA." Policy Brief #23. Waterloo, Canada: Centre for International Governance Innovation.

———. 2012b. "The IAEA and Fukushima: Best Laid Plans, Reality Checks and Doing It Better Next Time." Belfer Center for Science and International Affairs, International Security Program and Project on Managing the Atom, March 29. http://belfercenter.ksg.harvard.edu/publication/21957/iaea_and_fukushima .html.

———. 2012c. "Strengthening and Reform of the International Atomic Energy Agency." Waterloo, Canada: Centre for International Governance Innovation, Carleton University.

Finnemore, Martha. 1996. "Constructing Norms of Humanitarian Intervention." In *The Culture of National Security: Norms and Identity in World Politics,* ed. Peter J. Katzenstein, 153–85. New York: Columbia University Press.

Finnemore, Martha, and Kathryn Sikkink. 1998. "International Norm Dynamics and Political Change." *International Organization* 52, no. 4 (Autumn): 887–917.

Fioretos, Orfeo. 2011. "Historical Institutionalism in International Relations." *International Organization* 65:367–99.

Firmage, Edwin Brown. 1969. "The Treaty on the Non-Proliferation of Nuclear Weapons." *American Journal of International Law* 63, no. 4: 711–46.

Fischer, David A.V. 1997. *History of the International Atomic Energy Agency: The First Forty Years*. Vienna: International Atomic Energy Agency.

———. 2007. "Nuclear Safeguards: The First Steps." *IAEA Bulletin* 49, no. 1 (September) 7–11.

Franck, Thomas. 1990. *The Power of Legitimacy among Nations*. New York: Oxford University Press.

———. 1992. "The Emerging Right of Democratic Governance." *American Journal of International Law* 86, no. 1 (January): 46–91.

Frank, Gideon. 1997. "The IAEA at a Crossroads: An Israeli Perspective." In *International Atomic Energy Agency: Personal Reflections*, ed. Hans Blix, 271–86. Vienna: International Atomic Energy Agency. http://www-pub.iaea.org/MTCD/publications/PDF/Pub1033_web.pdf.

Freedman, Lawrence. 2003. *The Evolution of Nuclear Strategy*. New York: Palgrave Macmillan.

Frieden, Jeffrey A., David A. Lake, and Kenneth A. Schultz. 2009. *World Politics: Interests, Interactions, Institutions*. New York: W. W. Norton.

Frost, Robin M. 2005. *Nuclear Terrorism after 9/11*. New York: Routledge.

Frye, William R. 1961. "Characteristics of Recent Arms-Control Proposals and Agreements." In *Arms Control, Disarmament, and National Security*, ed. Donald P. Brennan, 68–85. New York: George Braziller.

Fuhrmann, Matthew. 2009a. "Spreading Temptation: Proliferation and Peaceful Nuclear Cooperation Agreements." *International Security* 34, no. 1: 7–41.

———. 2009b. "Taking a Walk on the Supply Side: The Determinants of Civilian Nuclear Cooperation." *Journal of Conflict Resolution* 53, no. 2: 181–208.

Funabashi, Yoichi. 2007. *The Peninsula Question: A Chronicle of the Second Korean Nuclear Crisis*. Washington, DC: Brookings Institution Press.

Gabel, Matthew. 1998. "Public Support for European Integration: An Empirical Test of Five Theories." *Journal of Politics* 60, no. 2: 333–54.

Gallini, Linda S. 1985. "The 1985 NPT Review Conference." In *The Nuclear Suppliers and Nonproliferation*, ed. Rodney W. Jones, Cesare Merlini, Joseph F. Pilat, and William C. Potter, 203–10. Lexington, MA: Lexington Books.

GAO. 1997. "Nuclear Nonproliferation and Safety: Concerns with the International Atomic Energy Agency's Technical Cooperation Program (GAO/RCED-97-192)." Washington, DC: US Government Accountability Office.

———. 2009. "Nuclear Nonproliferation and Safety: Strengthened Oversight Needed to Address Proliferation and Management Challenges in IAEA's Technical Cooperation Program (GAO-09-275)." Washington, DC: US Government Accountability Office.

———. 2013. "Nuclear Nonproliferation: IAEA Has Made Progress in Implementing Critical Programs but Continues to Face Challenges (GAO-13-139)." Washington, DC: US Government Accountability Office.

George, Alexander L., and Richard Smoke. 1974. *Deterrence in American Foreign Policy: Theory and Practice*. New York: Columbia University Press.

Goldschmidt, Bertrand. 1977. "A Historical Survey of Nonproliferation Policies." *International Security* 2, no. 1: 69–87.

———. 1981. "The Negotiation of the Non-Proliferation Treaty (NPT)." *IAEA Bulletin* 22, no. 3–4: 73–81.

———. 1982. *The Atomic Complex*. La Grange Park, IL, American Nuclear Society.

Goldschmidt, Pierre. 2008a. *IAEA Safeguards: Dealing Preventively with Non-Compliance*. Washington, DC: Carnegie Endowment for International Peace and Harvard Belfer Center.

———. 2008b. "The Nuclear Non-Proliferation Regime: Avoiding the Void." In *Falling Behind: International Scrutiny of the Peaceful Atom*, ed. Henry D. Sokolski. Carlisle, PA: Strategic Studies Institute of the US Army War College.

Gonzalez, Abel J. 2002. "International Negotiations on Radiation and Nuclear Safety." In *Containing the Atom*, ed. Rudolf Avenhaus, Victor Kremenyuk, and Gunmar Sjöstedt. Lanham, MD: Lexington Books.

Goodby, James E. 2005. "The Limited Test Ban Negotiations, 1954–63: How a Negotiator Viewed the Proceedings." *International Negotiation* 10:381–404.

———. 2006. *The Borderline of Armageddon*. Lanham, MD: Rowman and Littlefield.

Gould, Erica R. 2006a. "Delegating IMF Conditionality: Understanding Variations in Control and Conformity." In *Delegation and Agency in International Organizations*, ed. Darren Hawkins, David A. Lake, Daniel Nielson, and Michael J. Tierney, 281–311. Cambridge: Cambridge University Press.

———. 2006b. *Money Talks: The International Monetary Fund, Conditionality, and Supplemental Financiers*. Stanford, CA: Stanford University Press.

Greenhill, Brian. 2010. "The Company You Keep: International Socialization and the Diffusion of Human Rights Norms." *International Studies Quarterly* 54, no. 2: 127–45.

Greenwood, Ted, and Robert Haffa Jr. 1981. "Supply-Side Non-Proliferation." *Foreign Policy* 42:125–40.

Grey, Robert T., Jr. 1983. "United States Nuclear Weapons and Arms Control Policy in the Early 1980s." *New York Law School Journal of International and Comparative Law* 4, no. 2: 381.

Gromyko, Andrei A. 1947. "Statement by the Soviet Representative on the Security Council (Gromyko) Concerning the Report of the Atomic Energy Commission, March 5, 1947." *International Organization* 1, no. 2: 395–409.

Guarino, Douglas P. 2012. "US Official Rejects Call For International Nuclear Security Standards." *Global Security Newswire*, May 1. http://www.nti.org/gsn/article/us-official-rejects-call-international-nuclear-security-standards/.

Gummett, Philip. 1981. "From NPT to INFCE: Development in Thinking about Nuclear Non-Proliferation." *International Affairs* 57, no. 4: 549–67.

Guzman, Andrew T., and Jennifer Landsidle. 2008. "The Myth of International Delegation." Berkeley Program in Law and Economics, Working Paper Series. University of California, Berkeley. http://escholarship.org/uc/item/77j316zw.

Hafele, Wolf. 1974. "NPT Safeguards." In *Nuclear Proliferation Problems*, ed. Bhupendra Jasani, 142–50. Cambridge, MA: MIT Press.

Haggard, Stephan, and Marcus Noland. 2007. *Famine in North Korea: Markets, Aid, and Reform.* New York: Columbia University Press.

Harris, Richard. 2012. "Trauma, Not Radiation, Is Key Concern in Japan." *Morning Edition*, NPR, March 9. http://www.npr.org/2012/03/09/148227596/trauma-not-radiation-is-key-concern-in-japan.

Hathaway, Oona A. 2002. "Do Human Rights Treaties Make a Difference?" *Yale Law Review* 111:1935–2042.

Hawkins, Darren, and Wade Jacoby. 2008. "Agent Permeability, Principal Delegation and the European Court of Human Rights." *Review of International Organizations* 3, no. 1: 1–28.

Hawkins, Darren, David A. Lake, Daniel Nielson, and Michael J. Tierney. 2006a. *Delegation and Agency in International Organizations.* Cambridge: Cambridge University Press.

———. 2006b. "Delegation under Anarchy: States, International Organizations, and Principal-Agent Theory." In *Delegation and Agency in International Organizations*, ed. Darren Hawkins, David A. Lake, Daniel Nielson, and Michael J. Tierney, 3–38. Cambridge: Cambridge University Press.

Hecht, Gabrielle. 2006. "Negotiating Global Nuclearities: Apartheid, Decolonization, and the Cold War in the Making of the IAEA." *Osiris* 21, no. 1: 25–48.

Heinonen, Olli. 2011. "North Korea's Nuclear Enrichment: Capabilities and Consequences." *38 North*, June 22. http://38north.org/2011/06/heinonen062211/.

Herken, Gregg. 1980. "'A Most Deadly Illusion': The Atomic Secret and American Nuclear Weapons Policy, 1945–1950." *Pacific Historical Review* 49, no. 1: 51–76.

Hewlett, Richard G. 1985. "From Proposal to Program." In *Atoms for Peace: An Analysis after Thirty Years*, ed. Joseph F. Pilat, Robert E. Pendley and Charles K. Ebinger, 25–33. Boulder, CO: Westview Press.

Hibbs, Mark. 2014. "Deconstructing Sherman on PMD." *Arms Control Wonk*, February 19. http://hibbs.armscontrolwonk.com/archive/2527/deconstructing-sherman-on-pmd.

Hibbs, Mark, and Andreas Persbo. 2009. "The ElBaradei Legacy." *Bulletin of the Atomic Scientists* 65, no. 5 (September 2): 10–23. doi:10.2968/065005002.

———. 2014. "Handling Iran's Weaponization File." *Arms Control Wonk*, January 20. http://hibbs.armscontrolwonk.com/archive/2481/handling-irans-weaponization.

Hirdman, Sven, ed. 1972. *The Near-Nuclear Countries and the NPT*. Stockholm: Stockholm International Peace Research Institute.

Holt, Mark, Richard J. Campbell, and Mary Beth Nikitin. 2012. *Fukushima Nuclear Disaster*, January 18. Washington, DC: Congressional Research Service. http://fas.org/sgp/crs/nuke/R41694.pdf.

Holum, John D. 1994. "Statement of John D. Holum, Director of the U.S. Arms Control and Disarmament Agency, on Nuclear Test Ban Talks." *Congressional Record* 40, no. 1, http://www.gpo.gov/fdsys/pkg/CREC-1994–01–25/html/CREC -1994-01-25-pt1-PgS64.ht m.

Hooghe, Liesbet, and Gary Marks. 2005. "Calculation, Community and Cues Public Opinion on European Integration." *European Union Politics* 6, no. 4: 419–43.

Hooper, Richard. 1999. "The IAEA's Additional Protocol." *Disarmament Forum* 3.

———. 2003. "The Changing Nature of Safeguards." *IAEA Bulletin*, June, 7–11.

Hooper, Rich, and Tom Shea. 2007. "A Panel Discussion with Current and Former SAGSI Representatives, PNNL-SA-56894: Jim Casterton (Canada), Dieter Tillwick (South Africa), Roger Howsley (United Kingdom), Kaoru Naito (Japan), and Jim Tape (United States)." PNNL Foundations of International Safeguards Project, Tuscon, AZ. http://cgs.pnnl.gov/fois/doclib/5.0Tucsontranscript.pdf.

Huntington, Samuel P. 1991. *The Third Wave: Democratization in the Late Twentieth Century*. Norman: University of Oklahoma Press.

Hurd, Ian. 2007. *After Anarchy: Legitimacy and Power in the United Nations Security Council*. Princeton, NJ: Princeton University Press.

———. 2008a. "Myths of Membership: The Politics of Legitimation in UN Security Council Reform." *Global Governance* 14, no. 2: 199–217.

———. 2008b. "Theories and Tests of International Authority." In *The UN Security Council and the Politics of International Authority*, ed. Bruce Cronin and Ian Hurd, 23–39. New York: Routledge.

Hurrell, Andrew. 2005. "Legitimacy and the Use of Force: Can the Circle Be Squared?" *Review of International Studies* 31 (December): 15–32.

IAEA. 1957. Statute of the IAEA. Vienna: International Atomic Energy Agency.

———. 1960. INFCIRC/18: The Agency's Health and Safety Measures. Vienna: International Atomic Energy Agency.

———. 1972a. INFCIRC/153 (Rev.): The Structure and Content of Agreements between the Agency and States Required in Connection with the Treaty on the Non-Proliferation of Nuclear Weapons. Vienna: International Atomic Energy Agency.

————. 1972b. INFCIRC/209: Communication Received from Members Regarding the Export of Nuclear Material and of Certain Categories of Equipment and Other Material. Vienna: International Atomic Energy Agency.

————.1976a. The Agency's Accounts for 1975. Vienna: International Atomic Energy Agency.

————. 1976b. INFCIRC/18/Rev.1: The Agency's Health and Safety Measures. Vienna: International Atomic Energy Agency.

————. 1979. INFCIRC/267: The Revised Guiding Principles and General Operating Rules to Govern the Provision of Technical Assistance by the Agency. Vienna: International Atomic Energy Agency.

————. 1980. INFCIRC/274/Rev.1: The Convention on the Physical Protection of Nuclear Material. Vienna: International Atomic Energy Agency.

————. 1986a. INFCIRC/336: Convention on Assistance in the Case of a Nuclear Accident or Radiological Emergency. Vienna: International Atomic Energy Agency.

————. 1986b. INFCIRC/335: Convention on Early Notification of a Nuclear Accident. Vienna: International Atomic Energy Agency.

————. 1990a. Technical Cooperation Report for 1990 (GC(35)/INF/294). Vienna: IAEA.

————. 1990b. Thirty Fourth (1990) Regular Session Record of the 326th Plenary Meeting (GC/34/OR.326). General Conference. Vienna: International Atomic Energy Agency.

————. 1991. Resolution Adopted during the 342nd Plenary Meeting on 20 September 1991: Strengthening of the Agency's Main Activities. *General Conference*. Vienna: International Atomic Energy Agency.

————. 1992a. *INSAG-7: The Chernobyl Accident: Updating of INSAG-1*. Safety Series Safety Reports. Vienna: International Atomic Energy Agency.

————. 1992b. Thirty-Fifth (1991) Regular Session: Record of the 333rd Plenary Meeting, Statement by the Director General (GC/35/OR.333). General Conference. Vienna: International Atomic Energy Agency.

————. 1995. GC(39)/17: Strengthening the Effectiveness and Improving the Efficiency of the Safeguards System: Report by the Director General to the General Conference. Vienna: International Atomic Energy Agency.

————. 1996. Resolutions Adopted by the General Conference: Amendment of Article VI of the Statute. General Conference. Vienna: International Atomic Energy Agency.

————. 1997a. Letter dated 6 October 1997 from the Director General of the International Atomic Energy Agency to the Secretary-General (Security Council S/1997/779). Vienna: International Atomic Energy Agency.

————. 1997b. INFCIRC/540 (Corr.): Model Protocol Additional to the Agreement(s) between State(s) and the International Atomic Energy Agency for the Application of Safeguards. Vienna: International Atomic Energy Agency.

———. 1998. The Evolution of IAEA Safeguards. Vienna: International Atomic Energy Agency.

———. 1999a. Report of the External Auditor on the Agency's accounts for 1999. Board of Governors. Vienna: International Atomic Energy Agency.

———. 1999b. Technical Co-operation Report for 1998. Vienna: International Atomic Energy Agency.

———. 2002. IAEA Iraq Action Team Chronology of Main Events. Vienna: International Atomic Energy Agency.

———. 2003. GOV/2003/40: Implementation of the NPT Safeguards Agreement in the Islamic Republic of Iran. Vienna: International Atomic Energy Agency.

———. 2004. GOV/2004/11: Implementation of the NPT Safeguards in the Islamic Republic of Iran. Vienna: International Atomic Energy Agency.

———. 2006. Nuclear Security—Measures to Protect against Nuclear Terrorism (GOV/2006/46-GC(50)/13). Vienna: International Atomic Energy Agency.

———. 2007. "Fact Sheet on DPRK Nuclear Safeguards." *In Focus: IAEA and DPRK,* http://www.iaea.org/NewsCenter/Focus/IaeaDprk/fact_sheet_may2003 .shtml.

———. 2011a. Amendment of Article VI of the Statute: Decision. General Conference. Vienna: International Atomic Energy Agency.

———. 2011b. Draft IAEA Action Plan on Nuclear Safety: Report by the Director General (GOV/2011/59-GC(55)/14). Vienna: International Atomic Energy Agency.

———. 2011c. GOV/2011/65: Implementation of the NPT Safeguards Agreement and Relevant Provisions of Security Council Resolutions in the Islamic Republic of Iran. Vienna: International Atomic Energy Agency.

———. 2012a. "Experts Consider Fukushima Accident Causes (Statement of IAEA Deputy Director General, Department of Nuclear Safety and Security, Denis Flory)." March 19, from http://www.iaea.org/newscenter/news/2012/lessons -learned.html.

———. 2012b. IAEA Nuclear Security Achievements 2002–2011. Vienna: International Atomic Energy Agency.

———. 2013a. INFCIRC/856: Communication Dated 28 November 2013 Received from the Permanent Mission of the Islamic Republic of Iran to the Agency concerning the Text of the Joint Plan of Action. Vienna: International Atomic Energy Agency.

———. 2013b. Ministerial Declaration of International Conference on Nuclear Security: Enhancing Global Efforts. Vienna: International Atomic Energy Agency.

Iansiti, Enzo. 1976. "Safety Codes and Guides for Nuclear Power Plants." *IAEA Bulletin.* Vienna: International Atomic Energy Agency.

Ikenberry, G. John. 2001. *After Victory: Institutions, Strategic Restraint, and the Rebuilding of Order after Major Wars.* Princeton, NJ: Princeton University Press.

Imber, Mark F. 1989. *The USA, ILO, UNESCO and IAEA: Politicization and Withdrawal in the Specialized Agencies.* New York: St. Martin's Press.

International Energy Associates. 1984. "Review of the Negotiating History of the IAEA Safeguards Document Infcirc/153." *The Arms Control and Disarmament Agency under Contract No. AC2NCI03.* Washington, DC: International Energy Associates.

Jackson, Robert H. 1987. "Quasi-States, Dual Regimes, and Neoclassical Theory: International Jurisprudence and the Third World." *International Organization* 41, no. 4: 519–49.

Japan, Government of. 2011a. Executive Summary of the Interim Report (December 26). Tokyo, Investigation Committee on the Accident at Fukushima Nuclear Power Stations of Tokyo Electric Power Company. http://www.cas.go.jp/jp/seisaku/icanps/eng/120224SummaryEng.pdf.

———. 2011b. "Report of the Japanese Government to the IAEA Ministerial Conference on Nuclear Safety." Tokyo: Nuclear Emergency Response Headquarters.

Jenkins, Brian Michael. 1975. "International Terrorism: A New Mode of Conflict." In *International Terrorism and World Security*, ed. David Carlton and Caro Schaerf. London: Croom Helm.

Jensen, Lloyd. 1974. *Return from the Nuclear Brink.* Lexington, MA: Lexington Books.

Jentleson, Bruce W., and Christopher A. Whytock. 2005–6. "Who 'Won' Libya? The Force-Diplomacy Debate and Its Implications for Theory and Policy." *International Security* 30, no. 3: 47–86.

Jervis, Robert. 1978. "Cooperation under the Security Dilemma." *World Politics* 30, no. 2: 167–214.

Jo, Dong-Joon, and Erik Gartzke. 2007. "Determinants of Nuclear Weapons Proliferation." *Journal of Conflict Resolution* 51, no. 1: 167–94.

Johnson, Chalmers. 1982. *MITI and the Japanese Miracle.* Stanford, CA: Stanford University Press.

Johnstone, Ian. 2008a. "Law-Making through the Operational Activities of International Organizations." *George Washington International Law Review* 40:87–122.

———. 2008b. "Legislation and Adjudication in the UN Security Council: Bringing Down the Deliberative Deficit." *American Journal of International Law* 102, no. 2 (April): 275–308.

Jönsson, Christer, and Staffan Bolin. 1988. "The Role of the International Atomic Energy Agency in the International Politics of Atomic Energy." In *Politics in the United Nations System*, ed. L. S. Finklestein. Durham, NC: Duke University Press.

Joyner, Daniel H. 2011–12. "The Security Council as a Legal Hegemon." *Georgetown Journal of International Law* 43:225–57.

Joyner, Daniel H., Christopher A. Ford, and Andreas Persbo. 2012. "Roundtable on Iran and the bomb: The legal standards of the IAEA." *Bulletin of the Atomic Scientists*, December 12. http://thebulletin.org/iran-and-bomb-legal-standards -iaea-0.

Kahler, Miles. 2001. *Leadership Selection in the Major Multilaterals*. Washington, DC: Institute for International Economics.

Kahler, Miles, and David A. Lake. 2003. "Globalization and Governance." In *Governance in a Global Economy: Political Authority in Transition*, ed. Miles Kahler and David A. Lake, 1–32. Princeton, NJ: Princeton University Press.

Kahn, Herman. 1960. *On Thermonuclear War*. Princeton, NJ: Princeton University Press.

Kang, Jungmin, Peter Hayes, Li Bin, Tastujiro Suzuki, and Richard Tanter. 2005. "South Korea's Nuclear Surprise." *Bulletin of the Atomic Scientists* 61, no. 1: 40–49.

Kaplan, Fred. 1983. *The Wizards of Armageddon*. Stanford, CA: Stanford University Press.

Katzenstein, Peter J. 1996. "Introduction: Alternative Perspectives on National Security." *The Culture of National Security: Norms and Identity in World Politics*, ed. Peter J. Katzenstein, 1–32. New York: Columbia University Press.

Kennan, George Frost. 1947. "The sources of Soviet conduct." *Foreign Affairs*. http://www.foreignaffairs.com/articles/23331/x/the-sources-of-soviet-conduct.

Kennedy, John F. 1963. News Conference 52. Boston, MA: John F. Kennedy Presidential Library and Museum.

Kennedy, Richard T. 1997. "The Period 1980–1993." In *International Atomic Energy Agency: Personal Reflections*, ed. Hans Blix, 115–26. Vienna: International Atomic Energy Agency. http://www-pub.iaea.org/MTCD/publications/ PDF/Pub1033_web.pdf.

Keohane, Robert O. 1984. *After Hegemony: Cooperation and Discord in the World Political Economy*. Princeton, NJ: Princeton University Press.

Kerr, Paul. 2007. "ElBaradei: IAEA Budget Problems Dangerous." *Arms Control Today*, July/August.

Kerr, Paul, and Miles A. Pomper. 2005. "Tackling the Nuclear Dilemma: An Interview with IAEA Director-General Mohamed ElBaradei." *Arms Control Today*, February 4. http://www.armscontrol.org/act/2005_03/elbaradei.

Khan, Munir Ahmad. 1997. "Major Milestones in the Development of the IAEA." In *International Atomic Energy Agency: Personal Reflections*, ed. Hans Blix, 297–311. Vienna: International Atomic Energy Agency. http://www-pub .iaea.org/MTCD/publications/PDF/Pub1033_web.pdf.

Kiewiet, D. Roderick, and Mathew D. McCubbins. 1991. *The Logic of Delegation*. Chicago: University of Chicago Press.

Kindleberger, Charles P. 1973. *The World in Depression, 1919–1939*. Berkeley: University of California Press.

Kirk, Roger. 1997. "The Suspension of US Participation in the IAEA: 1982–1983." In *International Atomic Energy Agency: Personal Reflections*, ed. Hans Blix, 93–106. Vienna, International Atomic Energy Agency. http://www-pub.iaea .org/MTCD/publications/PDF/Pub1033_web.pdf.

Kislyak, Sergey I. 1985. "A Soviet Perspective on the Future of Nonproliferation." In *The Nuclear Suppliers and Nonproliferation*, ed. Rodney W. Jones, Cesare Merlini, Joseph F. Pilat, and William C. Potter, 211–18. Lexington, MA: Lexington Books.

Kolodziej, Edward A. 1992. "Renaissance in Security Studies? Caveat Lector!" *International Studies Quarterly* 36, no. 4: 421–38.

Koppell, Jonathan G. S. 2008. "Global Governance Organizations: Legitimacy and Authority in Conflict." *Journal of Public Administration Research and Theory* 18:177–203.

Koremenos, Barbara. 2001. "Loosening the Ties That Bind: A Learning Model of Agreement Flexibility." *International Organization* 55, no. 2: 289–325.

———. 2008. "When, What, and Why Do States Choose to Delegate." *Law and Contemporary Problems* 71, no. 1: 151–92.

Koremenos, Barbara, Charles Lipson, and Duncan Snidal. 2001. "The Rational Design of International Institutions." *International Organization* 55, no. 4: 761–99.

Krasner, Stephen D. 1991. "Global Communications and National Power." *World Politics* 43:336–66.

———. 1999. *Sovereignty: Organized Hypocrisy*. Princeton, NJ: Princeton University Press.

Kratzer, Myron, Rich Hooper, and Norman Wulf. 2005. *A Retrospective of INFCIRCs 153 and 540: A Panel Discussion with Myron Kratzer, Rich Hooper, and Ambassador Norm Wulf, PNNL-SA-48940*. PNNL Foundations of International Safeguards Project, Santa Fe, NM.

Krauthammer, Charles. 1990–91. "The Unipolar Moment." *Foreign Affairs* 70, no. 1: 23–33.

Kristensen, Hans M. 2014. "US Nuclear Weapons Stockpile Number Declassified: Only 309 Warheads Cut by Obama Administration." *FAS Strategic Security Blog*, April 29. http://fas.org/blogs/security/2014/04/nuclearstockpile/.

Kristensen, Hans M., and Joshua Handler. 1996. "The USA and Counterproliferation." *Security Dialogue* 27, no. 4.

Kroenig, Matthew. 2009a. "Exporting the Bomb: Why States Provide Sensitive Nuclear Assistance." *American Political Science Review* 103, no. 1: 113–34.

———. 2009b. "Importing the Bomb: Sensitive Nuclear Assistance and Nuclear Proliferation." *Journal of Conflict Resolution* 53, no. 2: 161–80.

Kydd, Andrew. 2001. "Trust Building, Trust Breaking: The Dilemma of NATO Enlargement." *International Organization* 55, no. 4: 801–28.

Lake, David A. 2009. *Hierarchy in International Relations*. Ithaca, NY: Cornell University Press.

Lake, David A., and Mathew D. McCubbins. 2006. "The Logic of Delegation to International Organizations." In *Delegation and Agency in International Organizations*, ed. Darren Hawkins, David A. Lake, Daniel Nielson, and Michael J. Tierney, 341–68. Cambridge: Cambridge University Press.

Lake, David A., and Robert Powell. 1999. "International Relations: A Strategic-Choice Approach." *Strategic Choice and International Relations*, ed. David A. Lake and Robert Powell, 3–38. Princeton, NJ: Princeton University Press.

Lavigne, Robert, Philipp Maier, and Eric Santor. 2009. "Renewing IMF Surveillance: Transparency, Accountability, and Independence." *Review of International Organizations* 4, no. 1: 29–46.

Layne, Christopher. 2006. "The Unipolar Illusion Revisited." *International Security* 31, no. 2: 7–41.

Le Guelte, Georges. 1997. "The IAEA Board of Governors during the Years 1978–1982." In *International Atomic Energy Agency: Personal Reflections*, ed. Hans Blix, 79–92. Vienna: International Atomic Energy Agency. http://www-pub .iaea.org/MTCD/publications/PDF/Pub1033_web.pdf.

Ledgerwood, Judy L. 1994. "UN Peacekeeping Missions: The Lessons from Cambodia." *Asia Pacific Issues*, no. 11 (March): 1–10.

Leslie, Russell, John Carlson, and Annette Berriman. 2007. "Ensuring Effective Safeguards Coverage of States with Small Quantities Protocols." Australian Government Department of Foreign Affairs and Trade.

Levi, Margaret. 1988. *Of Rule and Revenue*. Berkeley: University of California Press.

Levi, Michael. 2007. *On Nuclear Terrorism*. Cambridge, MA: Harvard University Press.

Lewis, Charles, and Mark Reading-Smith. 2008. "False Pretenses." *Center for Public Integrity*, January 23. http://www.iwatchnews.org/2008/01/23/5641/false -pretenses.

Lewis, Jeffrey. 2011. "The Case against ElBaradei." *Arms Control Wonk*, September 1, http://lewis.armscontrolwonk.com/archive/4427/the-case-against-elbar adei.

Liberman, Peter. 2001. "The Rise and Fall of the South African Bomb." *International Security* 26, no. 2: 43–86.

Linzer, Dafna. 2005. "Iran Is Judged 10 Years from Nuclear Bomb." *Washington Post*, August 2, A01.

Lipset, Seymour Martin. 1981. *Political Man: The Social Bases of Politics*. 1959, repr. Baltimore: Johns Hopkins University Press.

Lochbaum, David. 2012. "Nuclear 101: Nuclear Safety." Presentation to the seminar series *Project on Managing the Atom*, April 25, Belfer Center for Science and International Affairs.

Loeb, Benjamin S. 1991. "The Limited Test Ban Treaty." In *The Politics of Arms Control Treaty Ratification*, ed. Michael Krepon and Dan Caldwell, 167–227. New York: St. Martin's Press.

Loosch, Reinhard. 1997. "The Emergence of the Group of 77 as a Major Player in the Board of Governors." In *International Atomic Energy Agency: Personal Reflections*, ed. Hans Blix, 63–78. Vienna: International Atomic Energy Agency. http://www-pub.iaea.org/MTCD/publications/PDF/Pub1033_web.pdf.

Losquadro, Michael. 2007. "The 30th Anniversary of the US Support Program to IAEA Safeguards." Presentation to the USSP Annual Review Meeting. http://www.slideserve.com/obert/the-30th-anniversary-of-the-u-s-support-program-to-iaea-safeguards.

Lupia, Arthur, and Mathew D. McCubbins. 1994. "Designing Bureaucratic Accountability." *Law and Contemporary Problems* 57, no. 1: 91–126.

Lynch, Colum. 2005. "UN Faces More Accusations of Sexual Misconduct." *Washington Post*, March 13, A22.

Lyne, Mona, Daniel Nielson, and Michael J. Tierney. 2006. "Who Delegates? Alternative Models of Principals in Development Aid." In *Delegation and Agency in International Organizations*, ed. Darren Hawkins, David A. Lake, Daniel Nielson, and Michael J. Tierney, 41–76. Cambridge: Cambridge University Press.

Mackby, Jennifer, and Paul Cornish, eds. 2008. *US–UK Nuclear Cooperation after 50 Years*. Washington, DC: Center for Strategic and International Studies.

Manzione, Lara L. 2002. "Multinational Investment in the Space Station: An Outer Space Model for International Cooperation?" *American University International Law Review* 18, no. 2: 507–35.

March, James G., and Johan P. Olsen. 1999. "The Institutional Dynamics of International Political Orders." In *Exploration and Contestation in the Study of World Politics*, ed. Peter J. Katzenstein, Robert O. Keohane, and Stephen D. Krasner, 303–29. Cambridge, MA: MIT Press.

Mark, Clyde R. 2005. *Libya*. Washington, DC: Congressional Research Service.

Martin, Lisa L. 2003. "International Institutions in the New Global Economy." In *The International Library of Writings on the New Global Economy*, ed. Helen V. Milner. Cheltenham, UK: Edward Elgar Publishing.

———. 2006. "Distribution, Information, and Delegation to International Organizations: The Case of IMF Conditionality." In *Delegation and Agency in International Organizations*, ed. Darren Hawkins, David A. Lake, Daniel Nielson, and Michael J. Tierney, 140–64. Cambridge: Cambridge University Press.

Martinez, J. Michael. 2002. "The Carter Administration and the Evolution of Nuclear Nonproliferation Policy, 1977–1981." *Journal of Policy History* 14, no. 3: 261–92.

Matthews, Carrie, Laura Rockwood, and Rich Hooper. 2009. "The Path towards Strengthened Safeguards: Verification Challenges of the 90's with Jacques Baute, Rich Hooper, IAEA (Retired), and Dmitri Perrico." Presentation PNNL-SA-75433. PNNL Foundations of International Safeguards Project, Vienna, Austria.

May, Michael. 2008. "Nuclear Forensics: Role, State of the Art, and Program Needs." Washington, DC: Joint Working Group of the American Physical Society and the American Association for the Advancement of Science.

Mayr, Walter. 2006. "Chernobyl's Aftermath: The Pompeii of the Nuclear Age (Part III)." *Spiegel Online*, April 17. http://www.spiegel.de/international/spiegel/0,15 18,411684-3,00.html.

McBride, James Hubert. 1967. *The Test Ban Treaty: Military, Technological, and Political Implications*. Chicago: Henry Regnery.

McCubbins, Mathew, Roger Noll, and Barry Weingast. 1987. "Administrative Procedures as Instruments of Political Control." *Journal of Law, Economics and Organization* 3, no. 2: 243–77.

McCubbins, Mathew, and Thomas Schwartz. 1984. "Congressional Oversight Overlooked: Police Patrols versus Fire Alarms." *American Journal of Political Science* 28, no. 1: 165–79.

McKnight, Allan. 1971. *Atomic Safeguards: A Study in International Verification*. New York: United Nations Publications.

McNamara, Kathleen. 2010. "Constructing Authority in the European Union." *Who Governs the Globe?*, ed. Deborah Avant, Martha Finnemore, and Susan K. Sell, 153–80. Cambridge: Cambridge University Press.

Mearsheimer, John J. 1994. "The False Promise of International Institutions." *International Security* 19, no. 3: 5–49.

———. 2001. *The Tragedy of Great Power Politics*. New York: Norton.

Medalia, Jonathan. 1998. *Nuclear Weapons: Comprehensive Test Ban Treaty and Nuclear Testing* (CRS Issue Brief IB92099). Washington, DC: Congressional Research Service.

Meyer, John W., and Brian Rowan. 1977. "Institutionalized Organizations: Formal Structure as Myth and Ceremony." *American Journal of Sociology* 83, no. 2: 340–63.

Milanovic, Branko. 2003. "The Two Faces of Globalization: Against Globalization as We Know It." *World Development* 31, no. 4: 667–83.

Miller, Judith. 1981. "Disputes Growing in UN Atom Panel." *New York Times*, November 1. http://www.nytimes.com/1981/11/01/world/disputes-growing-in -un-atom-panel.html.

———. 2006. "Gadhafi's Leap of Faith." *Wall Street Journal*, May 17.

Miller, Judith, Stephen Engelberg, and William Broad. 2001. *Germs: Biological Weapons and America's Secret War*. New York: Simon & Schuster.

Milne, Roger. 1987. "Disastrous Plans for Nuclear Accidents." *New Scientist* 114, no. 1557: 54–57.

Mitchell, Sara McLaughlin, and Emilia Justyna Powell. 2011. *Domestic Law Goes Global: Legal Traditions and International Courts*. Cambridge: Cambridge University Press.

Mitrany, David. 1948. "The Functional Approach to World Organization." *International Affairs* 24, no. 3: 350–63.

Mjøs, Ole Danbolt. 2005. *Presentation Speech*. Nobel Peace Prize Award Ceremony, December 10, Oslo, Norway. http://www.nobelprize.org/nobel_prizes/peace/ laureates/2005/presentation-speech.html.

Moravcsik, Andrew. 2000. "The Origins of Human Rights Regimes: Democratic Delegation in Postwar Europe." *International Organization* 54, no. 2: 217–52.

Morgan, Patrick M. 2003. *Deterrence Now.* Cambridge: Cambridge University Press.

Morgenthau, Hans J. 1985. *Politics among Nations.* Boston: McGraw-Hill.

Nacht, Michael. 1981. "The Future Unlike the Past: Nuclear Proliferation and American Security Policy." *International Organization* 35, no. 1: 193–212.

Noland, Marcus. 2008. "The (Non)Impact of UN Sanctions on North Korea." Peterson Institute for International Economics Working Paper Series. Washington, DC.

NRC. 2011. "Recommendations for Enhancing Reactor Safety in the 21st Century." Washington, DC: US Nuclear Regulatory Commission.

Obama, Barak. 2009. "Remarks in Hradčany Square, Prague, Czech Republic on 5 April." Embassy of the United States, Prague, Czech Republic. http://prague .usembassy.gov/obama.html.

O'Donnell, Guillermo A. 1973. *Modernization and Bureaucratic-Authoritarianism.* Berkeley: University of California Berkeley.

Ølgaard, P. L. 1969. "The Soviet-American Draft Non-Proliferation Treaty: Will It Work? In *1st Pugwash Symposium: Preventing the Spread of Nuclear Weapons,* ed. C. F. Barnaby, 213–28. London: Souvenir Press.

Olson, Mancur, and Richard Zeckhauser. 1966. "An Economic Theory of Alliances." *Review of Economics and Statistics* 48, no. 3: 266–79.

OSD. 1997. "Proliferation: Threat and Response." Washington, DC: Office of the Secretary of Defense, US Department of Defense.

Pabian, Frank V. 1995. "South Africa's Nuclear Weapon Program: Lessons for US Nonproliferation Policy." *Nonproliferation Review,* Fall: 1–19.

Pastinen, Ilkka. 1977. "Safeguards and Non-Proliferation." *IAEA Bulletin.* Vienna: International Atomic Energy Agency. http://www.iaea.org/Publications/Maga zines/Bulletin/Bull194/19403 502039.pdf.

Patterson, Morehead. 1956. "Progress Report on Atoms-for-Peace Program." *US Department of State Bulletin* 34:8.

Patterson, Walt. 1987. "Nuclear Watchdog Finds Its Role." *New Scientist,* 50–53.

Peet, Richard. 2003. *Unholy Trinity: The IMF, World Bank and WTO.* New York: Zed Books.

Pendley, Robert E., Lawrence Scheinman, and Richard W. Butler. 1975. "International Safeguarding as Institutionalized Collective Behavior." *International Organization* 29, no. 3: 585–616.

Peterson, Cass. 1989. "A Decade Later, TMI's Legacy Is Mistrust." *Washington Post,* March 28. A01.

Pinkston, Daniel A. 2004. "South Korea's Nuclear Experiments." *CNS Research Story,* November 9. http://cns.miis.edu/stories/041109.htm.

Pollack, Mark A. 1997. "Delegation, Agency, and Agenda Setting in the European Community." *International Organization* 51, no. 1: 99–134.

Pollack, Mark A., and Gregory C. Shaffer. 2009. *When Cooperation Fails: The International Law and Politics of Genetically Modified Foods.* New York: Oxford University Press.

Portes, Alejandro. 1998. "On the Sociology of National Development: Theories and Issues." In *Development and Underdevelopment: The Political Economy of Global Inequality,* ed. Mitchell A. Seligson and John T. Passe-Smith, 241–48. Boulder, CO: Lynne Rienner.

Posen, Barry R., and Stephen Van Evera. 1983. "Defense Policy and the Reagan Administration: Departure from Containment." *International Security* 8, no. 1: 3–45.

Potter, William C. 1985. U.S.–Soviet Cooperative Measures for Nonproliferation. In *The Nuclear Suppliers and Nonproliferation,* ed. Rodney W. Jones, Cesare Merlini, Joseph F. Pilat, and William C. Potter, 9–16. Lexington, MA: Lexington Books.

Potter, William C., and Gaukhar Mukhatzhanova. 2012. *Nuclear Politics and the Non-Aligned Movement.* New York: International Institute for Strategic Studies.

Powell, Colin L. 2003. "Remarks to the United Nations Security Council," February 5, New York City. http://www.gwu.edu/~nsarchiv/NSAEBB/NSAEBB80/new/doc%2023/Remarks%20to%20the%20United%20Nations%20Security%20Council.htm.

Powell, Robert. 1990. *Nuclear Deterrence Theory: The Search for Credibility.* Cambridge: Cambridge University Press.

———. 2003. "Nuclear Deterrence Theory, Nuclear Proliferation, and National Missile Defense." *International Security* 27, no. 4: 86–118.

Power, Paul F. 1986. "The Mixed State of Non-Proliferation: The NPT Review Conference and Beyond." *International Affairs* 62, no. 3: 477–91.

Prawitz, Jan. 1969. "Safeguards and Related Arms Control Problems." In *1st Pugwash Symposium: Preventing the Spread of Nuclear Weapons,* ed. C. F. Barnaby, 113–26. London: Souvenir Press.

Pritchard, Charles L. 2007. *Failed Diplomacy: The Tragic Story of How North Korea Got the Bomb.* Washington, DC: Brookings Institution Press.

Prosser, Andrew. 2004. "Considering China as a Potential Member of the Nuclear Suppliers Group." Washington, DC: Center for Defense Information.

Purkitt, Helen E., and Stephen F. Burgess. 2002. "South Africa's Nuclear Decisions." *International Security* 27, no. 1: 186–94.

Quester, George H. 1970. "The Nuclear Nonproliferation Treaty and the International Atomic Energy Agency." *International Organization* 24, no. 2: 163–82.

Quihillalt, Oscar A., and Carlos L. Büchler. 1997. "The Fifth General Conference of the IAEA." In *International Atomic Energy Agency: Personal Reflections,* ed. Hans Blix, 53–62. Vienna: International Atomic Energy Agency. http://www-pub.iaea.org/MTCD/publications/PDF/Pub1033_web.pdf.

Rathjens, George. 1995. "Rethinking Nuclear Proliferation." In *Weapons Proliferation in the 1990s*, ed. Brad Roberts, 93–105. Cambridge, MA: CSIS and MIT Press.

Rauchhaus, Robert, Matthew Kroenig, and Erik Gartzke, eds. 2011. *Causes and Consequences of Nuclear Proliferation*. New York: Routledge.

Reagan, Ronald. 1983. "Remarks at the Annual Convention of the National Association of Evangelicals," March 8, Orlando, Florida. http://www.reagan.utexas.edu/archives/speeches/1983/30883b.htm.

Rector, Chad. 2009. *Federations: The Political Dynamics of Cooperation*. Ithaca, NY: Cornell University Press.

Redden, Kaleb J. 2003. "Inspecting the Inspectorate: A Look at Financial and Political Support for the IAEA." *The Nonproliferation Review*, Fall–Winter: 34–47.

Reiss, Mitchell. 1995. *Bridled Ambition*. Washington DC: Woodrow Wilson Center Press.

Richelson, Jeffrey T. 2004. "Iraq and Weapons of Mass Destruction," National Security Archive Electronic Briefing Book No. 80. http://www2.gwu.edu/~ns archiv/NSAEBB/NSAEBB80/.

———. 2006. "U.S. Intelligence and the South African Bomb," National Security Archive Electronic Briefing Book No. 181. http://www2.gwu.edu/~nsarchiv/NSAEBB/NSAEBB181/index.htm.

Risse, Thomas. 2000. "'Let's Argue!' Communicative Action in World Politics." *International Organization* 54, no. 1: 1–39.

Rockwood, Laura. 2002. "The IAEA's Strengthened Safeguards System." *Journal of Conflict and Security Law* 7, no. 1: 123–36.

Rogowski, Ronald. 1999. "Institutions as Constraints in Strategic Choice." In *Strategic Choice and International Relations*, ed. David A. Lake and Robert Powell, 115–36. Princeton, NJ: Princeton University Press.

Roosevelt, Franklin D., and Winston S. Churchill. 1943. Articles of Agreement Governing Collaboration between the Authorities of the USA and the UK in the Matter of Tube Alloys ("Quebec Agreement"), August 19. The Citadel, Quebec, http://www.atomicarchive.com/Docs/ManhattanProject/Quebec.shtml.

Rosand, Eric. 2004. "The Security Council as 'Global Legislator': Ultra Vires or Ultra Innovative?" *Fordham International Law Journal* 28, no. 3: 542–90.

Rosen, Steven. 1967. "Proliferation Treaty Controls and the IAEA." *Journal of Conflict Resolution* 11, no. 2: 168–75.

Rosenberg, Barbara Hatch. 2004. "The Cupboard Was Bare." *Los Angeles Times*, February 1. http://articles.latimes.com/2004/feb/01/opinion/op-rosenberg1.

Rosenthal, Michael D., Leslie Fishbone, Linda S. Gallini, Allan Krass, Myron Kratzer, Jonathan Sanborn, Barclay Ward, and Norman Wulf. 2013. "Deterring Nuclear Proliferation: The Importance of IAEA Safeguards." Brookhaven Science Associates. http://www.bnl.gov/gars/NNS/IAEAtextbook.php.

Rosenthal, Michael D., Lisa L. Saum-Manning, and Frank Houck. 2010. "Review of the Negotiation of the Model Protocol Additional to the Agreement(s) between State(s) and the International Atomic Energy Agency for the Application of Safeguards (INFCIRC/540 (Corrected))," vol. 2. Upton, NY: Brookhaven National Laboratory. http://www.bnl.gov/isd/documents/71014.pdf.

Rosenthal, Michael D., Lisa L. Saum-Manning, Frank Houck, and George Anzelon. 2010. "Review of the Negotiation of the Model Protocol Additional to the Agreement(s) between State(s) and the International Atomic Energy Agency for the Application of Safeguards (INFCIRC/540 (Corrected))," vol. 1. Upton, NY, Brookhaven National Laboratory.

Rostow, Walt W. 1960. *The Stages of Economic Growth: A Non-Communist Manifesto.* Cambridge: Cambridge University Press.

Royden, Alexa. 2008. "Legitimacy and International Public Authority: The Evolution of Iaea Safeguards." PhD diss., University of St. Andrews.

Rublee, Maria Rost. 2009. *Nonproliferation Norms: Why States Choose Nuclear Restraint.* Athens: University of Georgia Press.

Russert, Tim. 2003. Interview with Vice President Dick Cheney. *NBC News' Meet the Press*, March 16. https://www.mtholyoke.edu/acad/intrel/bush/cheneymeet thepress.htm.

Rycroft, Matthew. 2002. "Memo to [Foreign Policy Advisor] David Manning: Iraq: Prime Minister's Meeting, July 23." London. As originally reported in the *Sunday Times*, May1, 2005. http://downingstreetmemo.com/memotext.html.

Sagan, Scott D. 1996–97. "Why Do States Build Nuclear Weapons?" *International Security* 21, no. 3: 54–86.

———. 2002. "More Will Be Worse." In *The Spread of Nuclear Weapons: A Debate Renewed*, ed. Kenneth N. Waltz and Scott D. Sagan, 47–92. New York: Norton.

———. 2011. "The Causes of Nuclear Weapons Proliferation." *Annual Review of Political Science* 14:225–44.

Saikal, Amin. 2002. "The Coercive Disarmament of Iraq." In *Biological Warfare and Disarmament: New Problems/New Perspectives*, ed. Susan Wright, 265–83. Lanham, MD: Rowman and Littlefield Publishers.

Saleem, Farrukh. 2001. "War Americana." October 28. http://www.jang.com.pk/thenews/columnists/furrukh/furrukh16.htm.

Sanger, David E. 2004. "The Khan Network." Paper presented at the Conference on South Asia and the Nuclear Future, June 4–5, Stanford University, Stanford Institute for International Studies.

Scheinman, Lawrence. 1981. "Multinational Alternatives and Nuclear Nonproliferation." *International Organization* 35, no. 1: 77–102.

———. 1983. "An Evaluation of Non-Proliferation Policies: Retrospect and Prospect." *New York Law School Journal of International and Comparative Law* 4, no. 2: 355.

———. 1985. *The Nonproliferation Role of the International Atomic Energy Agency.* Washington, DC: Resources for the Future.

———. 1987. *The International Atomic Energy Agency and World Nuclear Order.* Washington, D.C.: Resources for the Future.

Schelling, Thomas C. 1960. *The Strategy of Conflict.* Cambridge, MA: Harvard University Press.

———. 1961. "Reciprocal Measures for Arms Stabilization." In *Arms Control, Disarmament, and National Security,* ed. Donald P. Brennan, 167–86. New York: George Braziller.

Schmidt, Fritz W. 1994. "The Zangger Committee: Its History and Future Role." *Nonproliferation Review* 2, no. 1: 38–44.

———. 1997. *The Role of the IAEA in Nuclear Export Controls.* Paper presented at the International Seminar on the Role of Export Controls in Nuclear Non-Proliferation, October 7–8, Vienna, Austria, Nuclear Suppliers Group.

Schneider, Christina J. 2011. "Weak States and Institutionalized Bargaining Power in International Organizations." *International Studies Quarterly* 55, no. 2: 331–55.

Schulte, Gregory L. 2009. DG ElBaradei Fuels the Budget Debate. USMISSION UNVIE VIENNA. Vienna.

———. 2010. "Strengthening the IAEA: How the Nuclear Watchdog Can Regain Its Bark." *Strategic Forum,* no. 253 (March): 1–6.

Schultz, Kenneth A. 1999. "Do Democratic Institutions Constrain or Inform? Contrasting Two Institutional Perspectives on Democracy and War." *International Organization* 53, no. 2: 233–66.

Scoblic, J. Peter. 2001. "Alive and Kicking: The Greatly Exaggerated Death of Nuclear Deterrence. A Response to Nina Tannenwald." *Ethics and International Affairs* 15, no. 1. http://www.carnegiecouncil.org/publications/journal/15_1/articles/487.html.

Shils, Edward. 1948. "The Failure of the United Nations Atomic Energy Commission: An Interpretation." *University of Chicago Law Review,* 855–76.

Shultz, George P., William J. Perry, Henry A. Kissinger, and Sam Nunn. 2007. "A World Free of Nuclear Weapons." *Wall Street Journal,* January 4. http://online.wsj.com/news/articles/SB116787515251566636.

Sigal, Leon V. 1998. *Disarming Strangers.* Princeton, NJ: Princeton University Press.

Simmons, Beth A., and Allison Danner. 2010. "Credible Commitments and the International Criminal Court." *International Organization* 64, no. 2: 225–56.

Sims, Jennifer E. 1990. *Icarus Restrained: An Intellectual History of Nuclear Arms Control, 1945–1960.* Boulder, CO: Westview Press.

Singer, J. David. 1987. "Reconstructing the Correlates of War Dataset on Military Capabilities of States, 1816–1985." *International Interactions* 14:115–32.

Smith, Terence. 1981. "US Frames Policy on Halting Spread of Nuclear Arms." *New York Times,* July 8. http://www.nytimes.com/1981/07/08/world/us-frames-policy-on-halting-spread-of-nuclear-arms.html.

Smyth, Henry DeWolf. 1945. *Atomic Energy for Military Purposes: The Official Report on the Development of the Atomic Bomb under the Auspices of the*

United States Government 1940–1945. Princeton, NJ: Princeton University Press.

Sole, Donald B. 1997. "Great Expectations: A Diplomat's Recollections of the Birth and Early Years of the IAEA." In *International Atomic Energy Agency: Personal Reflections*, ed. Hans Blix, 15–26. Vienna: International Atomic Energy Agency. http://www-pub.iaea.org/MTCD/publications/PDF/Pub1033_web.pdf.

Solingen, Etel. 2007. *Nuclear Logics: Contrasting Paths in East Asia and the Middle East*. Princeton, NJ: Princeton University Press.

Spector, Leonard S. 2007. "Iranian Nuclear Program Remains Major Threat Despite Partial Freeze of Weapons-Relevant Activities Described in New US National Intelligence Estimate." *CNS Feature Story*. Washington, DC: Center for Nonproliferation Studies.

Steinberg, Richard H. 2002. "In the Shadow of Law or Power? Consensus-Based Bargaining and Outcomes in the GATT/WTO." *International Organization 56*, no. 2: 339–74.

Steinwand, Martin C., and Randall W. Stone. 2008. "The International Monetary Fund: A Review of Recent Evidence." *Review of International Organizations* 3, no. 2: 123–49.

Stoiber, Carlton R. 1983. "Current United States Nuclear Non-Proliferation Policy." *New York Law School Journal of International and Comparative Law* 4, no. 2: 367.

Stone, Randall W. 2011. *Controlling Institutions: International Organizations and the Global Economy*. Cambridge: Cambridge University Press.

Stumpf, Waldo. 1995. "South Africa's Nuclear Weapons Program: From Deterrence to Dismantlement." *Arms Control Today* 25:3–9.

Subramanian, Ram R. 1985. "Second-Tier Nuclear Suppliers: Threat to the NPT Regime?" In *The Nuclear Suppliers and Nonproliferation*, ed. Rodney W. Jones, Cesare Merlini, Joseph F. Pilat, and William C. Potter, 95–103. Lexington, MA: Lexington Books.

Suschny, Otto. 1997. "The Agency's Laboratories at Seibersdorf and Vienna." In *International Atomic Energy Agency: Personal Reflections*, ed. Hans Blix, 211–20. Vienna: International Atomic Energy Agency. http://www-pub.iaea.org/MTCD/publications/PDF/Pub1033_web.pdf.

Suskind, Ron. 2004. *The Price of Loyalty*. New York: Simon & Schuster.

Tannenwald, Nina. 1999. "The Nuclear Taboo: The United States and the Normative Basis of Nuclear Non-Use." *International Organization* 53, no. 3: 433–68.

———. 2007. *The Nuclear Taboo*. New York: Cambridge University Press.

Tate, Trevor McMorris. 1990. "Regime-Building in the Non-Proliferation System." *Journal of Peace Research* 27, no. 4: 399–414.

Thompson, Alexander. 2006. "Coercion through IOs: The Security Council and the Logic of Information Transmission." *International Organization* 60, no. 1: 1–34.

Thorne, Carleton E. 1997. *Multilateral Nuclear Export Controls: Past, Present and Future*. International Seminar on the Role of Export Controls in Nuclear Non-Proliferation, Vienna, Austria, Nuclear Suppliers Group.

Thorne, Leslie. 1992. "IAEA Nuclear Inspections in Iraq." *IAEA Bulletin* 1:16–24. www.iaea.org/Publications/Magazines/Bulletin/Bull341/34102451624.pdf.

Trachtenberg, Marc. 1989. "Strategic Thought in America, 1952–1966." *Political Science Quarterly* 104, no. 2: 301–34.

Traub, James. 2004. "The Netherworld of Nonproliferation." *New York Times Magazine*, June 13. http://www.nytimes.com/2004/06/13/magazine/13NUKES.html.

Truman, Harry S. 1945. "The Decision to Drop the Atomic Bomb." *Truman Papers*. Truman Library, Independence, Missouri.

Truman, Harry S., Clement R. Attlee, and William King. 1945. Declaration on Atomic Bomb, November 15. *NuclearFiles.org*, Project of the Nuclear Age Peace Foundation. http://www.nuclearfiles.org/menu/key-issues/nuclear-energy/history/dec-truma-atlee-king_1945-11-15.htm.

Tucker, Jonathan B. 1996. "Monitoring and Verification in a Noncooperative Environment: Lessons from the UN Experience in Iraq." *Nonproliferation Review* 3, no. 3 (Spring/Summer): 1–14.

Unger, Craig. 2007. *The Fall of the House of Bush*. New York: Scribner.

United Nations. 1991. Report of the Secretary-General on Setting up a Special Commission (UNSCOM) to Carry Out On-Site Inspection of Iraq's Biological, Chemical and Missile Capabilities (S/22508).

Urpelainen, Johannes. 2012. "Unilateral Influence on International Bureaucrats: An International Delegation Problem." *Journal of Conflict Resolution* 56, no. 4. doi:10.1177/0022002711431423.

US Department of State. 1970. Treaty on the Non-Proliferation of Nuclear Weapons. Treaties and Other International Acts Series. Washington, DC.

US House of Representatives. 1981. Committee on Foreign Affairs. Israeli Attack on Iraqi Nuclear Facilities of June 17 and 25, 1981. Washington, DC: US GPO.

———. 1990. Committee on Foreign Affairs and Its Subcommittee on Arms Control, International Security and Science. Proliferation and Arms Control. Hearings before the United States House of Representatives Committee on Foreign Affairs and Its Subcommittee on Arms Control, International Security and Science, 101st Congr. 2nd Sess. (May 17 and July 11). Washington, DC: US GPO.

US Senate, Committee on Foreign Relations. 1957. Statute of the International Atomic Energy Agency. Committee on Foreign Relations and Senate Members of the Joint Committee on Atomic Energy, 85th Cong. 1st Sess. Washington, DC: US GPO, 260.

———. 1968. The Treaty on the Nonproliferation of Nuclear Weapons (Executive H). Washington, DC: US GPO.

———. 1969. The Treaty on the Nonproliferation of Nuclear Weapons (Executive H), Part 2. Washington, DC: US GPO.

————. 1977. Subcommittee on Arms Control, International Law and Organization of the Committee on Foreign Relations. Nonproliferation Issues. Hearings before The Subcommittee on Arms Control, International Law and Organization of the Committee on Foreign Relations, 94th Congr. 1st and 2nd Sess. (March 19, April 16 and 28, July 18 and 22, October 21 and 24, 1975; February 23 and 24, March 15, September 22, and November 8, 1976). Washington, DC: US GPO.

————. 1980. Subcommittee on Arms Control, Oceans, International Operations and Environment of the Committee on Foreign Relations. The Non-Proliferation Treaty Review Conference. Hearing before The Subcommittee on Arms Control, Oceans, International Operations and Environment of the Committee on Foreign Relations, 96th Congr. 2nd Sess. (July 24, 1980). Washington, DC: US GPO.

van Gorkom, Lodewijk. 1997. "Nuclear Safety: The Public Battle Lost?" In *International Atomic Energy Agency: Personal Reflections*, ed. Hans Blix, 169–84. Vienna: International Atomic Energy Agency. http://www-pub.iaea.org/MTCD/publications/PDF/Pub1033_web.pdf.

Vez Carmona, Maria de Lourdes. 2005. "The International Regime on the Physical Protection of Nuclear Material and the Amendment to the Convention on the Physical Protection of Nuclear Material." *Nuclear Law Bulletin* 76, no. 1: 31–46.

Voeten, Erik. 2000. "Clashes in the Assembly." *International Organization* 54, no. 2: 185–215.

————. 2004. "Resisting the Lonely Superpower: Responses of States in the UN to US Dominance." *Journal of Politics* 66, no. 3: 729–54.

————. 2011. "Unipolar Politics as Usual." *Cambridge Review of International Affairs* 24, no. 2: 121–28. doi:10.1080/09557571.2011.558492.

von Baeckmann, Adolf, Garry Dillon, and Demetrius Perricos. 1995. "Nuclear Verification in South Africa." *IAEA Bulletin*, 1, www.iaea.org/Publications/Magazines/Bulletin/Bull371/37105394248.pdf.

von Stein, Jana. 2005. "Do Treaties Constrain or Screen? Selection Bias and Treaty Compliance." *American Political Science Review* 99, no. 4: 611–22.

Wade, Robert. 1998. "The Asian Debt-and-Development Crisis of 1997–?: Causes and Consequences." *World Development* 26, no. 8: 1535–53.

Wæver, Ole. 1999. "The Sociology of a Not So International Discipline: American and European Developments in International Relations." In *Exploration and Contestation in the Study of World Politics*, ed. Peter J. Katzenstein, Robert O. Keohane, and Stephen D. Krasner, 47–87. Cambridge, MA: MIT Press.

Walker, J. Samuel. 2005. "Recent Literature on Truman's Atomic Bomb Decision: A Search for Middle Ground." *Diplomatic History* 29, no. 2: 311–34.

Walker, William. 2011. *A Perpetual Menace: Nuclear Weapons and International Order*. New York: Routledge.

Wallander, Celeste A. 2000. "Institutional Assets and Adaptability: NATO after the Cold War." *International Organization* 54, no. 4: 705–35.

Wallander, Celeste A., Helga Haftendorn, and Robert O. Keohane. 1999. Introduction to *Imperfect Unions: Security Institutions over Time and Space*, ed. Helga Haftendorn, Robert O. Keohane, and Celeste A. Wallander, 1–20. Oxford: Oxford University Press.

Waltz, Kenneth N. 1979. *Theory of International Politics*. New York: McGraw-Hill.

———. 1993. "The Emerging Structure of International Politics." *International Security* 18, no. 2: 44–79.

———. 2002. "More May Be Better." In *The Spread of Nuclear Weapons: A Debate Renewed*, ed. Kenneth N. Waltz and Scott D. Sagan, 1–46. New York: Norton.

Wampler, Robert A. 2003. "North Korea and Nuclear Weapons: The Declassified U.S. Record," Electronic Briefing Book No. 87. Washington, DC: National Security Archive. http://www2.gwu.edu/~nsarchiv/NSAEBB/NSAEBB87/.

Washington, Monica J. 1999. "Monitoring Compliance with Nuclear Safety Standards: Peer Review through the International Atomic Energy Agency and Its Convention on Nuclear Safety." In *Administrative and Expert Monitoring of International Treaties*, ed. Paul Szasz. Ardsley, NY: Transnational.

Weber, Max. 1978. *Economy and Society: An Outline of Interpretive Sociology*. Berkeley: University of California Press.

Weightman, Mike. 2011a. "Chairpersons' Summaries: IAEA Ministerial Conference on Nuclear Safety." Vienna: International Atomic Energy Agency.

———. 2011b. "Japanese Earthquake and Tsunami: Implications for the UK Nuclear Industry." Final Report of HM Chief Inspector of Nuclear Facilities. London: UK Health and Safety Executive Office for Nuclear Regulation

Wendt, Alexander. 1992. "Anarchy Is What States Make of It: The Social Construction of Power Politics." *International Organization* 46, no. 2: 391–425.

———. 1999. *Social Theory of International Politics*. Cambridge: Cambridge University Press.

Williams, Robert C., and Philip L. Cantelon. 1984. *The American Atom: A Documentary History of Nuclear Policies from the Discovery of Fission to the Present, 1939–1984*. Philadelphia: University of Pennsylvania Press.

Wilson, Michael. 1997. "Safeguards and the IAEA Board of Governors, 1991–1993: Iraq, a Necessary Stimulus for Handling the DPRK." In *International Atomic Energy Agency: Personal Reflections*, ed. Hans Blix, 127–40. Vienna: International Atomic Energy Agency. http://www-pub.iaea.org/MTCD/publications/PDF/Pub1033_web.pdf.

Wilson, Ward. 2008. "The Myth of Nuclear Deterrence." *Nonproliferation Review* 15, no. 3: 421–39.

Wittner, Lawrence S. 1993. *One World or None: A History of the World Nuclear Disarmament Movement through 1953*. Stanford, CA: Stanford University Press.

———. 1997. *Resisting the Bomb: 1954–1970*. Stanford, CA: Stanford University Press.

———. 2003. *Toward Nuclear Abolition*. Stanford, CA: Stanford University Press.

———. 2009. *Confronting the Bomb: A Short History of the World Nuclear Disarmament Movement*. Stanford, CA: Stanford University Press.

Wohlstetter, Albert. 1959. "The Delicate Balance of Terror." *Foreign Affairs* 37, no. 2: 211–34.

Wojcik, Tradesuz. 1997. "Introducing Changes into the Agency's Scientific and Technical Programmes." In *International Atomic Energy Agency: Personal Reflections*, ed. Hans Blix, 259–70. Vienna, International Atomic Energy Agency. http://www-pub.iaea.org/MTCD/publications/PDF/Pub1033_web.pdf.

Wright, Erik Olin. 1973. *Politics of Punishment: A Critical Analysis of Prisons in America*. New York: Harper and Row.

York, Herbert F. 1987. *Making Weapons, Talking Peace: A Physicist's Odyssey from Hiroshima to Geneva*. New York: Basic Books.

Zanders, Jean Pascal, Frida Kuhlau, John Hart, and Richard Guthrie. 2003. "Non-Compliance with the Chemical Weapons Convention: Lessons from and for Iraq," SIPRI Policy Report #5. Stockholm: Stockholm International Peace Research Institute.

Zunes, Stephen. 2005. "Undermining the Nuclear Non-Proliferation Treaty: It Didn't Start with the Bush Administration." *Foreign Policy in Focus*, June 1. http://stephenzunes.org/2005/06/01/undermining-the-nuclear-non-proliferation-treaty%E2%80%94it-didn%E2%80%99t-start-with-the-bush-administration/.

Index

Information in figures and tables is denoted by *f* and *t*.

235

North Korea and, 108–9; nuclear technology acquired by, 5, 53, 65n2; proliferation and, 5, 75, 78; safeguards promotion and, 89; superpower influence of, 75–76; test bans and, 47–48; US relations with, 102–3; verification and, 47–48, 50, 62, 69; and verification of nuclear weapons, 69. *See also* Russia
staffing, 60, 82–83
Standing Advisory Group on Safeguards Implementation (SAGSI), 132
START (Strategic Arms Reduction Talks), 74, 103, 121, 196. *See also* New START
Stone, Randall, 24
Strategic Arms Limitation Talks (SALT), 73, 97
Strategic Arms Reduction Talks (START), 74, 103, 121, 196. *See also* New START
Strategic Offensive Reduction Treaty (SORT), 142, 178n1. *See also* Moscow Treaty
Strauss, Lewis L., 53–54, 65n7
Straw, Jack, 171
structural constraints, 24–26
Sudan, 140
Suez Crisis, 49
superpower influence, 75–76
suppliers, nuclear, 71–72; G-77 and, 80; internationalization and, 54; Iraq and, 107; nonproliferation and, 79; power generation and, 71–72, 84–86; safety and, 85; security and, 196–97. *See also* Nuclear Suppliers Group (NSG); uranium
Suskind, Ron, 144
Sweden, 68, 132
Syria, 144, 148, 150, 178n8

taboo, nuclear weapons as, 25–26
Taiwan, 58, 141
Technical Cooperation: authority and, 186, 196; development programs and, 120–21, 157; G-77 and, 80;

growth of, 186; international development and, 157, 158; as international functionalism example, 120; in Iran, 146; Iran and, 146; management reforms and, 155; Millennium Development Goals and, 155; national development programs and, 120–21; in North Korea, 110; North Korea and, 110; proliferation and, 157, 158; safety and, 158; success of, 120. *See also* power generation
terrorism: in Russia, 162; of September 11, 142–43, 149. *See also* safety and security
test bans, 6–7, 47–48, 68, 97. *See also* Comprehensive Test Ban Treaty (CTBT); Limited Test Ban Treaty (LTBT)
testing: deterrence and, 182, 195; environmental movement and, 76; fallout from, 45, 65n7; Non-Proliferation Treaty and, 77–78; norms and, 114; proliferation and, 6, 182
Three Mile Island disaster, 67, 72–73, 88, 101n10, 104
Threshold Test Ban Treaty (TTBT), 97–98, 103
Treaty of Pelindaba, 132
Treaty of Rarotonga, 132
Treaty of Tlatelolco, 97, 99
Truman, Harry, 1, 4, 42
TTBT (Threshold Test Ban Treaty), 97–98, 103
Turkey, 44

Ukraine, 40n1, 105, 115, 147, 150, 166
uncertainty, 32–34, 167, 183
UN Conference on the Peaceful Uses of Atomic Energy, 55
Unger, Craig, 171
unipolarity, 149–51
United Kingdom: Atoms for Peace and, 45–46; Comprehensive Test Ban Treaty and, 47; Iraq and, 125–26; Libya and, 164–65; in Manhattan Project, 42; Non-Proliferation Treaty

CPSIA information can be obtained at www.ICGtesting.com
Printed in the USA
BVOW07*0438100315

390711BV00002B/8/P